L O G I C

Theoretical
and
Applied

BARUCH A. BRODY

Massachusetts Institute of Technology

PRENTICE-HALL, INC., *Englewood Cliffs, New Jersey*

Library of Congress Cataloging in Publication Data

BRODY, BARUCH A
  Logic.

  1. Logic. I. Title.
BC108.B724   160   72-11732
ISBN 0-13-540146-1

10 9 8 7 6 5 4 3 2 1

Printed in the United States of America

PRENTICE-HALL INTERNATIONAL, INC., *London*
PRENTICE-HALL OF AUSTRALIA, PTY. LTD., *Sydney*
PRENTICE-HALL OF CANADA, LTD., *Toronto*
PRENTICE-HALL OF INDIA PRIVATE LIMITED, *New Delhi*
PRENTICE-HALL OF JAPAN, INC., *Tokyo*

To Todd Daniel and Jeremy Keith

CONTENTS

Three Current
Controversies

In this book we will be primarily concerned with a theoretical study of the process of communication and the process of reasoning. In particular, we will inquire into the meaning and truth of symbols used in communicating and into the validity and soundness of reasonings. We will attempt to construct theories to analyze and explain these concepts.

Although our inquiry will be primarily theoretical, we do not want to lose sight of the fact that our theories have important practical applications. Indeed, people first began to probe into these theoretical issues in the belief that resolving them would lead to better communicating and thinking. Although the principles of logic have in the course of time become an independent study, nevertheless the practical applications of these theories should not be neglected.

To demonstrate the practical applications of logic, this text is arranged as follows: In this chapter we consider three real controversies in which seemingly good arguments can be advanced on both sides. In the last chapter, having gone through all the theoretical material, we return to the controversies and reexamine the arguments. Our studies will not resolve these controversies, but will at least shed light upon the validity of the arguments on both sides.

1.1 The Rationality of Faith

Throughout the ages many people have thought they could prove that God exists; conversely, others have thought they could prove that God does not exist. Both groups have advanced many arguments to prove either contention. According to which of these arguments works (i.e., is sound), there can be no question about what a rational man should believe. If the existence of God could be proved, then a rational man should believe that God exists. If the nonexistence of God could be proved, then a rational man should believe that God does not exist.

What is the impact of "should" in the statements above? Presumably it is the following: If it could be proved that God does (does not) exist, then a man who desires, more than anything else, to be rational should believe in the existence (nonexistence) of God. For if he believed otherwise, he would not be a rational man. Note, however, that if other goals were more important to the man than being rational, then perhaps in order to reach those other goals, he should believe in the nonexistence (existence) of God despite proof to the contrary.

Most philosophers and theologians think that none of the arguments on either side have actually succeeded in proving (or even making it likely) that God exists or that God does not exist. In this regard they share the popular conviction that religious issues are a matter of faith, and not of reason. We need not analyze here the traditional evaluation of the arguments for and against the existence of God. For our purpose let us assume it to be correct, and look instead into the implications of this assessment for the rational man—the man who desires, more than anything else, to be rational.

There are three options open to such a man: (1) he can believe in the existence of God even though there is no proof that God exists; (2) he can believe in the nonexistence of God even though there is no proof that God does not exist; or (3) he can hold no belief on this issue. If he adopts the first option, we shall say that he has a *theistic faith;* if he adopts the second option, we shall say that he has an *atheistic faith;* and if he adopts the third option, we shall say that he is an *agnostic.* The question that concerns us is, Which of these three options should a rational man adopt? So, our question is really about the rationality of faith.

There are two widely recognized positions on this issue. One, often attributed to William James, is that, given the failure of the arguments for or against the existence of God, it is equally rational to have a theistic faith, or to have an atheistic faith, or to be an agnostic. We shall call this the *permissive position.* The second, often attributed to William Clifford, maintains that, given the failure of the arguments for or against the existence of God, the only rational course is to be an agnostic. We shall call this the *strict position.*

The argument often advanced in favor of the permissive position runs as follows. Let us imagine that Joe believes that Mary loves him. Let us also imagine he knows that though she has refused to go out with him, she is dating others, and has told her friends how much she despises Joe. From these facts we would certainly be convinced that Joe is acting irrationally if he continues to believe that Mary loves him. The evidence of her behavior makes it highly unlikely that Mary loves Joe, and perhaps even proves conclusively that she does not. In general, then, it is irrational to believe something when there is evidence that proves, or at least makes it highly likely, that the belief in question is false. This is why it would be irrational to have an atheistic (theistic) faith if it could be proved that God exists (does not exist). But when the evidence is, so to speak, not against your belief, then your belief is perfectly rational. Now, regarding belief in the existence of God, since there is no evidence for or against the belief—inasmuch as the proofs on either side don't work—neither theism nor atheism is irrational; either faith is as rational as agnosticism.

The following argument has often been advanced in favor of the strict position. Whenever we consider a given proposition, there are always three options open to us: (1) we can believe that what it says is the case; (2) we can believe that what it says is not the case; or (3) we can believe neither. The rational man does not act capriciously or hastily. Until there is evidence proving, or at least making it highly plausible, that what the proposition says is the case (is not the case), he neither believes nor disbelieves it; he holds no beliefs. Thus, in our previous example, even if Joe had no evidence showing that Mary did *not* love him, it would still be irrational for him to believe that Mary *did* love him if he had no evidence showing that she loved him. Even if your evidence is not against your belief, your belief is still irrational; it becomes rational only when the evidence is for it. Now, in the case of belief in the existence of God, someone who adopts either a theistic or an atheistic faith is acting irrationally. Although it is true that the evidence is not *against* his belief, it is also true that, because of the failure of the proofs on either side, there is no evidence *for* his belief; and he who maintains a belief when there is no evidence for it is, as we have seen, irrational. So, the only rational option is agnosticism.

The arguments for the permissive position and for the strict position are both quite plausible. Which is correct? We shall return to that question in the last chapter. What is important to note here is that both arguments have a common structure. Each begins with some general claims about when beliefs are rational or irrational, and then goes on to apply these claims to the case of belief in the existence of God. Neither approach depends upon any particular claims about the spiritual significance of the belief in the existence of God. To be convincing, the defenders of the permissive position need not fall back upon the argument that the question of the existence of God is so important to us that it is rational to hold whatever beliefs we want as long as the evidence is not against us. And the defenders of the strict position need not fall back upon the argument that the question of the existence of God is so emotion charged that we have to be especially careful, if we want to be rational, not to hold any belief until we get strong or conclusive evidence either way. All of this strengthens both arguments and makes them more plausible, since they do not rest upon any dubious claims about the special status of the question of God's existence. So our task in the last chapter, when we attempt to see which argument is correct, is going to be very difficult.

1.2 *Marijuana and Heroin*

One of the most controversial issues in recent times concerns the legal status of marijuana. At present there are relatively strict laws against the possession and use of marijuana. Many feel that these laws are not justified, and should be modified or abolished. On the other hand, many believe that the laws in question are justified.

We will consider only one aspect of this very complex issue, that concerned with the relationship between marijuana and heroin use. One of the arguments for retaining the laws on marijuana is that the use of marijuana leads to the use of heroin. Even this argument is extremely complex. It breaks down into the following steps:

(1) Marijuana use leads to later heroin use.

(2) Heroin use is intrinsically bad, and not merely bad because of the existence of laws against it.

(3) We can cut down on marijuana use, and therefore on heroin use, by keeping our laws against marijuana.

(4) This benefit from retaining these laws outweighs any disadvantages of keeping the law.

(5) Therefore, we should retain our marijuana laws.

What we shall be concerned with is step (1) of this argument, the claim that the use of marijuana leads to, or causes, later use of heroin. We must remember, however, that even if step (1) is correct, it does not mean that we should retain our marijuana laws. It would still be an open issue as to whether steps (2)–(4) were also correct. And we must also remember that even if step (1) is false, it does not follow that we should revoke our marijuana laws, for there may be other arguments for retaining them that do not depend upon the truth of step (1).

The type of argument normally put forth to support the contention that marijuana use leads to heroin use runs something like this: If you study heroin users, you soon discover that a majority of them have used marijuana before using heroin. The percentage of heroin users who have previously used marijuana is much larger than the percentage of nonheroin users who have previously used marijuana. So there is every reason to believe that a causal connection exists between the use of marijuana and the use of heroin.

Let us examine this argument a bit more carefully. In a recent study, 2,213 opium addicts in the Lexington and Forth Worth hospitals were surveyed for previous use of marijuana.[1] Most addicts fell into two groups— those from 12 southern states who were primarily users of opiates other than heroin, and those from 16 northeastern and southwestern states who were primarily heroin users. Of the latter group, 80% had used marijuana before heroin, whereas 25% of the former group had a previous history of marijuana use. The data is summarized in the following table. Either of these percentages is, of course, much greater than the percentage of adult Americans who

	Northeastern heroin users	Southern opiate users
No previous marijuana use	20%	75%
Previous marijuana use	80%	25%

have a history of marijuana use. So, it might be concluded, there is a causal connection between the use of marijuana and the use of opiates, especially heroin.

Opponents of this argument generally offer two reasons for not accepting these statistics as proof that the use of marijuana causes later use of heroin. Reason one: These selfsame statistics show that many people who have become users of heroin (and opiates in general) have not previously used marijuana. And, certainly, most people who use marijuana do not go on to the use of addictive drugs. (Although this second claim is difficult to support with statistical evidence since few people are willing to give information which might subject them to criminal penalties, the view is generally held by many medical and law enforcement officials who are in close contact with the problem.) So, how can it be claimed that the use of marijuana causes heroin addiction?

Reason two: These statistics can be explained in many ways without supposing that marijuana use causes later heroin use. For example, the only way an addict can buy heroin in the United States is through a pusher. And since marijuana users also must resort to illegal suppliers of their drug, they are more likely to know where to obtain hard drugs such as heroin than are nonmarijuana users. That explains in part why most heroin users have previously used marijuana. More generally, smoking marijuana leads one into a subgroup of American society that is less inclined to obey the drug laws and that contains a fair number of heroin and opiate users who are willing to initiate the subgroup's nonusers. This, too, explains why most heroin

[1] J. C. Ball and C. D. Chambers, "Marijuana Smoking as a Precursor of Opiate Addiction in the United States," *Journal of Criminal Law, Criminology, and Police Science* (1968).

users have first used marijuana. Note that both these interpretations of the statistics, rather than establish a causal connection between marijuana and heroin use, offer explanations in terms of the current legal and sociological circumstances surrounding the use of marijuana. One might even conclude that the illegality of marijuana, rather than its use, is the real cause of eventual heroin addiction.

We have here, then, two persuasive positions. One claims that the statistical evidence of the type found in the Ball and Chambers study supports step (1), the idea that the use of marijuana does cause eventual heroin addiction. The other claims that it does nothing of the sort, by pointing out instances in which the two are not connected, and by showing that other explanations are possible. Which of these positions is correct? We shall return to this question in the last chapter and try to answer it.

1.3 *The Morality of Civil Disobedience*

One of the marks of the morally mature and rational person is his unwillingness to accept without questioning the judgments of people in political power. Such a person is inclined rather to thinking about issues and forming his own opinions. From independent thinking he sometimes draws the conclusion that certain governmental actions, laws, and policies are wrong or unjust or offensive, or perhaps all three. That being the case, the question facing the morally mature, rational person is, What should I do about the situation?

In some countries in which governmental policies, leaders, and political institutions are open to questioning and criticism, there are, sometimes, reasonably effective legal means available—such as lobbying, petitioning, voting—through which disagreement may be expressed and laws may be changed or abolished.

Under some political systems, however, no legal methods are available through which those dissatisfied with governmental actions can effect change. In still other systems the apparatus may be present but not functioning, whether because of discriminatory practices, public apathy, or various other reasons. When legal means are absent or ineffectual, other methods may be resorted to. Civil disobedience may be defined as illegal actions whose purpose is to correct the wrongs produced by those who possess political and legal power.

An an instrument of social change, civil disobedience relies on the dramatic impact of illegal actions to focus attention on the grievance. The objective is to change the condition; the means used are whatever steps provide effective pressure and provocation: strikes, protests, sit-ins, arrests, desertions, etc. Examples abound in the civil rights movement and the anti-war movement. Note that the strategy employed is a conscious, morally wrong act—breaking the law—in order to pursue a morally just goal. This is what makes such actions controversial.

The defenders of civil disobedience argue as follows: Let us imagine that everyone who felt that certain laws were wrong and that only through civil disobedience could changes be made decided nevertheless to obey the laws rather than to challenge them. The result would be that all forms of injustice, ranging from segregation to genocide, would continue indefinitely. They point out, for example, how long black people were legally persecuted in the United States, and how much change has been accomplished by acts of civil disobedience. If recourse to illegal action is the only way in which you can hope to change unjust laws, then such action is justified.

The critics of civil disobedience argue as follows: Since people often disagree about what is right and what is wrong, we would soon have a total breakdown in society if everyone violated the law in order to bring about change. Just as blacks in our country resorted to civil disobedience to gain their ends, so white segregationists could do likewise to prevent integration. Just as war resisters have gone to jail or deserted from the army in protest, so could those who do not want the United States to pull out of Vietnam mount protest demonstrations in favor of continuing the war. And so on. The net result would be anarchy and chaos—a jungle society in which each faction promotes its partisan viewpoint by deliberately violating the law. This is a terrifying prospect, and could lead to the destruction of civilization as we know it. We cannot, therefore, justify breaking the law in order to improve society. To produce changes for the better in our laws and social systems, we must do the best we can with the legal means available. So, although civil disobedience may seem to be the only way to effect desired changes, we should not resort to it.

The arguments for and against civil disobedience are highly charged and persuasive. We shall need to be well fortified by the solid theories of logic before we return to this controversial issue in the last chapter.

THE THEORY
of
LANGUAGE

CHAPTER
2

Meaning
and Definition

Human beings emit many types of sounds, but only some of them can be used in the process of communication. Similarly, human beings make many types of marks. Again, however, only some of them can be used in the process of communication. The sounds and marks that can be used for communicating can be so used because they mean something. What is it for a sound or mark to mean something? How do we go about letting other people know what they mean? This chapter will be concerned with these questions.

Before turning to these questions, however, we must consider one important distinction—that between a *natural sign* and a *symbol*. Both are sounds or marks that mean something. The difference between them is that symbols have meaning because of the existence of rules governing their use, whereas natural signs have meaning without the existence of such rules. Thus, a word has meaning only because of the existence of rules governing its use in a given language, rules that give it its meaning. The word itself has no intrinsic meaning. Therefore, a word is a symbol. Pictures (particularly realistic ones) are different in that they have meaning intrinsically— by virtue of their similarity to the objects symbolized—and do not require the existence of rules governing their use to give them meaning. Thus, pictures are natural signs. Since we are concerned now primarily with the meaning of linguistic objects (words, phrases, sentences), and since these are almost always symbols, we shall disregard any special questions about the meaning of natural signs, and confine ourselves to the meaning of symbols.

2.1 Meaning and Reference

Our first theory, the *referential theory of meaning*, is the simplest and most obvious. The theory states that a symbol has meaning when it stands for or represents some object, that the object is the meaning of the symbol, and that therefore two symbols mean the same thing (are *synonymous*) when they stand for the same object. Consequently, to explain what a symbol means, one needs merely to indicate what object the symbol stands for.

This theory derives its plausibility from the truism that symbols are often used to stand for or represent something other than themselves. Obviously, then, that something else is the meaning of the symbol.

Proponents of this theory point out an important difference between two types of standing-for relations. In one type, the symbol stands for only one object. Such symbols, called *singular symbols*, are said to *refer* to that object, and the object is called the *reference* of the symbol. Thus 'President Nixon' or 'the present Queen of England' are singular symbols, one referring to a particular man (that man is the reference of 'President Nixon') and the other referring to a particular woman (that woman is the reference of 'the present Queen of England'). In the second type, the symbol may stand for many different objects. Such symbols, called *general symbols*, are said to *denote* those objects, and those objects are called the *denotation* of the symbol. Thus, 'woman' and 'prime number' are general symbols, one denoting all women (who are, collectively, the denotation of that symbol) and the other denoting all prime numbers (which are, collectively, the denotation of that symbol).

Using our new terminology, we can formulate the main theses of the *referential theory of meaning* as follows:

(1) A symbol has meaning if and only if it has a reference or a denotation.

(2) The reference or denotation of a symbol is its meaning; consequently, two symbols are synonymous when they refer to, or denote, the same object or objects.

(3) One tells someone the meaning of a symbol when and only when one indicates to that person the reference or denotation of the symbol.

Although this theory is initially very plausible, there are good reasons for supposing that each of the preceding claims is false. Indeed, even if we confine ourselves to linguistic symbols, there are clear counterexamples for each of them. To begin with, some words or expressions are meaningful but have no reference or denotation; for example, 'the present king of France' or 'ghosts': neither term refers or denotes in actual fact (although there have been French kings, and there could be ghosts). Other words, however, such as 'it is not the case that' or the marriage vow 'I do', could have no reference or denotation, yet each of these phrases has a meaning. These examples show that thesis (1) of the referential theory of meaning is false.

Similarly, examples may be found of linguistic symbols having the same reference or the same denotation without being synonymous. 'George Washington' and 'the first President of the United States' both refer to the same man, but the two symbols do not mean the same thing. Again, the denotation of 'creature with a heart' is the same as the denotation of 'creature with a lung'; yet these two symbols do not mean the same thing. So thesis (2) of the referential theory of meaning is false.

Finally, it is possible to convey the meaning of a symbol without indicating the reference or denotation of that symbol. The most obvious examples, as we have seen, are symbols that have no reference or denotation. But we can also explain a symbol that does have a reference or denotation, without indicating either. Thus, 'the present Queen of England' can be explained as *a symbol used to refer to that woman who, at the time of the use of the symbol, is the titular ruler of England,* without actually identifying her. So thesis (3) of the referential theory is false.

It follows from this discussion that we must distinguish between the meaning of a singular symbol (which we shall call its *sense*) and the reference of that symbol, and between the meaning of a general symbol (which we shall call its *connotation*) and the denotation of that symbol. In summary we can state:

(1) There are singular symbols with sense but no reference and general symbols with connotation but no denotation.

(2) There are symbols with the same reference or denotation but with different senses or connotations.

Although the referential theory of meaning turns out to be false, it has called our attention to certain important truths about the meaning of symbols that any adequate theory of meaning must take into account. First, it reminds us that certain symbols do have references and denotations, and any adequate theory of meaning should explain that. But more importantly, it reminds us that there is a strong connection between the fact that a symbol has the meaning it does and the fact (if it is a fact) that it has a certain reference or denotation. After all, 'the first President of the United States' refers to George Washington because it means what it does. If it had a different sense—if it meant, say, what 'the most beautiful woman who ever lived' now means—then it certainly would not refer to George Washington. Any adequate theory of meaning must explain this strong connection between meaning and reference in the case of singular symbols and the equally strong connection between meaning and denotation in the case of general symbols.

2.2 Meaning and Ideas

The next theory of meaning we shall consider is the *ideational theory*. According to this theory, the meaning of a symbol is the idea accompanying that symbol in the mind of the user. For example, let us imagine that you ask someone where Joe is, and the reply is "at home." That phrase is a symbol used by the speaker to transmit from his mind to yours the idea that Joe is at home. Thus, we can state that symbols are used to convey ideas from one mind to another, and that these ideas are the meanings of the symbols. In other words, according to the ideational theory, the meaning of a symbol is that which is truly represented by the symbol, the idea in the mind of the user of the symbol.

In the example the idea in the mind of the user of the symbol is a complete belief; namely, the belief that Joe is at home. But symbols can be used in other ways. For example, the symbol 'house' might convey the concept of any dwelling place. Or the exclamation 'wowee' can express a multitude of emotions. The ideational theory includes all these different types of mental contents in the denotation of 'idea'.

It is important to keep in mind that when adherents of the ideational theory talk about ideas, they are not talking about images (mental pictures). If they were, their theory would be false, since there are many meaningful symbols for which there are no corresponding mental pictures (for example, 'six-dimensional space', 'ego') and there are other meaningful symbols whose corresponding mental pictures are clearly not the meaning of these symbols (for example, 'justice', which does not mean a blind lady holding a set of scales). But neither of these cases poses problems for the ideational theory, since its adherents are talking about nonpictorial ideas and not pictorial images.

We may now state more formally the main theses of the ideational theory:

(1) A symbol has meaning if and only if there is an idea that accompanies its use in the mind of the user.

(2) This idea is the meaning of the symbol; consequently, two symbols are synonymous when the identical idea accompanies their use in the mind of the user.

(3) One tells someone the meaning of a symbol when and only when one indicates to that person the idea that accompanies its use in the mind of its user.

We saw at the end of section 2.1 that any adequate theory of meaning would have to explain the close connection existing between the meaning (or sense) of a singular symbol and its reference, and between the meaning (or connotation) of a general symbol and its denotation. How does the ideational theory explain this connection? According to the ideational theory, there will be, for every singular symbol, a corresponding singular idea in the mind of the user of the symbol when he uses it. But this idea is the idea of a particular object. So that object is the reference of the singular symbol. Thus, corresponding to 'the present Queen of England' is an idea of a woman who is currently the titular ruler of England, and this idea occurs in the mind of the user when he uses 'present Queen of England'. But this idea is an idea of a particular reigning monarch; therefore, Queen Elizabeth II is the reference of 'present Queen of England'. Similarly, for every general symbol there will be a corresponding general idea in the mind of the user of the symbol when he uses it. But this idea is the idea of a particular group of objects. So these objects are the denotation of the general symbol. Thus, corresponding to 'prime number' is an idea of a number not divisible by any other number except one, and this idea occurs in the mind of the user when he uses 'prime number'. But this idea is an idea of a whole group of numbers; therefore, that group of numbers is the denotation of 'prime number'.

The ideational theory of meaning, furthermore, has no trouble explaining those facts that destroyed the referential theory; namely, the existence of symbols with meaning but with no reference or denotation, and the existence of nonsynonymous symbols with the same reference or denotation. The former phenomenon occurs when there is an idea in the mind of the user of the symbol but there is no object, the latter occurs when there are two different ideas that are ideas of the same object or objects.

Despite its initial plausibility and its advantages over the referential theory of meaning, the ideational theory must be rejected. The first problem that the theory encounters is with its claim that whenever a meaningful symbol is used, a corresponding idea occurs in the mind of the user. Many instances may be cited when this does not occur. For example, it is possible to read a previously prepared speech or to utter a pat formula without corresponding ideas occurring in one's mind. Nor can it be maintained that a corresponding idea always occurs in the mind of the user of the symbol every time he thinks about the symbol he is using. One might rather be thinking, How do I sound when I use a certain cliché. Do I sound sincere? So one can be thinking about the symbol and how it is being used without having the corresponding idea occur in one's mind. The only true thing that we can say is that the corresponding idea occurs in the mind of the user of a symbol whenever he thinks about the meaning of the symbol he is using. Thus, according to the ideational theory, the meaning of a symbol is that idea which occurs in the mind of the user of the symbol when he uses the symbol and thinks about the meaning of the symbol he is using. In other words, the ideational theory uses the notion of meaning to explain what meaning is, and this circularity rules the theory out.

The second difficulty with the ideational theory is that it merely pushes our problems one step back. Consider, for example, the question of why a given symbol refers to or denotes a given object or objects. The ideational theory tells us that it does so because the idea that is the meaning of the symbol is an idea of that object or objects. But what makes that idea an idea of that object or objects? Our problem has reappeared one step further back; so the ideational theory has not really explained anything. Similarly, we were trying to figure out when two symbols mean the same thing. The ideational theory tells us that they do so when their corresponding ideas are the same ideas. But when are two ideas the same idea? They are not, as we saw, the same idea just because they are ideas of the same object or objects. So when are they the same idea? Once more our problem has reappeared one step further back, and the ideational theory has not really explained anything. Thus, the ideational theory doesn't solve any problems in the theory of meaning, and we must look for a more helpful theory.

It is intuitively understandable that the ideational theory should fail. We were looking for an explanation of what makes a sound or a mark into a symbol. The ideational theory tells us that the answer lies in the presence of a certain mental object, an idea. But then we can equally well ask, What makes this mental object into anything more than that? The fact that we can still ask that question is ultimately responsible for the failure of the ideational theory of meaning.

2.3 Meaning and Operations

The *operationalist theory of meaning* starts from the truism that for many symbols, operations can be performed that enable us to determine whether the symbol is applicable to a given object, situation, event, and so on. Thus, we can determine whether '80°F' is applicable to water in a beaker or to the air in a room by measuring with a thermometer. If the thermometer reads exactly 80 degrees, then '80°F' is an applicable symbol for that water or that air, if not, it is not applicable. So by the simple expedient of a given operation, we can determine whether a given symbol is applicable. The easiest way to account for this, say the adherents of our theory, is to identify the meaning of the symbol with the rules governing the operation that enables us to determine whether the symbol is applicable in a given case.

We should note another motivation for the operationalist theory even though it raises issues beyond our present scope. Symbols such as 'real', 'good', 'beautiful' play a prominent role in some of the most fascinating but endless philosophical disputes about the nature of reality, goodness, beauty. Many thinkers, particularly scientists, have become suspicious of such controversies because, unlike other scholarly disputes, they do not seem to be resolvable by rational means. They began to suspect that some of the basic symbols involved in these disputes are really meaningless for the very reason that no objective procedure exists for deciding when they are applicable. This attitude has led such thinkers to adopt the operationalist theory as a general theory for the meaning of symbols.

The main theses of the operationalist theory of meaning can be set out as follows:

(1) A symbol has meaning if and only if there is an operation which could, in principle, be carried out in order for us to determine, in any given case, whether that symbol is applicable in that case.

(2) The meaning of the symbol is the rules governing that operation; two symbols are synonymous when the rules governing the operation for determining whether they are applicable are identical.

(3) One tells someone the meaning of a symbol when one tells him the rules for the operation for determining whether the symbol is applicable in a given case.

Note that the theory does not require actual performance of the operation; it requires only that the operation be possible in principle. There is a good reason for this. Consider the symbol 'weighs one million tons'. By a very simple operation—weighing—we could determine whether that symbol is applicable in a given case, but it would require larger scales than we actually have. So the operation could not be carried out in practice, although in principle (if a large enough scale were built) the operation could be carried out. Obviously, then, this is a perfectly meaningful symbol, and our theory requires only that the operation be possible in principle.

In section 2.1 we saw that any adequate theory of meaning would have to explain the close connection between the sense of a singular symbol and its reference, and that between the connotation of a general symbol and its denotation. How does the operationalist theory explain this connection? According to operationalism, for every singular symbol there will be a corresponding rule governing an operation that determines to what particular thing, state, event, etc., the symbol is applicable. The reference of the symbol is simply that to which the operation determines the symbol is applicable. Similarly, for every general symbol there will be a corresponding rule governing an operation that determines to what things, states, events, etc., the symbol is applicable. The denotation of the symbol is simply those objects, states, events, etc., to which the operation determines the symbol is applicable.

The operationalist theory of meaning, furthermore, has no difficulty in explaining those facts which destroyed the referential theory; namely, the existence of symbols with meaning but with no reference or denotation, and the existence of nonsynonymous symbols with the same reference or denotation. The former phenomenon occurs when there is a rule governing an operation that will determine to what the symbol is applicable but there is nothing to which it is applicable. The latter phenomenon takes place when each of the symbols has a different rule governing a different operation to determine its applicability but when it turns out that the symbols are applicable to the same object.

Finally, the operationalist theory of meaning does not have the disadvantages of the ideationalist theory. It involves no assumptions as to what is going on in the mind of the user of a symbol when he uses that symbol. And it does not involve any dubious notions (such as 'idea of') that merely reintroduce all our problems.

Despite its strong points, the operationalist theory presents a number of major defects. The first stems from its attempt to rule out certain symbols as meaningless even though they normally are thought of as having meaning. Now there are perfectly normal procedures for determining whether a given symbol has meaning; for example, seeing whether people are perplexed in certain ways that indicate lack of understanding when the symbol is used, seeing whether people can offer arguments for or against the applicability of the symbol in a given case, and so on. But the very symbols that the operationalist wants to and must rule out as meaningless seem to pass the ordinary tests for being meaningful. So what the operationalist must be doing is offering us a new conception of when a symbol has meaning, one that imposes stricter requirements than the ordinary conception. We leave aside for now the question of whether this new proposal is a beneficial tightening up of the requirements for a symbol's having meaning or an artificial and arbitrary ruling out as meaningless certain perfectly satisfactory symbols. The important point is that from the beginning of this chapter, we have construed 'meaning' in the ordinary sense; and the operationalist theory, precisely because it rules out satisfactory, meaningful symbols, is an incorrect theory of that conception of meaning.

A second major difficulty that the operationalist faces is in his theory of synonymy. We have seen how operationalists try to distinguish between having the same reference or denotation and being synonymous. Although 'creature with a heart' and 'creature with a lung' have the same denotation, the operation for determining whether one is applicable (does it have a heart?) is different from the operation for determining whether the other is applicable (does it have a lung?). Therefore, says the operationalist, the two symbols are not synonymous. But are the operations different? Since we now know that the symbols have the same denotation, we can use any operation that determines whether one is applicable to determine whether the other is applicable. So the operations that determine the applicability of the two symbols will be the same, and therefore, on the operationalist theory, the two are synonymous. But since they are not, operationalism is false.

Finally, the operationalist has trouble explaining symbols such as 'hurray', 'why', please', etc., that are not meant to refer or denote. According to operationalism, these symbols are meaningful only if there is some rule governing an operation that will determine their applicability in a given case. But that is an absurd theory in the case of these symbols (and the many others like them), which are not meant to be applicable to anything. The trouble with operationalism is that it doesn't even consider these types of symbols.

Although operationalism turns out to be an inadequate theory of meaning, it has one strong feature: it emphasizes the close connection between meaning and the rules governing the use of symbols. This emphasis will be important in our last theory of meaning.

2.4 *Meaning and Rules of Use*

Our last theory of meaning, the *rules of use theory*, departs from the definition of a symbol. Unlike natural signs, symbols have no intrinsic meaning. A symbol has meaning only because of the existence of rules governing its use; hence these rules are the meaning of the symbol.

In a way, this theory is an extension of the operationalist theory of meaning. The operationalist identified meaning with rules for operations to determine the applicability of the term. This new theory identifies meaning not only with this one type of rule but also with all types of rules governing the use of the word. For this reason it is known as the *rules of use* theory of meaning.

One important possible misconception about these rules must be cleared up immediately. The proponents of this theory do not make the absurd claim that for every symbol there is a set of rules of which we are all consciously aware and which was adopted by some sort of decision-making body at some earlier time. Such a claim would, of course, be false. All that is maintained is that there is such a set of rules followed by the users of the symbol by acting in accordance with them and by recognizing that a mistake has been made when someone does not act in accordance with them.

We can now set out the main theses of the rules of use theory as follows:

(1) A symbol has meaning if and only if there is a set of rules governing the use of the symbol.

(2) The meaning of the symbol is that set of rules governing its use; two symbols are synonymous when the rules governing their use are the same.

(3) One tells someone the meaning of a symbol when one tells him the rules governing its use.

To bring out fully the nature of this theory, let us give one or two examples of an analysis of the meaning of a symbol according to this theory.

Consider 'present Queen of England'. That symbol is a singular noun (this is a shorthand way of stating a lot of grammatical rules; we shall discuss this later) used to refer to that woman who, at the moment of the use of the symbol, is the titular ruler of England (this is a rule stating what the symbol is to be used to refer to). Consider 'it is not the case that'. This symbol can be put before whole sentences only (another grammatical rule) in order to form a new sentence that is true if and only if the original sentence was false (a rule about the truth of sentences beginning with this symbol).

As the previous two examples indicate, the rules governing the use of different symbols may be very different types of rules. Sometimes they are rules of reference; sometimes they are truth rules; sometimes they are. . . . This is a very important feature of this new approach: The rules of use theory has a flexibility that enables it to handle all different types of symbols—something the other theories simply could not do.

The rules of use theory has absolutely no trouble explaining the strong connection between the sense of a singular symbol and its reference, and that between the connotation of a general symbol and its denotation. For every singular symbol there presumably are rules indicating the reference of that symbol, and the object so indicated is its reference. Similarly, for every general symbol there are rules indicating the type of object denoted by that symbol, and the objects so indicated are the denotation of the symbol. The rules of use theory, furthermore, has no trouble explaining those facts that destroyed the referential theory of meaning; namely, the existence of symbols with meaning but with no reference or denotation, and the existence of nonsynonymous symbols with the same reference or denotation. The former phenomenon occurs when there are rules (perhaps even rules of reference or denotation) governing the use of the symbol but no object that the symbol refers to or denotes. The latter phenomenon occurs when there are, for each of the symbols, different rules indicating what object the symbol refers to or denotes, but, as a matter of fact, the object or objects so indicated are the same.

As it stands, the rules of use theory is not quite right. For there certainly are rules governing the use of a symbol that could not, by any stretch of the imagination, be considered part of the meaning of that symbol. For example, there are rules of politeness (certain symbols cannot be used in polite company or when ladies are present), rules of style (in writing poetry, do not use symbols of type A after symbols of type B because their sounds clash with each other), and so on. This objection is well taken, but not serious to the viability of the theory. As difficult as the task may be of setting out formally the differences between the rules that are part of the meaning of the symbols (rules of grammar, referring rules, etc.) and the rules that are not, we all can recognize the distinction and know which rules are being referred to by the adherents of the rules of use theory.

There are, of course, certain important distinctions even between those rules that are part of the meaning of the symbol, and we cannot leave our theory without noting at least one very central one; namely, the distinction between *syntactical rules* (or *grammatical rules*), *semantical rules*, and *pragmatic rules*. Syntactical rules are rules that govern the way a symbol can or cannot be combined with other symbols to form new symbols. Thus, when we said that 'present Queen of England' is a singular noun, we were simply using a shorthand way of expressing a lot of syntactical rules about it; for example, that it can combine with any symbol of the form is P (where P is replaced by any symbol that is an adjective) to form a new symbol of the type known as a sentence. These rules are syntactical rules since they simply prescribe how one can, or cannot, combine words to form sentences. Semantical rules are rules that indicate the thing(s) or type of thing(s) that are referred to or denoted by the symbol. Thus, when we said that 'the present Queen of England' is used to refer to that woman who, at the time of the use of the symbol, is the titular ruler of England, we were stating a semantical rule governing the symbol in question. Finally, pragmatic rules are rules that prescribe what should be true about the user of a symbol when he uses that symbol. Consider, for example, the use of the symbol 'why is it the case that'. If I ask 'why is it the case that Joe went home?' I should want to be given an explanation of the fact that he did go home; that is, the user of the symbol should want an explanation of the fact that p (where p is the fact described by the declarative sentence which immediately succeeds the use of the symbol 'why is it the case that').

It is sometimes thought that only semantical rules are really part of the meaning of a symbol. This is a great error, as is evident from the fact that there are many symbols (such as 'why is it the case that') which have no semantical rules governing their use because they are not used to refer to or to denote anything. The suspicion that only semantical rules are part of the meaning of a symbol is a vestigial legacy from the referential theory of meaning.

2.5 The Function of Definitions

We are often in a position of wanting to explain to someone else the meaning of a symbol. Let us call the process of explaining the meaning the process of *defining* that symbol, and let us call the explanation given the *definition* of the symbol offered. In this section, we shall consider a variety of conditions under which this process is carried out and the resulting standards of correctness for the definitions offered.

One thing is clear: Given the truth of the rules of use theory of meaning, any reasonable definition is going to be an account of the rules governing the use of the symbol. But doesn't that give us a simple account of when a definition is correct? Can't we simply say that a definition is correct when it states all those rules and only those rules that actually do govern the use of the symbol?

Although this seems obviously correct, further reflection reveals that it is only partially correct. There are, as we shall see, at least three different types of cases in which we offer definitions and this account is correct for only one of them. Let us look at each of these cases separately.

The simplest case, and the one for which this account is correct, is the case in which the symbol in question is already in use, there is nothing wrong with the way it is used, and the purpose of offering the definition is simply to explain its use to someone who does not know how the symbol is used. In such cases we are said to offer a *descriptive* definition of the symbol. And in such cases, the definition is correct when it does give all those rules and only those rules actually governing the use of the symbol in question.

Although it is easy enough to say when, in such cases, a definition is correct, it is not so easy to say, in a given case, whether the definition offered actually is correct, for it is often difficult to tell which rules actually govern the use of a particular symbol. Although you obviously examine how the symbol is used, you cannot merely look at that, for symbols are often misused (people do speak ungrammatically, etc.). What you must do is to look only at those cases in which the symbol is used correctly. But which cases are those? And do we count all uses of a symbol equally, or do we say that the way it is used by some people counts more than the way it is used by others? These questions, and others like them, pose many difficult practical problems for students of symbols (e.g., grammarians, lexicographers) trying to determine the rules actually governing the use of a given symbol. Nevertheless, as long as they are dealing with a descriptive definition, they know under what conditions a definition would be correct and under what conditions it would be incorrect.

A very different type of situation arises when the symbol in question is not already in use, and when the person defining the symbol is actually proposing or stipulating, depending upon his authority, that the new symbol be governed by a certain set of rules. Let us call the definitions offered in such cases *stipulative* definitions. There is really no notion of correctness involved here; so our simple theory of the correctness is not valid for this type of case.

Although stipulative definitions cannot be evaluated as correct or incorrect, there are standards for determining the appropriateness of proposals to adopt new symbols to be used in certain stipulated ways. In particular, such a proposal can be criticized on the grounds that it is:

(a) unnecessary—there may already be another symbol used in exactly the same way proposed for the new symbol, in which case there is no reason for preferring the new symbol to the old one;

(b) pointless—there are far too few cases in which there would be a need for a symbol to be used the way it is proposed that the new symbol be used; and for those few cases we have other ways of expressing what we want to express;

(c) cumbersome—the symbol is too long or too difficult to write, speak, or reproduce in some other manner;

(d) misleading—the symbol is so much like another one that if we adopt it, people are likely to confuse the two and think that one is being used when it is really the other that is being used;

(e) preempted—the symbol is already in use, governed by a different set of rules.

These are only some of the major ways in which stipulative definitions can be criticized. Thus, even if they are not open to the challenge of incorrectness, this does not mean that any stipulative definition is as good as any other.

As we look over this list and see the various conditions that must be met by any stipulative definition, we can see why they are needed in some cases. If there is something we want to express, and if there is no convenient way to do it with the symbols currently in use, and if we encounter this problem often enough, then we have a situation in which a new symbol, to be defined stipulatively, is called for.

There is, finally, a third type of definition, offered in a third type of case, with a third set of standards for evaluation. This is the *explicative* definition, which is offered for symbols whose use is not entirely satisfactory. The person offering the explicative definition is attempting to redefine the symbol in such a way as will correct the faults in its present use but will preserve as much as possible of the rules currently governing its use. Since this is the least familiar type of definition, it may be helpful to give a few examples.

One of the rules that seem to govern the use of 'true' is that all declarative sentences that can be used to assert that something is the case are either true or false. Now consider the following sentence:

> The sentence in this box is false.

Is it true or is it false? If it is true, then it is false, and if it is false, then it is true. The paradox we have here is due to the rules governing the use of 'true'. To avoid this paradox we must change the rules governing the use of 'true', redefining it by an explicative definition so that there can be sentences that are neither true nor false (thereby avoiding the paradox).

One of the rules that seem to govern the use of 'fish' is that it denotes all those creatures that normally live in water. This means that whales are fish. This conclusion is most inconvenient because, unlike most fish, whales are mammals, and laws that seem to hold for most fish do not hold for whales. It makes life much easier for biologists if 'fish' is redefined, by an explicative definition, so that it no longer includes whales in its denotation. So redefined, it is much easier to state scientific laws about all fishes.

As these two examples indicate, there can be many different types of shortcomings in the current use of a given symbol. These shortcomings range from leading to paradoxes to mere inconvenience. But all these different shortcomings may justify the use of an explicative definition. These examples also indicate that the rules to be changed may be syntactical, semantical, or pragmatic rules.

Obviously the standard of correctness for descriptive definitions— that it give all the rules and only those rules actually governing the use of the symbol in question—is not appropriate for explicative definitions. After all, the whole purpose of an explicative definition is to provide us with a new and better set of rules. How, then, do we evaluate such definitions?

Since their whole purpose is to avoid certain problems inherent in the current use of a symbol, we can certainly say that one requirement is that the problem which necessitated such a definition must be solved by the introduction of the new definition; that is, that the change in the rules governing the use of the symbols must be sufficient to ensure that the same problem does not recur. However, we must also remember that by offering an explicative definition, we are trying to fix up our symbol, not create a new one. So our second requirement for a satisfactory explicative definition is that it preserve as much as possible of the old rules governing the use of the symbol. Putting these two requirements together, we may state that the best explicative definition is the one that makes the fewest changes in the rules governing the use of the symbol while still solving the problem which necessitated the redefinition of the symbol.

2.6 Methods of Definition

In section 2.5 we looked at three different types of definitions and at the different standards for evaluating each type. In this final section we shall look at the methods employed in defining symbols. In a way, any method that can work, any method that enables you to satisfy the standards of the previous section, is satisfactory. But there are certain standards, frequently employed methods, and we will want to look briefly at each of them.

The most obvious method for defining a symbol is to say that it is synonymous with another symbol. What happens in such a case is that the person offering the definition is aware that the people to whom he is offering his definition of a symbol *A* know the rules governing the use of some symbol *B* that is synonymous with *A*. So he tells them that *A* is synonymous with *B*, and they then know what rules govern the use of *A* (they are the familiar rules governing the use of *B*).

One good example of the use of this method for defining symbols occurs when we learn a foreign language. When our teacher wants to define for us a symbol in that foreign language, he tells us what symbol in our own language it is synonymous with, and we then know the meaning of and the rules governing the use of that symbol in the foreign language.

This also occurs in our own language when there are two synonymous symbols in it. We can then define one by reference to the other. For instance, my dictionary defines 'touchdown' as 'a scoring play in football in which the ball is held on or over the opponent's goal line'.

There are, naturally, two requirements that must be met if this method of defining a symbol is to be successful in a given case. First, the two symbols must actually be synonymous. Unfortunately, there are many cases in which two symbols seem to be synonymous, and in which many people use one to define the other, but in which their definition (which is meant as a descriptive definition) is incorrect because the two symbols are not really synonymous. Even dictionaries are not immune to this type of error. Many dictionaries define 'bachelor' as 'unmarried male', thereby implying incorrectly that two-day-old males are bachelors. The two symbols are not really synonymous, since the latter is used to denote all unmarried males, whereas the former is only used to denote unmarried adult males. Second, the person to whom the definition is being offered must be aware of the meaning of the synonymous symbol. You cannot learn the meaning of *A* by being told that it is synonymous with *B* unless you already know what *B* means.

It is this second requirement that explains what is wrong with *circular definitions*, definitions of a symbol in terms of itself. One good example of such a definition is the ideational theory of meaning, which defines 'meaning of a symbol' as 'that idea which occurs in the mind of the user of the symbol when he is thinking about the meaning of the symbol'. The trouble with such definitions is that the person for whom the definition is being offered (who does not, therefore, know the meaning of the symbol being defined) will not be aware of the meaning of the synonymous symbol, since it contains the very symbol being defined. In our example the person for whom we are trying to define 'meaning of a symbol' would not understand 'that idea which occurs in the mind of the speaker when he is thinking about the meaning of the symbol' since it contains the mysterious phrase 'meaning of the symbol'. Consequently, such a definition is useless.

A second method of defining a symbol is simply to offer a description of the rules governing its use. This method raises few theoretical issues, but there are many problems about the form such descriptions must take. These issues are technical ones involving the study of syntax and semantics, and we shall not consider them now.

A third technique of defining symbols, on the other hand, raises many theoretical issues. What is distinctive about this technique is that in the course of offering the definition, one points to, or uses some other method to call attention to, the object referred to by the symbol or an object which is part of the denotation of the symbol. When one uses this technique, one is said to have offered an *ostensive* definition of the symbol.

Let us imagine that we were trying to define 'red'. How would we do this? Since there doesn't seem to be a synonym for it, we can't use our first technique. And we cannot simply describe the rules governing its use. If we tried, we would come up with a statement such as 'it is an adjective that denotes all . . . ', in which it is unclear what should finish the sentence. What we must do is define it as follows: 'red' is an adjective denoting all objects that have the same color as *a*, *b*, *c* (pointing to, or indicating by some other means, the objects *a*, *b*, and *c*). In other words, to define symbols like 'red', we seem to need ostensive definitions.

But the use of ostensive definitions need not be confined to cases in which it is clearly needed; we often seem to use that technique even when others are available, simply because it seems more convenient or because we think that the person for whom the word is being defined will get the point quicker that way. There is nothing wrong with this; we are, as I mentioned at the outset of this section, entitled to use any technique of defining that works.

Several important misconceptions about ostensive definitions should be avoided. These include the following:

(1) that the essential thing which makes this method work is the physical pointing. Actually, the physical pointing is only one way of indicating which objects are the *a*, *b*, and *c* being used as your example of the denotation of the symbol. Any other method of indicating this will also work. Thus, my dictionary, which defines red as 'of a bright color resembling blood', is defining 'red' ostensively; it indicates which objects are the examples of the denotation, not by pointing but simply by saying that they are the color of blood (drops of blood, etc.).

(2) that it is possible to define any symbol ostensively, that we could learn our whole language that way. Actually, the only symbols that can be so defined are symbols used to refer to or denote a specific thing(s). For it is only of such symbols that one can indicate either the object referred to by the symbol or a part of the denotation of the symbol. The view that all symbols can be defined ostensively is based upon the mistaken belief that all symbols are used to refer to or denote objects.

We said previously that many important theoretical issues were raised by this technique of defining symbols. Let us see what these are. First, we have seen that only some symbols—those used to refer to or to denote objects—can be defined ostensively. Among those that can, there seem to be some (such as 'red') that must be so defined, whereas there seem to be others (such as 'house') that could be defined otherwise. Why is this so? Second, many thinkers have claimed (with some plausibility) that ostensive definitions play a fundamental role in language learning—that we must first learn the meaning of many symbols ostensively before we can learn the meaning of symbols by other means. Is this so; and if it is, why? Finally, and this is intimately connected with our first two questions, how much of our language could we learn without the use of ostensive definitions? We cannot enter into all these questions here; our purpose now is merely to note their existence.

It is not surprising that so many questions of this type have been raised about ostensive definitions. To many it seems intuitively to be the one technique of definition that "hooks up," that connects, our symbols to the world around us. But such issues belong more to the fields of psychology and theories of knowledge than to logic; from the perspective of logic, ostensive definitions are just one way of defining a symbol, of describing the rules governing the use of a symbol.

EXERCISES FOR CHAPTER 2

Part I

A. Which of the following are natural signs and which are symbols?

1. a photograph of a house
2. a realistic picture of that house
3. an abstract picture of that house
4. the architect's blueprint for the house
5. a scale model of the house
6. the name by which the house is usually called

B. Which of the following are singular symbols and which are general symbols?

1. the first astronaut
2. an astronaut
3. astronaut
4. the class of astronauts
5. state
6. the state of Massachusetts
7. the United States
8. the cattle
9. the herd of cattle
10. snow
11. the pile of snow

C. Do the following pairs of symbols have the same reference or the same denotation or the same sense or the same connotation or none of the above?
   1. bachelor—an adult male who has never married
   2. George Washington—first President of the United States
   3. creature with a heart—creature with a lung
   4. present Queen of England—woman who now occupies the throne of Great Britain
   5. human being—animal
   6. three—odd number
   7. logic text book—book I am now reading
   8. unicorn—centaur

D. Let us say that a symbol fails to refer if it has no denotation or no reference. Which of the following symbols fail to refer?
   1. Pegasus
   2. centaur
   3. the concept of a centaur
   4. the first number
   5. the last number
   6. the only American President
   7. square circle
   8. the belief that a square circle is square
   9. ghost
   10. picture of a ghost

E. What images, if any, are found in your mind in connection with the following symbols? What ideas, if any, are found in your mind in connection with the symbols? How and why do they differ?
   1. blue
   2. house
   3. run
   4. two
   5. justice
   6. hello
   7. electron
   8. George Washington

F. What operations can be performed to determine whether the following symbols are applicable to a given object, situation, event, etc.? In light of your answer, explain why, according to the operationalist theory of meaning, the symbol in question has the reference or denotation that it does.
   1. blue
   2. six feet tall
   3. very intelligent
   4. sympathetic
   5. breakable
   6. true
   7. beautiful

8. just
9. chair
10. atom
11. gene
12. ego

G. What are the rules governing the use of the following symbols? Does the account of these rules seem to be a satisfactory account of the meaning of these symbols?
1. tall
2. pungent
3. house
4. atom
5. hits
6. loves
7. beauty
8. righteousness
9. why
10. how
11. is
12. all
13. please
14. no
15. George Washington
16. the United States

H. Which of the following are syntactic rules, which are semantic rules, and which are pragmatic rules?
1. 'house' is a noun.
2. 'I command' should be used only by people in positions of authority.
3. '2' refers to the number that follows one.
4. 'George Washington' is a name of any man of the Washington family who is called 'George'.
5. 'it is not the case' can be placed before certain sentences to form a new sentence.
6. 'please' is used when one wants to be polite.
7. 'why' is used in forming questions.
8. 'horse' names horses.

I. Are the following definitions most plausible when understood as descriptive definitions, as stipulative definitions, or as explicative definitions?
1. 'just' has the same meaning as 'proportional to what is deserved'.
2. 'handy' has the same meaning as 'convenient'.
3. 'blue' has the same meaning as 'of a color similar to the color of the sky on a clear day'.
4. 'sentence', in this context, will have the same meaning as 'a string of words'.
5. 'word' means the same thing as 'any single symbol which has a meaning'.

J. Consult your dictionary to see how it defines the following symbols. Determine, in each case whether it defines it by offering a synonym, by describing the rules governing its use, or by using an ostensive definition.
1. bachelor
2. why
3. yellow
4. and
5. house
6. just
7. kinetic energy
8. indeed
9. government
10. soft
11. thing
12. cause

K. Which, if any, of the following definitions are circular definitions?
1. 'horseman' is used to refer to any man who regularly and expertly rides horses.
2. 'wooden Indian' is used to refer to any sculpture of an Indian in wood.
3. 'man' is used to refer to all animals that have the characteristic features of men.
4. 'underpay' means the same thing as 'pay under that amount that one should pay'.

L. Which, if any, of the following symbols can only be defined ostensively?
1. pungent
2. house
3. thing
4. yellow
5. justice
6. man
7. love
8. number

Part II

1. It is often believed that although practically all words are symbols, there are a few words, such as 'hiccup' and 'cuckoo', that are natural signs. Is this belief true?

2. The following street sign in Pisa might seem like an obvious example of a natural sign saying which direction you go to reach the Leaning Tower:

But is it really? After all, it is only a convention that says that it is the head of the arrow, and not its tail, that indicates the direction in which you should travel. Is this argument correct?

3. In the text we argued against the referential theory on the grounds that there are symbols with different meaning but with the same reference (or denotation). Critically evaluate the following reply to that objection. All that we must do to save the referential theory is to modify it so that it claims that the meaning of a symbol is its ordinary reference (or denotation) and its secondary reference or denotation where the secondary reference or denotation of a symbol is the pictures of its ordinary reference (or denotation).

4. If, as we have seen, an idea is not an image (a mental picture), then what makes an idea of some property *P* an idea of that property and not an idea of something else?

5. Critically evaluate the following *behavioral theory of meaning:* The meaning of a symbol is those common features of the situation in which the symbol is used.

6. How would you draw the distinction between those rules governing the use of a symbol which are part of the meaning of the symbol and those rules (e.g., rules of politeness) which are not?

7. Consider the following rule governing the use of 'and': When 'and' is placed between two declarative sentences to form a new declarative sentence, the statement expressed by the new sentence is true if and only if the statement expressed by both of the original sentences is true. Is this rule a syntactical rule, a semantical rule, or a pragmatic rule?

8. We saw that in trying to determine what rules actually govern the use of a symbol, one only examines cases in which the symbol is correctly used. How do we determine, before we know the rules governing the use of the symbol, which cases those are?

9. In scientific texts one finds a great many stipulative definitions. Why is this so?

10. Critically evaluate the following argument: A symbol, unlike a natural sign, has no intrinsic meaning; we are free to give it any meaning we want. Hence, all our talk in the text about correct and incorrect definitions is really meaningless.

11. Consider the following argument that purports to prove that it is impossible to define a symbol: When we define a symbol, we have to use other symbols. In defining those symbols, we have to use still other symbols. Eventually, since the number of symbols is limited, we will have to return to our original symbols. Consequently, the whole set of definitions will be circular and therefore useless.

12. Can you explain why some symbols can only be defined ostensively, whereas others can be defined both ostensively and nonostensively?

CHAPTER

3

Problems about

Meaning

In Chapter 2 we set out a theory about the meanings of symbols and about the way we can explain those meanings to others. It all seemed very simple. For every meaningful symbol there was a set of rules governing its use (these rules are the meaning of the symbol), and one explained the meaning of a symbol when one explained the rules governing its use.

Actually, it is not that simple. For some symbols, there seem to be different and even conflicting rules governing their use. For other symbols, the rules don't seem to be adequate, since they leave it unclear, in many cases, whether the symbol is correctly used. For still other symbols, the rules don't seem to capture all that is expressed by the use of the symbol. In this chapter we shall examine these problems about meaning, find their causes and effects on our thinking, and see whether we can devise methods to ensure that we will not be misled by these shortcomings in our symbols.

3.1 Ambiguity and Equivocity

Let us imagine that someone asked you for a definition of 'fork'. What would you tell him? You might say that 'fork' is a noun denoting all instruments with a handle and two or more prongs used for handling food. This seems right. But what about the fork in the road? If it is a piece of silverware that someone dropped, okay. But if, as is more likely, it is a place where the road branches, then it isn't an instrument with a handle and two

32

or more prongs; yet it seems to be part of the denotation of 'fork'. Should we conclude that your account is wrong? Should we conclude that 'fork' is being misused when it denotes a fork in the road? Neither of these seems like the right move.

The obvious way to describe the situation is as follows: The symbol in question, 'fork', is *equivocal* (it has two or more meanings). This is so because there are more than one set of rules governing its use. According to one set of rules, it is a noun denoting an instrument with a handle and two or more prongs used for handling food. According to the other set of rules, it is a noun denoting the place at which a road, stream, and so on, splits into two roads, or streams, which continue on in different directions.

Although the symbol is equivocal, we usually know, when it is used in a given case, what is meant. Thus, when my wife says that we're missing one of our good forks, I know what she means by 'fork' (which rules govern that use of the symbol). Hence, we can say that her use of the symbol in that case is unambiguous: The use of an equivocal symbol is *unambiguous* when it is clear which meaning of the symbol the user intends it to have in that case; the use of an equivocal symbol is *ambiguous* only when it is unclear which meaning of the symbol the user intends it to have in that case. In the case of 'fork', one has to use some imagination to construct an ambiguous usage. For example, I have just moved into a new apartment, doing the job myself, and quite a number of things have dropped in the road. My wife is helping me bring them in, but she has to stop to take the kids to a friend's house. She's not too sure about the way. Suddenly she says to me, "Are there any forks in the road?" In this case the use of 'fork' is ambiguous, for it is unclear whether, worried about getting lost, she wants to know if there are any forks in the road she has to take to the friend's house, or, worried about her silverware, she wants to know if I dropped her good forks in the road.

It should be clear, once the distinction between equivocity and ambiguity is noted, that equivocity per se is not a problem. If a symbol is equivocal but its every use (or practically every use) is unambiguous, then we have practically no problems in communicating when using this symbol. Thus, although 'fork' is equivocal, we have practically no problem using this symbol in communication, since, in the overwhelming majority of cases in which it is used, it is unambiguous. The only time we have problems with equivocal symbols is when their uses are ambiguous. In other words, it is ambiguity, not equivocity, that causes problems for communication and should be eliminated. We should be bothered by, and attempt to eliminate, equivocity only if it is likely to lead to ambiguity.

The problems into which ambiguity can lead us should not be underestimated. Besides the difficulties in communication already discussed, we are often misled by ambiguity into accepting proofs that are really fallacious. Consider the following "proofs" of disputed claims, none of which prove anything but all of which have seemed plausible:

Everything has a cause.
So there is some object that causes everything else.
This cause is God.

My sensations exist only while I exist.
What I experience is my sensations.
Therefore, what I experience exists only while I exist.

That building across the way is one of the things that I have experienced.
Therefore, that building exists only while I exist.

In the first argument the first statement is ambiguous. It might mean that for everything that occurs, there is something (not necessarily the same thing) that caused it to occur. Or it might mean that there is some one thing that caused everything else to occur. We all agree with the first statement in the argument because we have in mind the first meaning. But then the proponents of the argument switch to the second meaning and claim that there is therefore one thing which causes everything else. If they had kept to the first meaning, we would never assent to their drawing their conclusion. In other words, we assent to the first statement thinking it means one thing, and assent to the move from it to the second statement because we think it means something else. If the first statement were not ambiguous in this case, we would never be fooled by this argument.

A similar thing happens in the second argument. 'Sensation' is an equivocal symbol: it might mean 'the act of sensing', or it might mean 'that which is sensed'. When we are presented with this argument, we cannot be sure which is meant; 'sensation' is ambiguous here. Now, when we agree with the first claim, we do so because we think it means that if I don't exist, then none of my acts of sensing exist either. But we agree with the second claim only because we think it means that what I experience is that which I sense. Once more, we would never be fooled by this argument if 'sensation' were not used ambiguously.

Because ambiguity can lead to problems in communication, and because it can also lead us to accept arguments and proofs that really prove nothing, it would apparently be a good idea to eliminate all ambiguities. But that is not such an easy task, for some types of ambiguities are more difficult to get rid of than others.

To see why this is so, let us consider the following proposal to eliminate ambiguities: We will eliminate ambiguity by getting rid of all equivocal symbols (or perhaps only those which might be used ambiguously). Now, let us divide symbols into two groups, the simple symbols (those not made up of other symbols—in ordinary languages these are usually the words) and the complex symbols (those made up of other symbols—in ordinary languages these are such things as phrases, clauses, and sentences). It would seem that if we simply got rid of all equivocal simple symbols, replacing them with a different symbol for each meaning of the old symbol, then we would have no equivocal symbols left, and there would be no possible ambiguous uses of symbols.

The intuitive idea behind this proposal is very simple. The equivocity of complex symbols, such as, 'Are there any forks in the road?' and 'My sensations exist only when I exist' is due to the equivocity of simple symbols in them ('fork' and 'sensations'). Thus, if we make sure that all simple symbols are not equivocal, then we will have no equivocal complex symbols either. Then, since there will be no equivocal symbols at all, there will be no possibility of ambiguity.

Unfortunately, this proposal will not do, because there are complex equivocal symbols the uses of which are often ambiguous and all of whose constitutent simple symbols are unequivocal. One good example is 'everything has a cause'. Although it is equivocal, and, in the context of the argument we were considering, ambiguous, none of its symbols are equivocal. Or, as another example, consider the equivocity of 'I would like either to go home or to go the movies and meet John'. None of the simple symbols in it are equivocal; yet the whole symbol is, for it might mean that I would like to do one of the first two and the last of the things mentioned, or it might mean that I would like to do either the first or the second and the third things mentioned. And, in a given case in which that symbol is used, it might be unclear which meaning is intended.

In other words, there are two very different types of equivocal complex symbols: One type, which would be eliminated by our proposal, consists in the equivocal complex symbols whose equivocity is due to the equivocity of simple symbols occurring in them. The other type consists in those complex equivocal symbols all of whose constituent simple symbols are unequivocal, and whose equivocity is due rather to the way the simple symbols are put together to form the complex symbol. It is this second type of equivocity that is not so easy to get rid of; the best that we can do is to handle it one case at a time. Thus, we can get rid of the equivocity of 'I would like either to go home or to go to the movies and meet John' by eliminating it as a symbol and replacing it with the following two different, and unequivocal, substitutes: 'I would like to go home or (go to the movies and meet John)' and 'I would like to (go home or go to the movies) and meet John'.

Of course, we will need a different technique to handle the equivocity of 'everything has a cause'. We might eliminate it as a symbol and replace it with the following two different, and unequivocal, substitutes: 'There is one thing that causes everything else', and 'everything is caused, but not necessarily by the same thing'.

We can summarize our discussion of ambiguity and equivocity so far as follows:

(1) Not every use of an equivocal symbol is ambiguous.

(2) Only the ambiguous uses of equivocal symbols lead to difficulties in communication and mistakes in reasoning.

(3) We could avoid many of these difficulties and mistakes by eliminating all equivocal simple symbols, but some will remain because of the existence of equivocal complex symbols, which can be used ambiguously and all of whose constituent simple symbols are unequivocal.

3.2 The Equivocity of Use and Mention and of Referential Opacity

In section 3.1 we were concerned with the type of equivocity that one symbol might have and another symbol might not. In this section, we will deal with two types of equivocity that seem to be present in all symbols ordinarily used.

Consider the following two sentences:

Cicero was a Roman author.
Cicero has six letters in it.

It is clear that 'Cicero' does not mean the same thing in these two sentences. In the first case 'Cicero' is a symbol referring to a famous Roman orator who was also called Tully. In the second case 'Cicero' is a symbol referring to a name of a famous Roman orator who was also called Tully. So 'Cicero' is equivocal.

What we see in this case is a symbol sometimes used in its normal way and sometimes used to refer to itself. We shall say that when used with its normal meaning, the symbol is being *used*, but that when used to refer to itself, the symbol is being *mentioned*.

This phenomenon is very common. Indeed, this type of equivocity seems to be present in every symbol. For when we want to talk about the symbol, we always seem to have the option of indicating which symbol we mean by mentioning it.

There is an important convention for eliminating this type of equivocity; indeed, we have been using it so far throughout this book. The convention is that we never mention a symbol—we only use it. When we would ordinarily mention the symbol, following this convention, we refer to it by the use of a different symbol: the ordinary symbol with single quotes around it. Thus, according to this convention, we must replace:

Cicero has six letters in it

(in which 'Cicero' is mentioned) by:

'Cicero' has six letters in it

where no symbol is mentioned. "Cicero", the new symbol in that sentence, is being *used* since its normal use is to refer to 'Cicero'. It is not being *mentioned*, since it refers not to itself but to 'Cicero'.

Let us consider one more example to help make the convention clear. Consider the following normal symbol:

John went home is an English sentence.

In this symbol 'John went home' is being mentioned and not used, since it is not being used normally but to refer to itself. According to our convention, this should not occur. So we replace that symbol with:

'John went home' is an English sentence.

In this new symbol all the constituent symbols are being used and not mentioned. Even the first constituent symbol ("John went home") is being used and not mentioned, since it refers not to itself but to our original equivocal symbol ('John went home').

So the equivocity of use and mention can be eliminated: But why should we care about this equivocity? In the section 3.1 we saw that there was nothing wrong with equivocity per se—that equivocity was bad only if it was likely to lead to ambiguity. And it seems unlikely that the equivocity of use and mention will lead to any ambiguity. After all, in all our examples, it was clear whether the symbol was being used or mentioned; there was no ambiguity about that.

This objection is good. It shows that the purpose of eliminating the use–mention equivocity cannot be the same as the purpose of eliminating ordinary equivocities. In ordinary communiation, there are few (if any) cases in which it is ambiguous whether a symbol is being used or mentioned. There are, however, special reasons, connected with certain vexing philosophical issues, for wanting to eliminate that equivocity.

Some of the most puzzling philosophical issues are the metaphysical issues. For example, in mathematics we constantly talk about numbers, their properties, and so on. Philosophers and mathematicians who have reflected upon the nature of mathematics have found all this talk very puzzling, especially the nature of these numbers. Are they things, like chairs and tables, except that they are not visible and not in space or time? Or are they something else (mental constructs, symbols, etc.)? Despite whatever has been said about such metaphysical questions they remain as puzzling as ever. Now it is in connection with just this type of problem that many philosophers have felt it important to clear up the equivocity of use and mention. They believe that two very different types of questions are being confused here. One is the question of whether numbers are things. The other is the question of whether 'the number four' (and other symbols used to refer to numbers) is a thing-symbol, governed by the same type of rules as those governing the use of words clearly referring to ordinary things. The former question, according to these philosophers, is a dubious question because it is unclear how we should go about answering it, whereas the latter question is a perfectly reasonable question for linguists to investigate.

In other words, the purpose of systematically eliminating the equivocity between use and mention is to help systematically draw the line between talk about symbols and talk about something other than symbols. Once this line is drawn, then, we will be able to distinguish between the meaningful linguistic issues and the dubious metaphysical issues.

Not all philosophers agree with this view that the nonlinguistic metaphysical issues are somehow dubious. But they all agree that it is extremely important to distinguish these two issues, so that each can be dealt with in the way appropriate to it.

The equivocity of use and mention, as we have just seen, is one that rarely confuses us; in ordinary cases we almost always know whether the symbol is being used or mentioned. In our second type of pervasive equivocity, the equivocity of referential opacity, the situation is very different. If it exists, this equivocity is so subtle that we are practically never aware of it.

The easiest way to explain this type of equivocity is to begin with an example. Let us imagine that Joe, who is in trouble with the college administration, is looking for his best friend on the faculty, Professor Hinckledink. Let us also imagine that Joe is not looking for the head of the college disciplinary committee. Finally, let us imagine that, unbeknown to Joe, Professor Hinckledink has recently been appointed the head of that committee. Then in our case, it is true that:

(1) Joe is looking for Professor Hinckledink.
(2) Joe is not looking for the head of the college disciplinary committee.
(3) Professor Hinckledink is the head of the college disciplinary committee.

Something is wrong here. After all, according to (1), there is a certain person for whom Joe is looking. According to (2), there is a certain person for whom Joe is not looking. But according to (3), those persons are the same person. So it looks as though it is both true and false that Joe is looking for a certain person, which seems puzzling.

Now, it has been suggested that the solution to this problem is to recognize that in (1) and (2) neither 'Professor Hinckledink' nor 'head of the college disciplinary committee' is being used to refer to some person. In the contexts of (1) and (2), such symbols are not used to refer to what they ordinarily refer. This solves the problem [although it leaves open the question, which we shall not now consider, of what those symbols are used for in (1) and (2)], because, according to this view, (1) and (2) are not talking about that professor, and they do not therefore say that it is either true or false that Joe is looking for him.

In this type of case, in which there occurs a symbol *A* normally used to refer to (or to denote) a certain object (or objects) and in which—if you substitute for *A* another symbol *B* that normally refers to (or denotes) the same object (or objects)—the resulting sentence may have a different truth-value than the original sentence, we say that this occurrence of the symbol *A* is *referentially opaque*.

What has all this to do with equivocity? Let's consider 'head of the college disciplinary committee'. We would normally and accurately say that this symbol refers to a certain person. But if we adopt the solution that in referentially opaque occurrences of the symbol it is not used to refer to that person, then 'head of the college disciplinary committee' will be an equivocal symbol, sometimes used in one way and sometimes in another.

Let us look at another example that helps bring out this point. 'Nine' is a symbol used to refer to that number greater than eight and smaller than ten. However, in referentially opaque occurrences of this symbol, it cannot be so used. After all, consider, the following three true sentences:

(1') Nine is necessarily greater than seven.
(2') The number of planets is not necessarily greater than seven.
(3') The number of planets is nine.

Once more, (1') seems to say that it is true that a certain number is necessarily greater than seven; (2') seems to say that it is not true that a certain number is necessarily greater than seven; and (3') tells us that those numbers are the same number. So it seems as though it is both true and false that that number is necessarily greater than seven, which seems puzzling.

It is clear enough that in both (1') and (2') the occurrence of 'nine' and of 'the number of planets' is a referentially opaque occurrence of those symbols. Now, we can solve the problem posed by the truth of (1')–(3') by saying that in these referentially opaque occurrences neither 'nine' nor 'the number of planets' refers to that number greater than eight and smaller than ten. Therefore, neither (1') nor (2') is talking about that number, and neither says that this number is either necessarily greater or not necessarily greater than seven. Again this leaves open the problem of how those symbols are being used in those contexts, but we leave that problem aside for now. In any case if we adopt that solution, then 'nine' and 'the number of planets' will be equivocal symbols, sometimes used to refer to a certain number and sometimes used in some other way.

There are several important differences between the equivocity of use and mention and the possible equivocity of referential opacity:

(a) There is no doubt about the existence of the use–mention equivocity. But there is some doubt as to whether symbols do have a different meaning when used in referentially opaque contexts. They do have a different meaning if the solution we are considering to the problem posed by opaque contexts is correct. But there may be a better solution—one that does not presuppose the symbols to mean something else in that context, but rather supposes that, in referentially opaque contexts, the symbols refer to (or denote) what they ordinarily refer to (or denote). If there is such an alternative superior solution, then the equivocity of referentially opaque concepts might not exist at all.

(b) The use–mention equivocity exists in the case of every symbol, for every symbol can be used in its normal way and can be mentioned; that is, used to refer to itself. But the referential opacity equivocity, if it exists at all, can only exist in the case of symbols used to refer to (or to denote) things, for only such symbols can occur in referentially opaque contexts.

3.3 Vagueness

We turn now to another feature of symbols that complicated the discussion in Chapter 2 about the meaning of symbols. According to our previous picture, for each symbol there are rules governing its use that indicate to what object it refers. If there is any question about the reference of the symbol, it exists only because we have not yet determined, by the appropriate means, which object is so indicated. Thus, 'present Queen of England' refers, according to the rules governing its use, to that woman who at the time the symbol is used is the titular ruler of England; if there is any question of who is referred to by 'present Queen of England', it can be resolved by an empirical investigation that determines who that woman is. Similarly, we previously supposed that every symbol which denotes some objects has a rule governing its use, indicating what objects the symbol denotes. If there is any question about the denotation of the symbol, it exists only because we have not yet determined, by the appropriate means, which objects are so indicated. Thus, 'prime number' denotes all numbers divisible only by themselves and one; if there is any question about whether some number is really a prime number, it exists only because we have not yet carried out the appropriate tests (attempting to divide it by other numbers) to determine whether it is prime.

This picture is oversimplified. As we shall see in this section, it is a feature of many symbols which denote or refer that the denotation or reference of those symbols is not fixed entirely by the rules governing their use, that there are cases in which, no matter what tests we run, we cannot determine whether something is part of the denotation of the symbol nor whether something is the reference (or part of the reference) of the symbol. This feature of these symbols is known as their *vagueness*.

Let us begin by considering the case of general symbols that denote many objects. Consider 'blue'. It denotes all objects having a color similar to the color of the sky on a clear day. And, of course, it does not denote objects that are purple in color. But aren't there many objects whose color somewhat resembles the color of the sky but whose color also somewhat resembles the color of clearly purple objects? Are these objects blue, or are they purple? Are they part of the denotation of 'blue', or are they part of the denotation of 'purple'? Do we have means other than an artificial fiat to answer this question? If the answer to the latter question is no, as it seems to be, then we can conclude that symbols such as 'blue' and 'purple' are vague.

Let us take as another example 'liberal' (in the political sense). In that sense 'liberal' denotes those people who favor extensive governmental intervention to aid the underprivileged and who believe that the government should take strong steps to eliminate discrimination and other social ills. On the other hand, 'conservative' denotes those people who believe that the ending of discrimination can only be accomplished through changes in individual attitudes and that governmental intervention in that area is inappropriate, and who believe that the underprivileged are ultimately better aided by the operation of a free economy and the freely granted help of individuals.

Now let us consider Senator Jones, who usually behaves like a liberal except on issues of discrimination. We can certainly say about him that he is a liberal on some issues and a conservative on others, but is he a liberal or a conservative? What further tests can we run to answer this question? Or do we have here, once more, a question that cannot be answered except by artificial fiat? If the answer to the latter question is yes, as it seems to be, then we can conclude that symbols such as 'liberal' and 'conservative' are vague.

Both 'blue' and 'liberal' have rules governing their use that indicate which objects are part of their denotation. In many cases, after the appropriate tests, there is no doubt that the object in question is blue or is liberal. But in other cases doubt still remains, which is why these symbols are vague.

There is, however, an important difference between these two types of vagueness. In the case of 'liberal', there are many conditions a person must satisfy to be called a liberal. The symbol 'liberal' is vague because given the rules governing the use of the symbol, it is not clear how many and/or which of these conditions you can fail to satisfy and still be a liberal. Senator Jones fails to meet only one condition, but it is an important one; therefore, it is unclear whether he can be considered a liberal. In the case of 'blue', the cause of vagueness is different. An object need not satisfy several conditions if it is to be part of the denotation of 'blue'; it merely has to have a color that sufficiently resembles that of the sky on a clear day. But resemblance is not an all-or-nothing affair. The color of some objects more closely resembles the color of a sky on a clear day than does that of some others. How closely does the color of an object have to resemble the color of a sky on a clear day before the object is blue? Because the answer to that question is not given precisely and exactly by the rules governing the use of 'blue', 'blue' is vague.

So much for the vagueness of general symbols denoting many objects. Let us now begin our consideration of the vagueness of singular symbols, which refer to only one object, by considering an example—'the oldest liberal senator'. According to the rules governing the use of that symbol, it refers to that member of the United States Senate who is a liberal and who was born before all other liberal members of the United States Senate. Given the vagueness of 'liberal', it is easy to see how this term might also be vague. If the oldest member of the Senate who is not clearly a conservative, Senator *A*, is one of those people about whom one cannot say, because of the vagueness of 'liberal', whether he is a liberal, then it is unclear whether 'the oldest liberal senator' refers to Senator *A* or to someone else. Moreover, given the fact that there are no tests which will enable us to determine whether Senator *A* is a liberal, there will also be no tests which will enable us to determine whether it is he that is referred to by 'the oldest liberal senator'. In such a case, then, the singular symbol is vague.

The vagueness of 'the oldest liberal senator' is clearly due to, and dependent upon, the vagueness of a general symbol, 'liberal'. It is a vagueness about what object is referred to by the symbol. Yet there is another type of vagueness, not based upon the vagueness of a general symbol, in which the reference of the symbol is clear. In this second type the vagueness is based upon an unclarity about the extent of the reference of the symbol. Let us begin once more by considering some examples.

To what does 'Midwest' (when used to refer to a region of the United States) refer? According to the rules governing its use, it refers to a region of the United States that certainly includes Illinois, Indiana, Iowa, and Kansas. But what about Kentucky? Or Missouri? Again, to what does 'modern history' refer? It certainly refers to the course of events from 1600 on, but does it include the Reformation as well? If so, does it include the whole Renaissance (from its first stirrings centuries before the Reformation)? In these cases we know, in one sense, the reference of the symbol, but we don't know how far that reference extends spatially or temporally.

There are still other cases of the vagueness of singular symbols. Consider 'the watch I bought fifteen years ago'. Does it refer to the watch I now use? I've never bought a new watch, but at one time or another, I've re-placed almost every part of the watch I bought fifteen years ago. Is this watch I now use the same watch I bought fifteen years ago? The answer to that question is unclear, so it's unclear whether the watch I now use is the reference of 'the watch I bought fifteen years ago'. In other words, in this case (and others like it), I know to what the symbol refers but there are still questions about the reference of the symbol which there are no means to answer because there are unanswerable questions about what is identical with the reference of the symbol.

It is clear by now that there are many different types of vagueness. Some symbols may be vague in one way but not in another. The question that we must now consider is whether this feature of symbols is good or bad. Vagueness is often considered an undesirable feature of symbols; perhaps we would be better off if none of our symbols were vague. It is easy to see, more-over, why people think that this is true. When we use vague symbols in communicating, we leave many unanswered questions about what we are saying. When, for example, I read an advertisement asking me to contribute to a fund supporting the reelection of liberal senators, I do not know whether it will be helping Senator Jones in his reelection campaign. Or if I want to study early Renaissance history, and I am told that a certain school specializes in all aspects of modern history, I do not know whether that school will be good for my interests. Wouldn't it be much better if these questions were not left unanswered? If you think they should not be left unanswered, then you see why we should eliminate vague symbols; it is the only way we can get rid of the unanswered questions.

Although this argument seems persuasive, further reflection shows that the situation is not so simple. There are many cases in which we prefer that some of the questions be left unanswered. In disciplining a child, for example, a parent may want to say, 'If you do this again, you will be punished severely', but not be pinned down as to exactly what 'severely' means. Indeed, this is true of all types of warnings, demands, requests, and so forth. In all these cases, a little vagueness allows one to have a way out, to have some options, if things don't work out exactly as planned.

Once we remember that precision is not always desirable, that there may be many cases in which it is better if we leave questions unanswered, our whole approach to vagueness changes. We now realize that it is only in some contexts that it should be eliminated, that whether or not it should be eliminated (and the extent to which it should be eliminated) depends upon whether (and the extent to which) we need to be more precise in a given con-text, and that a wholesale reform of our language to eliminate all vagueness would not be desirable.

How does one go about eliminating vagueness? There doesn't seem to be one answer to this question. It depends upon the nature of the vagueness and the degree of precision desired. But if we look at how one might eliminate those types of vagueness we have been discussing, we find certain recurring features.

In the case of 'liberal', one could eliminate the vagueness by specifying what positions the man must hold on certain key issues and/or in what percentage of the cases he must agree with the positions associated with liberalism. Thus, one might specify that no one could be called a liberal unless he holds certain views and/or unless, on a given (percentage) of issues, he holds views associated with liberalism. More generally, when the vagueness is due to an unclarity about how many of a set of conditions an object must satisfy in order to be part of the denotation of the symbol, one can eliminate that vagueness by specifying precisely which, if any, of these conditions the object must satisfy and/or what percentage of the rest it must fulfill.

In the case of 'blue', a different technique is required, for we have to find a way of specifying the extent to which the color of an object must be like the color of a clear sky before the object is part of the denotation of 'blue'. How can this be done? Scientists have discovered that objects of different colors reflect light of different wavelengths. Therefore, to eliminate the vagueness of 'blue', we need only specify the extent to which the wavelength of the light reflected by an object can differ from the wavelength of the light reflected by a clear sky and still remain blue. More generally, when the vagueness of a symbol is due to the unclarity about the extent to which an object can deviate from a standard example of the denotation and still remain part of the denotation of the symbol, we can eliminate this vagueness by finding a way to measure the extent of the deviation and by specifying what degree of deviation is allowed.

The vagueness of 'Midwest' and 'modern history' can be eliminated by specifying more precisely the spatial and/or temporal extent of their reference. The degree of preciseness with which these boundaries should be specified is a function of the degree of precision that you require. More generally, you can eliminate the vagueness of symbols due to unclarities in the spatio-temporal extent of their reference by specifying more precisely the boundaries of its extent.

Perhaps the most difficult vagueness to eliminate is the type we found present in 'the watch I bought fifteen years ago'. We must specify the conditions under which another watch is identical with that watch. Must it have the same parts as that watch had? If so, my watch now is not identical with it and is not the reference of that symbol. If that overly strict requirement is dropped, then my watch now may be identical with it and may be the reference of the symbol. More generally, if the vagueness in the reference of a symbol is due to an unclarity about questions of identity, then it can be eliminated by stating these conditions precisely. But because this is a very difficult job, such vagueness is notoriously hard to eliminate.

3.4 Meaning and Communication

One of the reasons for using symbols is to communicate information. It is, of course, not the only reason for using symbols; one also uses symbols to ask questions, to threaten people, to make promises, and so on. It is an open question whether, whenever one uses symbols for these other reasons, one is also using them to communicate information (or, at least, whether information is being communicated regardless of the user's intention). But whether the answer to that question is yes or no, there is no doubt that the communication of information is a central reason for the use of symbols. In this final section we will want to consider the relationship between the meaning of a symbol and the information conveyed by its use.

There is no doubt that there is a strong connection between the two. The meaning of a symbol obviously helps determine what is communicated by its use. When I say to you, 'John went home', the information that I convey to you is so conveyed because of what that symbol means; if that symbol meant what 'John stayed here' now means, then I would not have been able to communicate the information to you by use of that symbol.

The question we will want to consider is whether there are other factors, besides the meaning of a symbol, that help determine what information is conveyed to you by my use of the symbol. If there are such other factors, what are they and how do they operate?

Consider the symbol 'John is opposed to America's foreign policy' and the differences between the information conveyed by its use in 1938 and in 1968. In 1938 one would have learned from its use that John was opposed to America's isolationist stand vis-á-vis the growing crisis in Europe. In 1968 one would have learned that John was opposed to America's military intervention in Southeast Asia. Although the meaning of that symbol hasn't changed, the information conveyed by its use has. Why is this so? Obviously, it has something to do with the change in the reference of 'America's foreign policy.' In 1938, that symbol referred to America's isolationist stand toward Europe; in 1968 it referred to America's intervention in Southeast Asia.

Generalizing from this example, we can say the following: There are many symbols whose reference, or the reference of one of their constituent symbols, can change from one context in which it is used to another without any change in the meaning of the symbol. For this reason the information conveyed by one use of the symbol may differ from that conveyed by another use of the symbol, even though the symbol has not undergone a change of meaning.

Closely related to this case is the following one: Consider the difference in the information conveyed by the use of the symbol 'there is peace in the world' in 1954 and by its use in 1964. The symbol did not change its meaning during the period in question, and yet the information about the state of the world conveyed by the use of the symbol in 1954 is different from the information about the state of the world conveyed by the use of the symbol in 1964. Now, this difference cannot be due to a change in reference, since neither the symbol nor any of its constituents have changed their reference. But something very similar to that has happened here. Because this symbol is in the present tense (as is indicated by its having as a constituent 'is' rather than 'was' or 'will be'), there is a covert indication of the time period which is being talked about. In the first use the time in question is that moment in 1954 at which this use of the symbol occurred. In the second use the time in question is that moment in 1964 at which the second use of the symbol occurred. Since the times covertly indicated are not the same, the two uses of that symbol can and do communicate different information.

Generalizing from this example, we can say the following: *Tensed* symbols contain covert indicators of the time period being talked about. When these indicators indicate different times for different uses of the same symbol, then the information conveyed by one use of the symbol may differ from that conveyed by another use of the symbol, even though the symbol has not undergone a change of meaning.

It is helpful to contrast the two symbols we have considered so far with '2 + 2 = 4'. If '2 + 2 = 4' is used more than once, there is no change in reference from one use to the other. Moreover, it is not a tensed symbol (the 'is' is not an indicator of present tense, as can be seen from the absurdity of '2 + 2 = 4 now')—that is, it is not the case that what is claimed to be true is claimed to be true at a given time. Therefore, the information conveyed by one use of '2 + 2 = 4' cannot differ from the information conveyed by another use of it, in the way in which the information conveyed by one use of 'John is opposed to America's foreign policy' (or by one use of 'there is peace in the world') *can* differ from the information conveyed by another use of the same symbol.

These differences between '2 + 2 = 4', on the one hand, and 'John is opposed to America's foreign policy' and 'there is peace in the world', on the other hand, lead to another important difference between these symbols. In the case of symbols such as '2 + 2 = 4', if the statement they express when used one time is true (false), then the statement they express when used every other time will also be true (false). On the other hand, in the case of symbols such as 'there is peace in the world' or 'John is opposed to America's foreign policy', they may express true (false) statements when used one time and false (true) statements when used some other time. This change in the truth-value of the statements they express is, of course, connected to the change in the information conveyed.

Symbols which are such that the statements they express, on different occasions, must have the same truth-value are known as *eternal symbols*, whereas those which are such that the truth-values of the statements they express can change from one use to another are known as *ephemeral symbols*. We shall return to this important distinction in Chapter 4.

We turn now to the consideration of very different factors, ones that have nothing to do with reference, but rather affect the information conveyed by the use of the symbol. These new factors have to do with the knowledge on the part of the hearer or reader of the symbol about the beliefs and attitudes of the user of the symbol and about the circumstances surrounding the use of the symbol.

When asked to describe one of my new neighbors, my janitor, a sixty-year-old white former policeman, said that the husband has long hair. What information was conveyed to me by his use of the symbol 'the husband wears long hair'? Obviously, much more than would be indicated by an account of the meaning of the symbol. Knowing the attitudes and beliefs of my janitor, I learned that he does not trust my new neighbor, but rather believes that he is probably a Communist or a homosexual. I also learned that my new neighbor is likely to be interested in rock and folk music, and will probably be sympathetic to the political insurgents in our town. Now, none of this was part of the meaning of 'the husband wears long hair' yet it was conveyed to me (although my janitor did not necessarily realize that he was conveying it to me) by his use of the symbol. How? Partially because I know what my janitor thinks and feels about men with long hair, and partially because I have some knowledge about the likely tastes and beliefs of a man in our society who has long hair.

Obviously, this type of phenomenon occurs all the time. Although its occurrence is easy enough to understand, it does raise one very important question about the meaning of the symbols involved. Consider the symbol 'wife beater'. Certainly, when you tell me that John is a wife beater, I learn that you think John is a terrible person. This is not only true when you say it; it is true when most people say it. Now, there are two alternative accounts of my ability to acquire that information from your use of 'John is a wife beater'. The first is that although it is no part of the meaning of 'John is a wife beater' that the person who uses the symbol thinks that John is a terrible person, I can nevertheless learn that he holds that opinion from his use of the symbol because I know what he thinks of wife beaters. The other is that, given our commonly shared attitude toward wife beaters, it is part of the meaning of 'John is a wife beater' that the user of the symbol thinks that John is a terrible person. If you do not so evaluate John, then, according to the rules governing the use of 'John is a wife beater', you should not use that symbol.

What this example illustrates is that it is often difficult to draw the line between the meaning of a symbol and the information conveyed by its use.

Or, to put it another way, it shows that the reference of 'meaning of the symbol *A*' can be vague. Even 'meaning' suffers from problems about its meaning.

EXERCISES FOR CHAPTER 3

Part I

A. Which of the following symbols are equivocal? For each of the equivocal symbols, indicate their different meanings.
1. day
2. horse
3. yellow
4. mind
5. zero
6. number
7. true
8. table
9. book
10. night

B. Construct situations in which the following words could be used ambiguously:
1. hole
2. hot
3. or
4. knight
5. library
6. maiden
7. scraped
8. stamp

C. Expose the ambiguity in one of the key symbols involved in each of the following possibly fallacious arguments that makes them seem plausible:
1. Our mind is what we think with.
   Our mind is a part of our body.
   _____
   A part of our body is what we think with.

2. We do not know that *P* is true unless we are certain about *P*.
   Since we cannot absolutely rule out the possibility that we are mistaken about *P*, we cannot be certain about *P*.
   _____
   We do not know that *P* is true.

3. A man is responsible for his action only if he is free to do otherwise.
   Given our background, heredity, etc., we are not free to do otherwise.
   _____
   A man is not responsible for his action.

D. Is the equivocity of each of the following complex symbols due to the equivocity of some simple symbol that occurs in them or to something else? If the latter is so, what is this something else?
   1. John or Frank will take you for a ride.
   2. Bring me the handsomest knight.
   3. I called up the man that you told me about and said that he is a fink.
   4. The shooting of the hunters was over rapidly.
   5. He has a big library.

E. In each of the following sentences, is the italicized symbol used or mentioned?
   1. *Nine* contains four letters.
   2. *Nine* is greater than seven.
   3. *Nine* is a number.
   4. *Nine* is an adjective.
   5. There are seven occurrences of *nine* on this page.
   6. There are *nine nines* on this page.
   7. It is easy to count until *nine*.
   8. *Nine* children counted until *nine*.

F. To what does each of the following symbols refer?
   1. 'horse'
   2. horse
   3. "horse"
   4. 'the reference of "horse" '
   5. the reference of 'horse'
   6. the first word on this page
   7. 'the first word on this page'

G. In which, if any, of the following sentences is the occurrence of the italicized symbol referentially opaque?
   1. I believe that *nine* is greater than seven.
   2. It may be the case that *nine* is greater than seven.
   3. *Nine* is greater than seven.
   4. I am pleased by the fact that *nine* is greater than seven.

H. Each of the following symbols is at least somewhat vague. In each case explain the cause of its vagueness and how you would go about correcting it.
   1. green
   2. the tallest mountain in the Alps
   3. the Missouri River
   4. courageous
   5. the same color as this chair
   6. the oldest statesman
   7. this child
   8. hard

I. Which of the following symbols are eternal symbols and which are ephemeral symbols?
   1. Man is a rational animal.
   2. I believe that man is a rational animal.
   3. Joe is a rational animal.

4. I believe that Joe is a rational animal.
5. The Yankees won the pennant.
6. The Yankees won the pennant in 1970.
7. The oldest man alive died in 1970.
8. The oldest man who ever lived died in 1970.
9. The first astronaut is dead.
10. All men are mortal.

J. In each of the following cases, explain why the use of the symbol usually conveys information that is not part of the meaning of the symbol.
1. Seven is my favorite number.
2. John loves Mary.
3. Frank is a member of the Ku Klux Klan.
4. The shortest student in our class is now at home.
5. She teaches a class on current affairs.
6. All politicians wore little flags in their lapels during the last election.

Part II

1. Looking at the examples of equivocity in Exercise A of Part I of these exercises, can you offer any suggestions about how these words came to be equivocal in the way that they are?

2. Looking at those same examples, explain how, in a given case, we determine which meaning is intended. On the basis of these examples, can you construct a theory of how we understand what is meant when an equivocal symbol is used?

3. Explain what is wrong with the following claims: (a) when a symbol S_1 is used to refer to a symbol, it (S_1) is being mentioned and not used; (b) when a symbol S_1 is used to refer to itself, it (S_1) is being mentioned and not used; (c) a symbol and that same symbol with single quotes around it can never be used to refer to the same thing.

4. Consider the following analysis of 'nine is necessarily greater than seven': It is really equivalent to 'the statement expressed by the sentence 'nine is greater than seven' is necessarily true'. Explain (a) how, according to this analysis, all referring symbols are not referentially opaque; (b) why 'nine' does not refer to anything in this context.

5. Consider the following alternative analysis of 'nine is necessarily greater than seven': It is really equivalent to 'that number which is the number nine is necessarily greater than seven', and 'the number nine' is not referentially opaque, since if we substitute for 'the number nine' the expression 'the number of planets' the resulting statement expressed by 'that number which is the number of planets is necessarily greater than seven' is true. What are the main differences between this analysis and the analysis discussed in question 4? Are there any reasons for preferring one over the other?

6. If you eliminate some of the vagueness of a symbol by the methods employed in Chapter 3, would that mean that you had changed the meaning of the symbol?

7. Propose and defend a principle that eliminates, as much as possible, the vagueness in 'the watch I bought fifteen years ago'.

8. Are there any symbols used to denote or refer which have absolutely no vagueness? If so, give some examples and explain why they are that way. If not, explain why this is so.

9. Consider an ephemeral symbol such as 'John is opposed to America's foreign policy.' In light of your answer to Exercise I of Part I, can you think of any eternal symbol which, on a given occasion, could be used instead of it?

10. What criteria would you use in determining whether something is part of the meaning of a symbol or whether it is just information normally conveyed when the symbol is used?

CHAPTER 1

Meaning
and Truth

The two great questions that always arise in connection with the use of symbols are the question of their meaning and of their truth. In Chapters 2 and 3 we have been primarily concerned with questions about meaning. In this chapter we will be primarily concerned with questions about truth, although at the end of the chapter, we will return to meanings and talk about truth by meaning alone.

Truth is not related merely to symbols and their use. There are such things as true friends, true blue, and true grit. There are many fascinating questions that can be raised about the relationship between truth as related to symbols and their use and this other type of truth. But in this chapter we will be concerned only with the former type of truth.

We will consider three major questions: Of what is truth a property? Under what conditions is that thing true? Are some things true solely by virtue of the meaning of symbols?

4.1 The Bearer of Truth-values:
Sentences, Propositions, or Statements

It is helpful to begin by looking at a few examples of the way in which we use 'true' and 'truth':

Is it true that John killed his brother?
It is true that he killed his brother.
That's true.
Everything the speaker said is true.
There isn't a word of truth in what he said.
The truth is hard to find.

Philosophers and linguists have quite naturally assumed that it is the second example that shows the most basic way of using 'true'. All uses of 'true' and 'truth' are derived from symbols, beginning with 'it is true that'. For example, if I say that p and you say "that's true", then we can quite naturally say you have used an abbreviated form for saying that it is true that p. Similarly, if Jones says that p and q, and you say "there isn't a word of truth in what he said", then we can quite naturally say you have used an abbreviated form for saying that it is not the case that it is true that p and it is not the case that it is true that q.

For this reason we will now concentrate upon symbols, beginning with 'it is true that'. Now, the very simplest theory about such symbols is that they are attributing the property of truth to another symbol. Thus, 'it is true that he killed his brother' can very naturally be viewed as attributing the property of truth to 'he killed his brother'. In other words, according to this theory, it is symbols that are true (or false).

Naturally, not every symbol can be true or false. For example, 'hello', 'are you at home?', 'shut the door!', and so on, are symbols, but they are neither true nor false. Only some symbols have the property of being true or false. Which ones? The standard answer to this question is declarative sentences. But what about 'I hereby promise to come to your aid in time of trouble' or 'watch out for the fork in the road'. Grammatically, both of these are declarative sentences, but neither seems to be either true or false. The trouble with the traditional category of declarative sentences it that it includes symbols used to give advice, make promises, and so forth, and such symbols are neither true nor false. A much better answer is that only those symbols used to assert that something is the case are either true or false. This answer is much better than the first because not every declarative sentence is used to assert that something is the case. In particular, those declarative sentences which are neither true nor false, such as the ones used to make promises, give advice, and so on, are not used to assert that something is the case. So this answer avoids the difficulties faced by the answer that it is declarative sentences that are true or false.

Let us call truth and falsehood *truth-values*, and let us call that which is true or false the *bearer of truth-values*. Then, according to this first theory, the bearers of truth-values are symbols used to assert that something is the case.

Philosophers have hesitated to adopt this view for several reasons. First, it seems that it is not the symbol per se but only the symbol with a certain meaning that is true or false. After all, consider any equivocal symbol that can, given either of its meanings, be used to assert that something is the case. Is it true or false? That question cannot be answered. All that we can say is that if it is being used to assert one thing, then it has one truth-value, but if it is being used to assert something else, then it has another truth-value. The symbol itself has no truth-value.

Now, not all symbols are equivocal. Therefore, the preceding argument shows, at best, that equivocal symbols are not the bearers of truth-values. But if we want to have a unified theory of what is the bearer of truth-values, it seems best to conclude that symbols, whether equivocal or unequivocal, are never the bearers of truth-values.

If we follow this line of thought, we are led to the idea that it is the meaning of the symbol that is true or false. After all, equivocal symbols have two meanings, and we can therefore say that one might be true whereas the other might be false. Let us call the meaning of a symbol used to assert that something is the case the *proposition* expressed by use of that symbol. Then the natural suggestion is that propositions are the bearers of truth-values.

A second line of thought seems to lead to the same conclusion. Consider 'it is true that it is raining' and '*c'est vrai qu'il pleut*'. Now, intuitively, we would say that these two symbols assert the same thing. But according to the view that symbols are the bearers of truth-values, they would not. After all, one is understood, according to this theory, as being equivalent to 'it is raining is true', whereas the other is equivalent to '*il pleut est vrai*'. That is to say, according to that theory, one would be talking about an English sentence, whereas the other would be talking about a French sentence. So they could not be saying the same thing. Since, however, they obviously are, the theory that symbols are the bearers of truth-values must be wrong.

The theory that propositions are the bearers of truth-values, however, easily avoids this problem. After all, 'it is raining' and '*il pleut*', since they have the same meaning, express the same proposition. Therefore 'it is true that 'it is raining' and '*c'est vrai qu'il pleut*' assert the same thing, since they both say that the same proposition is true.

However, this view also runs into serious problems. Consider 'it is true that I am tired' as uttered by Jones and 'it is true that I am tired' as uttered by Smith. Now, 'I am tired' is not equivocal: it always has the same meaning; it always expresses the same proposition. Therefore, according to the theory that propositions are the bearers of truth-values, both utterances assert the same thing (that it is true) about the same thing (the proposition expressed by 'I am tired'). So they should both be true or both be false. And yet it is obviously the case that one can be true and the other be false. All that is required is that Jones be tired but Smith not be tired. So the theory that propositions are the bearers of truth-values must be mistaken.

Another example helps bring out the same point. Let us say that, both yesterday and today, I say that Joe is at home. Now, 'Joe is at home' is not equivocal; so the proposition expressed by its use yesterday is the same as the proposition expressed by its use today. Let us suppose that you had said, after each time I said that Joe is at home, 'it is true that Joe is at home'.

If the theory that propositions are the bearers of truth-values is correct, then in both cases you would have said the same thing (that it is true) about the same thing (the proposition expressed by 'Joe is at home'). But then, according to that theory, either both of your utterances should be true or both should be false. Clearly, however, one can be true while the other can be false. All that is required is that Joe be at home one day but not the other. So the theory that propositions are the bearers of truth-values must be mistaken.

The problem in both these cases is really the same. The symbols involved are ephemeral, not eternal, symbols; therefore their truth-value can change from one use to another. But the symbols have not changed their meaning; they express the same proposition in both uses. So if propositions are the bearers of truth-values, why do the truth-values change from one use of the symbol to another?

If we could eliminate all ephemeral symbols by finding ways of saying everything we want to say by using eternal symbols only, then there would be no problem. But since that does not seem possible, it seems as though we must give up the view that propositions are the bearers of truth-values.

What, then, are the bearers of truth-values? Perhaps the answer is *statements*. What is a statement? Well, two sentences express the same proposition if they mean the same thing; two sentences express the same statement if they mean the same thing and assert that the same thing is true of the same thing(s) at the same time. Thus, although 'Joe is at home' as uttered yesterday and 'Joe is at home' as uttered today express the same proposition (they mean the same thing), they do not express the same statement (since they say that Joe is at home at different times). Consequently, if statements are the bearers of truth-values, then the statement expressed by one use of that symbol could be true, whereas the statement expressed by another use of the symbol would be false. Similarly, although 'I am tired' as used by Smith and 'I am tired' as used by Jones express the same proposition (they mean the same thing), they do not express the same statement (since one says that Jones is tired while the other says that Smith is tired). Consequently, if statements are the bearers of truth-values, then the statement expressed by one use of that symbol could be true while the statement expressed by another use of that symbol would be false. So the theory that statements are the bearers of truth-values avoids the difficulties faced by the theory that propositions are the bearers of truth-values.

Let us see where we now stand. We began with the view that certain symbols, certain types of declarative sentences, were the bearers of truth-values. The trouble was that the same sentence could mean two different things (and so be both true and false). So we switched to the view that the propositions expressed by those symbols were the bearers of truth-values. But even that didn't do, since a symbol expressing the same proposition might be used to express two different statements (and so be both true and false). So we finally came to the view that statements are the bearers of truth-values.

4.2 *Simple Conditions of Adequacy for Theories about Truth*

In section 4.1 we considered what it is that is true, and we concluded that it is statements that are true. In this section we will deal with the question of what it is for a statement to be true—the question of what truth is. But rather than turn directly to that question we will first consider some obvious truths about truth; for if we have a list of some obvious truths about truth, then we can use this list as a way of checking our theories about truth. If any of our theories of truth entail the falsehood of some obvious truth about truth, then we will conclude that that theory about truth is mistaken. In other words, a condition for a theory of truth being adequate is that, according to it, all these truths about truth are true.

Let us first list the three obvious truths:

(1) For any statement p, either p is true or p is false.
(2) No statement p is both true and false.
(3) For any statement p, p is true if and only if p.

The first of these truths is known as the *law of bivalence* (the law of two values, since it says that there are only two truth-values); the second is known as the *law of noncontradiction;* and the third will be called *Tarski's law* (since it bears some resemblance to a law about sentences first formulated by the Polish logician Alfred Tarski).

The law of bivalence really says two things: that every statement has a truth-value, and that there only are two truth-values, true and false. It does not say that we always know whether the statement is true or false, it simply states that, whether or not we know it is true or false, it is one or the other.

The law of bivalence has been challenged on both its claims. A number of logicians have asserted that certain types of statements have some other truth-value besides truth or falsehood. They have constructed logics known as *many-valued logics* (logics that recognize more than two truth-values) in which they study these many different truth-values and the problems they pose. These issues, however, are beyond the scope of our investigation, and since none of these logicians have ever succeeded in producing really convincing arguments for the existence of these additional truth-values, we shall disregard their claims for now.

However, there is another type of objection that we must consider. It is the claim that there are statements, vague statements, that have no truth-value. Consider, for example, the statement that Communism is a religion.

Now 'religion' is a vague symbol. Established religions have many things in common, and Communism has some, but not all, of them. Is it true or false, then, that Communism is a religion? Actually, in light of the vagueness of 'religion' and the consequential vagueness of the statement that Communism is a religion, many people have been inclined to say that the statement is neither true nor false, and have therefore concluded that the law of bivalence is false.

This objection, however, is not entirely convincing, for is there really a statement expressed by 'Communism is a religion'? After all, in light of the vagueness of 'religion', what exactly are we saying when we say that Communism is a religion? Perhaps it would be better to say that vague sentences do not express statements rather than to say that they do but that the statements are neither true nor false.

We turn now to the law of noncontradiction. There has been little controversy about it. Occasionally, people have suggested that vague statements such as the claim that Communism is a religion are both true and false. But surely that is a confusion. What is true is that if 'religion' is made precise in one way, then 'Communism is a religion' will express a true statement, but that if it is made precise in another way, then 'Communism is a religion' will express a false statement. But none of this means that there is some one statement that is both true and false.

Tarski's law is a particularly important principle. Of our three principles it is the only one that asserts that there is some connection between the truth of a statement and what is the case in the world. It tells us, for example, that the statement that snow is white is true if and only if snow actually is white, or that, as another example, the statement that George is either at home or at the movies is true if and only if George is either at home or at the movies. But although it does make a claim about the relationship between the truth of statements and what is the case in the world, the claim made by Tarski's law is so innocuous that it, too, has not been challenged.

Although two of these obvious truths are so innocuous that they are not even open to challenge and the third is only a bit less innocuous, their truth rules out several important theories of truth that have been proposed. The first theory that it rules out is the so-called *verifiability theory of truth*. Let us say that we have *verified a statement* when we have collected overwhelming evidence that what it says is the case. According to the verifiability theory of truth, a statement is true if and only if we have verified it, and a statement is false if and only if we have verified its denial. It is easy to see why someone would propose such a theory about the meaning of 'true'— why someone would claim that the truth of a statement consists in its being verified. After all, we decide that a statement is true when we verify it; so shouldn't we conclude that its truth consists in its being verified? Nevertheless, the verifiability theory of truth entails that the law of bivalence and

Tarski's law are false. Hence, the verifiability theory of truth must be mistaken.

How does the verifiability theory of truth entail that the law of bivalence is false? Consider the statement that smoking marijuana can lead to taking heroin. As we stated earlier, neither the evidence for nor the evidence against this statement is overwhelming. (In this way it is like many other important statements at this stage in the process of inquiry.) Therefore, according to the verifiability theory, none of these statements are either true or false. They are not true because we have not verified them, and they are not false because we have not verified their denial. So the verifiability theory of truth entails that the law of bivalence is false.

How does the verifiability theory of truth entail that Tarski's law is false? Consider the statement that there are 48 chromosomes in every human cell. According to Tarski's law, that statement is true if and only if there are 48 chromosomes in every human cell. Actually, there are, and always have been, 46 chromosomes in every human cell. So, according to Tarski's law, the statement that there are 48 chromosomes in every human cell is and always has been false. However, for a long period of time, there was overwhelming evidence that there are 48 chromosomes in every human cell. Therefore, according to the verifiability theory, during all that time, the statement that there are 48 chromosomes in every human cell was true. So the verifiability theory of truth entails that Tarski's law is false.

A second theory of truth ruled out by the truth of our three innocuous laws is the *pragmatic theory of truth*, the theory that true statements are the ones for which belief in them works. Now, it is not entirely clear what the pragmatists mean by 'works'. Sometimes, they seem to mean that belief in a statement works if and only if the statement is supported by all the evidence. If that is what they mean, then the pragmatic theory is simply a version of the verifiability theory of truth, and we have already seen that such theories are mistaken.

Sometimes, however, the pragmatists seem to mean something else by 'works'—that belief in a statement works if and only if one is successful in acting upon the belief. Thus, belief in the statement that it is raining works when, acting upon it by taking an umbrella, one is successful in that he does not get wet. Although this version of the pragmatic theory of truth is not a type of the verifiability theory, and is not therefore open to the objections raised against that theory, it must also be rejected, for it entails that Tarski's law is false.

It is easy to see how this second version of the pragmatic theory entails that Tarski's law is false. Consider the statement that it is raining outside now. According to Tarski's law, that statement is true if and only if it is raining outside now; if it is not raining outside now, that statement is false. But even if it is not raining outside now, there may still be conditions in which one could be successful in acting upon that belief. If, for example, someone had put a bucket of water over my front door, then I would have acted successfully if, acting upon my belief that it is raining outside, I had used my umbrella as I left the house. In such a case, according to the second version of the pragmatic theory, the statement is true. So the second version of the pragmatic theory entails that Tarski's law is false, and therefore this theory is mistaken.

Speaking more generally, we clearly see what is wrong with the pragmatic theory of truth. It forgets that there are many cases in which one acts successfully by acting upon false beliefs. In each of these cases, there are special circumstances that make it advantageous to act upon a false belief. But these special circumstances do not turn the false statement into a true statement. There is a difference, after all, between what is expedient and what is true.

There is a third theory of truth that is ruled out because it entails that one or more of our laws are false. This is the *coherence theory of truth*. It takes its point of departure from the fact that we often judge a statement to be true because it fits in with the other statements in which we believe, and we often judge a statement to be false because it clashes with the other statements in which we believe. This truism has led some philosophers to propose the coherence theory, which states that a statement is true if it fits in with the statements that we already believe to be true, and false if it clashes with these beliefs.

We must also reject this theory, for it entails the falsity of Tarski's law. For example, let us imagine that I have many false beliefs and that there is some statement p that fits in with them. Then, according to the coherence theory, p would be true. But it might also be the case that it is not the case that p. Then, according to Tarski's law, p would be false. So the coherence theory entails that Tarski's law is false, and it must be rejected.

It also seems to be the case that the coherence theory entails that the law of noncontradiction is false. If, for example, I hold (as most people do) contradictory beliefs, then there will be some cases in which both p and not-p will fit in with my other beliefs. So, according to the coherence theory, both p and not-p will be true. But if not-p is true, p is false. So, according to the coherence theory, in such cases the statement p is both true and false. Therefore, the coherence theory entails that the law of noncontradiction is false, which is still another reason for rejecting the coherence theory.

4.3 Redundancy, Performative, and Correspondence Theories of Truth

In a way, Tarski's law is the point of departure for all the theories of truth that we will consider in this section. This is not surprising. Each of the theories considered in section 4.2 was open to the challenge that it allowed some p's to be true when it was not the case that p; that is, each of them was open to the challenge that it allowed violations of Tarski's law. So it seems safest, in attempting to construct a theory of truth, to begin by ensuring that the definition of truth does not allow any violations of that law.

The first theory that we will consider, the *redundancy theory of truth*, does this in the simplest way. According to this theory, the statement that p is true is the same as the statement that p. Thus, for example, 'it is true that snow is white' expresses the same statement as does 'snow is white'. In a strong sense, therefore, the addition of 'it is true' is superfluous.

The intuitive motivation for this theory is clear: As Tarski's law indicates, any statement p is true if and only if it is also true that p is true; if one of these statements is false, so is the other. The simplest explanation of this is to suppose that these two statements have the same truth-value because they are not really two different statements, but the same statement.

It is important to realize just how radical the redundancy theory is. We normally think of statements such as 'it is true that snow is white' as attributing the property of truth to something (to statements, we decided). But if the redundancy theory is right, then we are mistaken. After all, if the redundancy theory is right, that entire statement is the same statement as the one expressed by 'snow is white'; that is, the two statements attribute the same property (being white) to the same thing (snow), and neither attributes truth to anything.

We can put this last point in still another way: What is truth? We normally think of it as a property of something. According to the redundancy theory, it is nothing at all. All that exists is the superfluous symbol 'true' and the misleading symbol 'truth'—misleading because it suggests that there is such a thing as truth.

Many adherents of the redundancy theory feel, however, that there is more to be said about truth than this. Consider, for example, 'snow is white' and 'it is true that snow is white'. Even if we grant that these two symbols express the same statement, there still seems to be some difference between the ways in which the two are used (and therefore, according to our theory of meaning, there still seems to be some difference in their meaning). To emphasize this difference, let us imagine two conversations. In the first one you are talking to a child and he asks you to name something that is white. Would you say 'snow is white' or 'it is true that snow is white'? Obviously, the former. In the second conversation your friend has drawn the conclusion that because snow is white, it is always a soothing thing to look at. You want to grant that it is white, but want to challenge that it is soothing. Would you begin by saying 'although snow is white', or 'although it is true that snow is white'? The latter is certainly as appropriate as (if not more so) than the former.

What has changed in the second case? What you are trying to do, by saying 'although it is true that snow is white', is to concede the truth of 'snow is white' but prepare to challenge something else that the other person has said. In the first case, however, you are simply trying to assert that snow is white. So, generalizing from this case, one might say that sentences beginning with 'it is true that' are used when one wants to concede, endorse, and so on, what has been said before (or, to generalize further, what one anticipates would most likely be said presently if one did not say it now), but are not used when one simply wants to assert that something is the case.

Some adherents of the redundancy theory would, therefore, replace it with another theory, the *performative theory of truth*, which maintains that although the statements expressed by a sentence and by the same sentence prefaced by 'it is true that' are the same statement, one uses the latter sentence to express that statement only when one wants to concede it, endorse it, and so on. Consequently, if one leaves aside cases in which one is anticipating the utterance of that sentence by someone else, one only uses sentences beginning with 'it is true that' and followed by some other sentence when someone else has already asserted the statement expressed by that other sentence.

The name of this theory calls attention to its most striking feature. It is the one theory that attempts to explain the meaning of sentences beginning with 'it is true that', not only in terms of the conditions under which the statements expressed by such sentences are true, but also by considering the linguistic acts performed when one utters such sentences.

There is actually some doubt about the universality of the phenomenon called to our attention by the adherents of the performative theory. Consider, for example, 'if it is true that John is at home, then Matilda is there as well' and 'if John is at home, then Matilda is there as well'. Is there really any difference in the linguistic acts performed by uttering these two sentences? It would seem that there is none; so their meaning seems to be the same. Now, two things follow from this. First, the difference in performed linguistic acts noted by the adherents of the performative theory is a difference found when the sentences are simple categorical sentences, but not necessarily in other cases. Second, this leads one to suspect that this difference in linguistic acts performed is not, therefore, part of the meaning of 'it is true that'.

Whether in its simple version or in its modified version (the performative theory), there is much to be said for the redundancy theory, and many philosophers and logicians think that it is the correct theory of truth. However, there is another theory of truth, the *correspondence theory of truth*, that also has many adherents, and we turn now to its consideration.

Consider once more 'snow is white'. Corresponding to it, there is the fact that snow is white. On the other hand, there is no analogous fact—that snow is black—corresponding to 'snow is black'. Isn't this why the statement expressed by 'snow is white' is true whereas that expressed by 'snow is black' is false?

It is just this type of reflection that gives rise to the correspondence theory of truth. It says that a statement is true if and only if its corresponding fact exists, and to say that a statement is true is to say that its corresponding fact does exist, whereas to say that a statement is false is to say that its corresponding fact does not exist.

There are several important differences between the correspondence theory, on the one hand, and the redundancy and performative theories on the other. According to those latter theories, the statements expressed by 'snow is white' and 'it is true that snow is white' are really the same statements; according to the correspondence theory, they are not. The former express the statement that a certain type of thing (snow) has a certain color (white); the latter asserts the existence of a certain fact; namely, the fact corresponding to the statement that snow is white. Or, to put it another way, the former does not presuppose the existence of a special type of entity—facts—whereas the latter does. There is another difference between these theories. As we saw previously, the redundancy (and performative) theories assume that there is no special property of truth. However, according to the correspondence theory, there is such a property. Truth is the property possessed by statements when their corresponding facts exist.

In expounding the correspondence theory, we have spoken of the fact that corresponds to a given statement. But what makes one fact correspond to one statement and another fact correspond to a different statement? For a long time, this issue was highly controversial. Attempts were made to explain the notion of correspondence in terms of structural similarity, and a great debate raged as to whether this could be done. But we now see that all this is irrelevant. The fact that corresponds to a given statement is indicated by the rules governing the use of the symbol used to express that statement. Thus, there is a rule governing the use of 'snow is white', which indicates that the fact that corresponds to the statement expressed by the symbol, and whose existence makes that statement true, is the fact that snow is white.

We saw previously that the redundancy theory is set up to ensure the truth of Tarski's law, but Tarski's law is also true according to the correspondence theory. If a statement p is true, then, according to the correspondence theory, its corresponding fact exists. But its corresponding fact is that the object that p is talking about has the property that p says it has. So if p is true, then p. Similarly, it can be shown that if p, then, according to the correspondence theory, p is true. So Tarski's law holds if the correspondence theory is true.

How are we to choose between the redundancy (and performative) theory, on the one hand, and the correspondence theory, on the other? From the logician's point of view, both of them, unlike the verifiability, pragmatic and coherence theories, are satisfactory. So a choice between these theories must be made on other grounds. The choice seems to come down to the following: The redundancy theory has a simpler universe without strange entities, such as facts and the property of truth. So those who prefer theories that presuppose the existence of as few entities as possible will prefer either the redundancy theory or its modification, the performative theory. Those who prefer to stick to their intuitions that truth is a property, predicated to statements in sentences beginning with 'it is true that' will—even at the cost of presupposing the existence of these additional types of entities—prefer the correspondence theory. The choice between these two theories depends, therefore, on one's metaphysical views.

4.4 The Analytic–Synthetic Distinction and Logical Truths

We have not yet considered the question of the possible connections between meaning and truth; in this final section, we will discuss this aspect. It might seem as though there is no room for such a connection. After all, it is symbols that have meaning, but symbols are neither true nor false. As we have seen, it is statements that are true or false. Remember, though, that we assert statements by the use of symbols. So we can certainly ask whether there is any connection between the meaning of the symbol used in asserting a statement and the fact that that symbol expresses a true statement.

Certainly there is some connection. Let us say that I want to assert that snow is white and do so by using 'snow is white'. Obviously, 'snow is white' can be used to assert this truth only because it means what it does; if it meant what 'snow is black' now means, it could not be used to assert any true statement. Consequently, the meaning of a symbol helps determine whether the symbol is used to assert a true statement or a false statement. Of course, it only *helps* determine this, for this question is also determined by what is the case in the world (in this case, by the color of snow).

One must not confuse the existence of this connection with the existence of a connection between the meaning of 'snow is white' and the truth of the statement that snow is white. The meaning of 'snow is white' does not help determine whether that statement is true; its truth depends solely upon the color of snow. All that the meaning of 'snow is white' helps determine is whether that true statement is expressible by use of 'snow is white'.

In this connection there is an important difference between symbols that has generated much discussion. Consider the following difference between 'snow is snow' and 'snow is white'. Given the meaning of the symbol 'snow is snow', there is no question about the truth of any statement that it can be used to assert. The same thing is not true about 'snow is white'. Given the meaning of this symbol, there is still some question about the truth of the statement that it asserts; it could, under certain circumstances, be used to assert a false statement. This distinction, as we saw previously, can also be put as follows: Whether 'snow is white' is used to assert a true statement or a false statement is dependent, at least partially, upon the facts, for it could, in some circumstances (snow's being white), be used to assert a true statement, and, under other circumstances (snow's being black), to assert a false statement. On the other hand, there are no circumstances in which, given its meaning, 'snow is snow' could be used to assert a false statement.

In the last example, the two symbols are, in fact, used to assert true statements. But a similar distinction can be drawn between symbols that are used to assert false statements. After all, given the meaning of 'snow is not white', there are some circumstances under which it can (snow's being black), be used to assert a true statement. However, given the meaning of 'snow is not snow', there are no circumstances under which it could be used to assert a true statement.

We shall say that a symbol is an *analytic symbol* when, given its meaning, it can only be used to assert true statements (there are no circumstances under which it could be used to assert a false statement) or when, given its meaning, it can only be used to assert false statements (there are no conditions under which it could be used to assert a true statement). We shall say that a symbol is a *synthetic symbol* when, given its meaning, there are circumstances under which it could be used to assert a true statement and there are circumstances under which it could be used to assert a false statement.

Keep in mind that in these definitions there is repeated reference to the meaning of the symbols being fixed; otherwise, no symbol would be analytic. After all, if we drop that condition, even 'snow is not snow' could, under some circumstances, be used to assert a true statement. Those conditions would be that it means what 'snow is snow' means now. Given our definition, however, this type of case does not count, because it would involve a change in the meaning of the symbol in question.

Let us now turn to an important distinction between two types of analytic statements, beginning by considering an example. Both 'all bachelors are bachelors' and 'all bachelors are males' are analytic symbols. Given their meanings, there are no conditions under which either could be used to assert a false statement. However, there is an important difference between them. Let us take any symbol in them that denotes or refers to anything and replace every occurrence of that symbol with some other such symbol. For example, let us replace 'bachelor' with 'baseball fans'. Then, 'all bachelors are bachelors' becomes 'all baseball fans are baseball fans', and this symbol is also analytic. On the other hand, 'all bachelors are males' becomes 'all baseball fans are males', and this is not analytic. What this example shows is the following: In the case of some analytic symbols, such as 'all bachelors are males', it is possible to replace every occurrence of a symbol used to refer to or denote something with some other symbol used in such a way that the resulting symbol will not be analytic. This does not seem to be so, however, in the case of other analytic symbols, such as 'all bachelors are bachelors'.

Let us call this second type of analytic symbol *logically true* (or *logically false*) *symbols*, or simply *logical truths* (*falsehoods*). A symbol is logically true (false) if it is an analytic symbol that can only be used to express true (false) statements. It remains that way if, for any symbol occurring in it that is used to refer to or denote something, you replace every occurrence of that symbol with some other symbol (the same one in each case).

Now, to clarify this definition, let us see what is wrong with the following three arguments purporting to show that 'all bachelors are bachelors' is not really a logical truth.

(1) If we replace every occurrence of 'are' in 'all bachelors are bachelors' with 'are not', the resulting symbol, 'all bachelors are not bachelors', is no longer a symbol that can only be used to express true statements. This argument is faulty because 'are' is not used to refer to or denote anything. Consequently, the symbol must not remain analytic (and usable to express only truths) after 'are' is systematically replaced in order for the symbol to be a logical truth.

(2) If we replace the second occurrence of 'bachelor' in 'all bachelors are bachelors' with 'baseball fans', the resulting symbol, 'all bachelors are baseball fans', is no longer a symbol that can only be used to express true statements. This argument is faulty because it was required simply that the resulting statement be usable only to express true statements when you replace all occurrences of 'bachelor', and we replaced only the second one.

(3) If we replace one occurrence of 'bachelor' with 'men' and the other with 'six feet tall', the resulting 'all men are six feet tall', is no longer a symbol that can only be used to express true statements. This argument is faulty because it merely required that the resulting sentence be usable to express true statements only when you replace all occurrences of one symbol with the same symbol; we did not, since we replaced one occurrence of 'bachelor' with 'men' and the other with 'six feet tall'.

What is the intuitive idea behind the distinction between ordinary analytic symbols and logical truths (falsehoods)? There is the idea that some symbols are analytic because they are only usable to say about a certain thing(s) that it has a certain property. Thus, 'all bachelors are males' is analytic solely because it can only be used to say about bachelors that they are males. There seems to be a different reason for the analyticity of 'all bachelors are bachelors'. It is analytic because of its structure, because it says that all *A*'s are *A*'s, which is revealed by the fact that you can systematically substitute some other symbol for 'bachelor' and still have a symbol that can only be used to assert true statements. In other words, the analyticity of 'all bachelors are bachelors' is not due to the fact that it is used to say something about bachelors. It is this intuition that we are trying to capture by our distinction between logical truths and falsehoods, on the one hand, and ordinary analytic statements, on the other.

It would be a mistake to suppose that it is always clear whether a given symbol is analytic. Consider 'all ravens are black'. Could it be used to assert a false statement? To answer that we must ask whether there are circumstances in which there would be nonblack ravens; and whether there are depends upon whether a bird could count as a raven if it were not black. There is a certain vagueness in 'raven' that makes the answer unclear; as a result it is also unclear whether 'all ravens are black' could be used to assert a false statement. Hence the vagueness of 'analytic'. As we saw in an earlier chapter, however, this situation should not bother us, partly because a great many other symbols are also vague, and partly because being vague is not necessarily undesirable.

EXERCISES FOR CHAPTER 4

Part I

A. Do the following pairs of sentences necessarily express the same proposition, or the same statement, or neither? If they do not necessarily express the same statement, can they sometimes do so?

1. Six is the sum of three plus three. The number after five is the sum of three plus three.
2. Six is my favorite number. Six is the favorite number of the person using this sentence.
3. The author of this book is six feet tall. The man who wrote this book is six feet tall.
4. The author of this book is six feet tall. B. A. Brody is six feet tall.

B. Show, by use of our three laws about truth, that the following subjective theories of truth are false:

1. If I believe that something is true, then it is true.
2. What is true or false depends upon what society agrees upon.
3. If I believe one thing and you believe the opposite, both of our beliefs can be true.
4. What is true has nothing to do with how the world is.

C. Under what conditions, if any, could we be said to have verified the following statements?

   1. John is at home.
   2. All men are at home.
   3. Someone is at home.
   4. No one is at home.
   5. John loves her.
   6. Caesar crossed the Rubicon in 44 B.C.
   7. Justice is worthy of pursuing.
   8. There are forces in nature about which we know almost nothing.

D. Give examples of cases in which acting upon each of the following beliefs would be successful even though these beliefs are false:

   1. Everyone hates me.
   2. The good are always rewarded.
   3. It is raining outside.
   4. The shortest way home is down this street.
   5. The race is fixed and Lucky Star must win.
   6. Judy will know the solution to my problem.

E. Consider the following pairs of symbols. Explain, in light of the performative theory of truth, when we would use one and when we would use the other.

   1. While Joe is at home. While it is true that Joe is at home.
   2. Joe is certainly at home. It is certainly true that Joe is at home.
   3. Is Joe at home? Is it true that Joe is at home?
   4. Joe may be at home. It is true that Joe may be at home.

F. Which of the following symbols are analytic and which are synthetic?

   1. Joe is a man.
   2. A man is a man.
   3. A bachelor is a man.
   4. A woman is a man.
   5. A man is at home.
   6. The oldest man at home is at home.
   7. All men are rational.
   8. All ravens are black.
   9. All horses have four legs.
  10. All Presidents are male.
  11. All those who have been President until now are males.
  12. All male Presidents are male.

G. All of the following are analytic symbols, but some are logical truths (or falsehoods) and others are not. Which ones are and which are not?

   1. All squares have four sides.
   2. All quadrangles have four sides.

3. All squares are square.
4. All four-sided figures larger than six square feet have four sides.
5. All bachelors are females.
6. All males are females.
7. All males are not males.
8. All males are not females.

Part II

1. Without using the notion of truth and falsehood, can you give an account of when it is that a symbol can be used to assert that something is the case?

2. When are two propositions identical?

3. We introduced "statement" by saying that two sentences express the same statement if they have the same meaning and assert that the same thing is true of the same thing at the same time. Other logicians use "statement" in such a way that the requirement that the two sentences have the same meaning is dropped. Do the following: (a) give examples of cases in which two sentences express the same statement according to their use but not according to ours; (b) explain which of these uses are preferable if we want to treat statements as the bearers of truth-values.

4. Some philosophers claim that the bearers of truth-values are particular instances of the use of a symbol. Would this view be open to any of the objections we raised against the view that it is propositions or symbols that are the bearers of truth-values? If so, to which objections? If not, is it more or less preferable than the view that statements are the bearers of truth-values?

5. Using our three conditions of adequacy, criticize the following theories of truth:

   (a) A statement is true if there is no evidence against it.
   (b) A statement is true if there is some evidence for it.
   (c) A statement is true if it is one of the fundamental assumptions upon which our society is based.
   (d) A statement is true if belief in it advances the cause of the progressive forces in the world.

6. Consider the following objection against the redundancy theory: According to the redundancy theory, all uses of 'true' and all references to truth can be eliminated from our language. That's okay in cases such as 'it is true that it is raining', in which we can simply say 'it is raining'. But what can we use to replace 'everything Joe said is true' or 'the truth is hard to find'? Since there is no answer to that question, the redundancy theory is false.
   Is this a conclusive objection?

7. In what way does the performative theory of truth emphasize the pragmatic rules governing language?

8. Attempt to construct an account of correspondence in terms of structural similarity. What are the major difficulties you encounter?

9. Critically evaluate the following argument: Whether it is true or false that snow is white is a matter of convention. After all, it depends upon the meaning of 'snow is white'. So, in general, truth is conventional.

10. Is the symbol '7 + 5 = 12' an analytic symbol or a synthetic symbol? What about 'the sum of the angles of a triangle is 180°'? If the answer to these questions is not the same, explain why not.

11. In our definition of 'logical truth', we have presupposed that the symbols used to refer or denote are not part of the structure of a symbol, whereas the symbols that are not so used *are* part of the structure. Explain the rationale for this presupposition.

THE THEORY
of
DEDUCTION

CHAPTER

5

The Nature of

Deductive Inferences

Many times, when we know that something is true, we try to use that knowledge as a basis for coming to know that something else is the case. What we claim is that if what we know is true, then this other thing must also be true. This process of deriving the truth of one from the other is known as the process of *inferring* the truth of this new statement (the *conclusion*) from the old statement (the *premise*); the derivation of one from the other is known as the *inference* from one to the other.

Inferences are not statements; they are derivations of statements from other statements. Consequently, inferences are neither true nor false. Thus, although the statements that all men are mortal is either true or false, that Socrates is a man is either true or false, and that Socrates is mortal is either true or false, the inference of the truth of the last from the truth of the first two is not true or false.

This is not to say, however, that inferences cannot be qualitatively evaluated. Indeed, the rest of this book will be concerned with evaluating inferences. But the way in which we evaluate inferences is different from the way in which we evaluate statements; that is, we do not evaluate them as true or false.

5.1 *Validity of Inferences*

The purpose of an inference, again, is to prove the truth of its conclusion from the truth of its premises. When can it do this? Let us imagine that we have premises and a conclusion such that if the premises are true then the conclusion must be true, and such that the conclusion cannot be false when the premises are true. In such cases we can prove the truth of the conclusion from the truth of the premises.

As an example, consider the following inference (in which the premises are the statements expressed by the sentences above the line and the conclusion is the statement expressed by the sentence below the line):

> All men are mortal.
> Socrates is a man.
> _____
> Socrates is mortal.

Can the premises be true and the conclusion false? Obviously not, hence, if we know that these premises are true, then we can justifiably infer from their truth the truth of the conclusion.

Let us call inferences which are such that their conclusions cannot be false when their premises are true *valid inferences*, and inferences which are such that their conclusions can be false when their premises are true *invalid inferences*. Then we can say that one is always justified in making valid inferences from true premises. Notice that we did not say that one is always unjustified in invalidly inferring the truth of some conclusion from some premises. We shall see later that there are some perfectly acceptable invalid inferences. For now, we need only say that all valid inferences are acceptable.

We need to look more carefully at the definition of 'validity'. Consider the following inference:

> All men are immortal.
> Socrates is a man.
> _____
> Socrates is immortal.

Is this inference valid? One is immediately inclined to say that it is not, since its conclusion is false, but actually it is. Could its premises be true and its conclusion false? No. The truth of its premises would guarantee the truth of its conclusion. So the inference is valid. This is not to say, however, that this argument can be used to prove that its conclusion is true. But this is so because the premises are false, not because the inference is invalid.

Let us now look at a third inference:

> All men are Greeks.
> Socrates is a man.
> _____
> Socrates is a Greek.

This inference is once more valid. If its premises are true, then its conclusion would have to be true. And, as a matter of fact, its conclusion is true. Nevertheless, you still could not use this inference to prove the truth of its conclusion—not because it is invalid but because one of its premises is false.

So far we have had three examples of valid inferences, one with true premises and a true conclusion, one with false premises and a false conclusion and one with false premises and a true conclusion. This leaves only one more possibility. Can we have a valid inference with true premises and a false conclusion? No. Why not? Well, an inference is valid only if, when its premises are true, its conclusion must be true as well; therefore, there cannot be a valid inference with true premises and a false conclusion. This is ruled out by the definition of 'valid'.

Let us also look more carefully at the definition of 'invalidity'. Consider the following inference:

All men are mortal.
***
All mortals are men.

This inference is obviously invalid since it has a true premise but a false conclusion. However, examine the following inference:

All creatures with a heart are creatures with a lung.
***
All creatures with a lung are creatures with a heart.

In this case both the premise and the conclusion are true. Nevertheless, the inference is invalid because the premises could be true and the conclusion false. This would be the case if there were creatures with lungs but no heart.

Therefore, there are invalid inferences with true premises and a true conclusion as well as invalid inferences with a false conclusion and true premises. There can also be invalid inferences with false premises and true conclusions and invalid inferences with false premises and false conclusions. An example of the former is:

All men are married.
All mortals are married.
***
All men are mortal.

Besides having false premises, this inference is invalid. Even if its premises were true, its conclusion could be false since the premises do not rule out the possibility of immortal men. An example of the latter is:

All men are married.
All Greeks are married.
***
All men are Greeks.

Besides having false premises and a false conclusion, this inference is invalid. Even if its premises were true, its conclusion could be false since the premises do not rule out the possibility of non-Greek men.

What we have seen so far about validity and invalidity may be summarized in the following table:

	Inference can be valid	Inference can be invalid
True premises True conclusion	Yes	Yes
True premises False conclusion	No	Yes
False premises True conclusion	Yes	Yes
False premises False conclusion	Yes	Yes

All of this means that, even when you know the truth-value of all the premises and of the conclusion of an inference, you cannot tell, from that alone, whether the inference is valid or invalid. The only exception occurs when the premises of the inference are true and the conclusion is false. Or, put in another way, the validity of an inference is not directly determined by the truth-value of its premises or conclusion.

This does not mean that there is no connection between truth and validity. There is one, but it is indirect. The connection is between the possible truth-values (as opposed to the actual truth-values) of the premises and conclusion and the validity of the inference. An inference is valid if, and only if, it is not possible that its premises are true and its conclusion false.

Consider the following inference:

The pressure of a gas doubled while its temperature remained the same.

The volume of the gas was halved.

Is it valid or invalid? Or, to put the question another way, could its premises be true and its conclusion false? One's first inclination is to say that the premise could be true but the conclusion false. On further reflection, however, one remembers that this possibility seems to be ruled out by Boyle's law, which says that, providing that the temperature is constant, the pressure and volume of a gas are inversely proportional. Still further reflection, however, reveals that our original inclination was right—that the premises could be true and the conclusion false. Of course, this would require that Boyle's law be false, but that is surely possible.

Note, however, that there is an inference somewhat similar to the preceding one that is valid:

> The pressure of a gas doubled while its temperature remained the same.
> When the temperature of a gas is constant, the pressure is inversely proportional to the volume.
> _____
> The volume of the gas was halved.

Unlike the last case this inference is valid because when its premises (including Boyle's law) are true, its conclusion must be true.

Two points emerge from this example. (1) When determining whether the premises of an inference can be true while the conclusion is false, one must consider the possibilities that various laws of nature might not be true and that, therefore, the premises could be true and the conclusion false. (2) In such cases, when the inference is invalid, it is possible to construct a new valid inference simply by adding to the premises of the original inference premises asserting that the laws of nature in question do hold.

In many of the cases in which we have an invalid inference that would be valid if certain additional premises were added, it is rather clear from the context that the person who offered the inference really intended that these additional premises be included. In such cases we shall say that he offered a *valid enthymematic inference*, an inference which is invalid as it stands but which would be valid if the additional premises, understood but not stated, were taken into account.

As a matter of fact, most of the valid inferences that we offer are really only enthymematically valid. Few people would say 'all men are mortal and Socrates is a man; so he must be mortal', rather than simply 'Socrates is mortal since he is only a man'. That is to say, the convenience offered by leaving out premises, and the fact that we can usually count on the missing premises being understood, lead people to leave out premises when inferring conclusions. We must always keep this in mind since it woud be foolish to evaluate an inference as invalid when it is rather clear that it is enthymematically valid.

5.2 Valid Inferences
and Logically True Conditionals

In section 5.1 we saw one important connection between truth and validity. In this section we will consider the connection between valid inferences and true conditional statements.

What is a *conditional statement*? It is a statement asserting that if one statement (called the *antecedent statement*) is true, then another statement (called the *consequent statement*) is also true. Thus, the statement expressed by 'If you put salt in water, the salt will dissolve' is a conditional statement whose antecedent statement is expressed by 'you put salt in water' and whose consequent statement is expressed by 'the salt will dissolve'.

When are conditional statements true? We will return to this difficult question later on; for the moment let us simply say that they are false if and only if their antecedent statement is true and their consequent statement is false.

Every inference has its *corresponding conditional statement*, a conditional statement whose antecedent is the joint assertion of all the premises of the inference and whose consequent is the conclusion of the inference. Thus, for the inference:

All men are mortal.
Socrates is a man.

Socrates is mortal.

the corresponding conditional statement is the statement that if all men are mortal and Socrates is a man, then Socrates is mortal. Similarly, for the inference:

All creatures with a heart are creatures with a lung.

All creatures with a lung are creatures with a heart.

the corresponding conditional statement is the statement that if all creatures with a heart are creatures with a lung, then all creatures with a lung are creatures with a heart.

There is a very important connection between the validity of inferences and the truth of their corresponding conditional statements. An inference is valid if and only if its corresponding conditional statement must be true. Let us prove that this connection holds. Assume that some inference is valid, in which case it is not possible that its premises be true and its conclusion false. Therefore, it is not possible that the antecedent statement of the corresponding conditional statement is true and the consequent statement is false; that is, the corresponding conditional statement must be true. Now assume that some corresponding conditional statement cannot be false, in which case it is not possible that its antecedent statement is true while its consequent statement is false. So it is not possible that the premises of the corresponding inference are true while its conclusion is false—that is, the inference is valid. We have therefore proved that an inference is valid if and only if its corresponding conditional statement must be true.

This connection has a special importance worth discussing. The branch of logic that studies valid inferences is known as *deductive logic* (and these inferences are often known as *deductively valid* inferences). As one might expect, deductive logicians have traditionally concerned themselves with classifying the different types of valid inferences and showing that these inferences are valid. This last connection suggests, however, that there is another way of going about the study of deductive logic. One can, instead, simply study the necessarily true statements, classify them, and show that they are necessarily true. Then, if someone wants to know whether a given inference is valid, he simply has to check the theory of necessarily true statements and see whether the conditional statement that corresponds to the inference in question is necessarily true.

There is a definite advantage to proceeding in this second way. We saw previously that for every valid statement, there is a corresponding necessarily true statement (its corresponding conditional statement). But there are some necessarily true statements for which no corresponding valid inferences exist. These are nonconditional statements, such as the statement that either Joe is at home or he is not at home. Although that statement must be true, it has no corresponding valid inference. This means that studying deductive logic by studying necessarily true statements teaches us more than studying deductive logic by studying valid inferences.

Nevertheless, to acquire an easier theory, we should study the validity of inferences. To make our theory more extensive, we shall, in a later chapter, extend it to deal with the case of those necessarily true statements which are not conditional statements.

5.3 *Proving Conclusions True*

In an earlier section of this chapter, we studied several examples of valid inferences with false premises. We said that we cannot use these inferences to prove that their conclusions are true. In this final section we want to say more about this process of proving that certain conclusions are true and about the process of coming to know, on the basis of these proofs, that these conclusions are true.

What is it to *prove that some statement is true*? It is to show that the statement must be true. We can do this by validly inferring that statement from some other true statements. After all, since the inference is valid when its premises are true, its conclusion must also be true. And since the premises are true, the conclusion must be true.

We now see why we cannot prove that something is true by validly inferring it from some false premises. After all, the validity of the inference means only that the conclusion must be true when the premises are true. It does not mean that the conclusion must be true even when the premises are false.

So to prove that a statement is true, we need an inference that:

(1) is valid;
(2) has true premises.

But even if these two conditions are met, it does not follow that we can come to know, on the basis of this proof, that the conclusion is true. To do that, we would also have to know that these two conditions are met. In other words, to come to *know on the basis of some proof* that a statement is true, it must also be the case that:

(3) we know that (1) and (2) are satisfied.

We are now in a position to explain what is wrong with *circular inferences* (ones whose conclusion is one of the premises), such as the following:

John is at home.
_____
John is at home.

This inference is certainly valid, for if its premise is true, then its conclusion must also be true. And if John is at home, so that the premise of this inference is true, then this inference even proves the truth of its conclusion. What, then, is wrong with it? We can never use it to come to learn that something which we did not know was true is true. After all, to come to know, on the basis of this inference, that John is at home, we would first have to know that its premises are true; that is, we would already have to know that John is at home. In other words, to come to know, on the basis of a circular inference, that some statement p is true, we would first have to know that p is true. So we can never use circular inferences to come to know that something is true.

In summary, to use an inference to come to know that some statement p is true, (1) the inference must be valid, (2) its premises must be true, and (3) we must know that the inference is valid and the premises are true. These requirements have led some philosophers to suppose that we could never come to know, on the basis of some proof, that a statement is true. After all, to do that, we first have to know that some inference is valid and that some other statement (the premise) is true. So we would have to prove that each of these is true. To do that, we would have to know that the premises of these additional inferences are true, and that these additional inferences are valid, and so on. It turns out, then, that to come to know, on the basis of some proof, that a statement is true, we would first have to know the truth of an infinite number of other statements. Since we cannot do this, we cannot come to know, on the basis of a proof, that a statement is true.

This is a very powerful skeptical challenge to the very possibility of knowledge. We cannot here enter into the variety of suggested solutions to this problem. We merely wanted to show how this challenge arises the second we distinguish, as we must, between valid inferences and inferences that prove conclusions true, and between the latter and those inferences on the basis of which we can come to know that some statement is true.

EXERCISES FOR CHAPTER 5

Part I

A. What are the premises of each of the following inferences and what is its conclusion?

1. Since all men are mortal and Socrates is a man, Socrates must be mortal.
2. John must be unhappy; after all, he just saw Mary and he's always unhappy after he sees her.
3. All men are animals, so all animals must be men.
4. That bachelor must be unhappy; after all, all happy men are married.
5. If all men are mortal, then Socrates is mortal. So not all men are mortal, since Socrates is immortal.
6. All men are unhappy. So John is unhappy because John is a man.
7. There will be at least three people here today; after all, John will come, Mary will come, and Frank will come.
8. While many of our friends are at home, John must be at work because his job requires him to work at night.

B. Which of the following are inferences and which are statements?

1. If John goes home, he will find Mary there.
2. John went home; therefore, he will find Mary there.
3. Since John went home, it must be the case that he will find Mary there.
4. John will find Mary at home because he went home.
5. It follows from the fact that all men are animals that all animals are men.
6. All men are animals; therefore, all animals are men.
7. Since all men are animals, it must be the case that all animals are men.
8. All men are animals and all animals are men.
9. Because all men are animals, all animals are men.

C. Show that all of the following inferences are invalid by explaining how their conclusion could be false while their premises are true:

1. All creatures with a heart are creatures with a lung. Therefore, all creatures with a lung are creatures with a heart.
2. All men are mortal. All mortals are unhappy. Therefore, all unhappy things are men.
3. All men are immortal. Therefore, all nonmen are mortal.

4. Some men love everyone. Therefore, everyone loves someone.
5. No one hates everyone. So everyone loves everyone.

D. By supplying the missing premise that makes these invalid inferences valid, show that they are valid enthymematic inferences:

1. All men are animals; therefore, all men are mortal.
2. All men are mortal; therefore, no man is perfect.
3. Some men are unhappy; therefore, some animals are unhappy.
4. No man is immortal; therefore, some creatures are not men.
5. There are three men in this room; therefore, there are three mortal creatures in this room.
6. Everyone loves someone; therefore, everyone is loved by someone.

E. What is the antecedent and what is the consequent of each of the following conditional statements?

1. If John went home, he will have dinner and meet Mary.
2. John will meet Mary if he went home.
3. John will meet Mary or Susan if he went home and had dinner.
4. If John went home, he will not have dinner unless he is nice to Mary.
5. John went home and John had dinner if he met Mary or was nice to Susan.

F. Provide, for each of the following inferences, their corresponding conditional statement:

1. John went home, so he had to meet Mary.
2. Either John will go home or he will eat out. In either case he will be unhappy. Therefore, he will be unhappy.
3. John went home and had dinner. After all, Mary wanted him to do so, and he always does what Mary wants.
4. Since John went home, it must be the case that there will be someone at home now.
5. John went home; therefore, he has to be unhappy since he's always unhappy when he goes home.

G. Which of the following inferences are valid, which prove that their conclusion is true, and which do neither?

1. All men are immortal. No immortal creature is an animal. Therefore, no man is an animal.
2. All men are mortal. No mortal creature is a god. Therefore, no man is a god.
3. All men are mortal. No mortal creature is a god. Therefore, no god is a mortal creature.
4. Everyone loves someone; therefore, someone loves everyone.
5. Everyone loves someone; therefore, no man loves no one.
6. Someone loves everyone; therefore, everyone loves someone.
7. Either all men are good or all men are evil. But not all men are good. So all men must be evil.
8. Some men are good and some men are evil. No one loves evil men. So some men are loved by no one.

H. Which of the following inferences are circular.

1. Everyone loves someone; therefore, for every person, there is some person whom he loves.
2. Everyone loves someone; therefore, everyone is loved by someone.
3. Someone loves everyone; therefore, everyone is loved by someone.
4. Everyone loves someone; therefore, for every person, there is some other person whom he loves.

Part II

1. It is easy to understand how one can tell whether a premise or a conclusion actually is true or false. But how can one tell whether the conclusion must be true when the premises are true?

2. We have seen that in deciding about validity, we have to take into account the possibility that certain laws of nature might be false. Are there any statements which are such that we don't have to take into account, when deciding about validity, the possibility that they might be false?

3. By what criterion would we decide whether certain additional premises were understood, even if not explicitly stated, to be part of the inferences?

4. Given the parallelism that we have found between inferences and conditional statements, is there any reason that justifies distinguishing them?

5. Some logicians say that there is a valid inference that corresponds to the necessarily true statement that either Joe is at home or he is not at home. The inference is from no premises to that conclusion. Critically evaluate this claim.

6. If you cannot use every valid inference to prove that its conclusion is true, why does the logician study validity? Why doesn't he concentrate on only those inferences that can be used to prove the truth of their conclusion?

7. Are there any noncircular valid inferences which prove the truth of their conclusion but which are such that one can never use them to come to learn that something which one did not know was true actually is true? If there are such inferences, explain why they are that way.

8. What is wrong with the argument given in the text that purports to show that one can never come to know, on the basis of some proof, that some statement is true?

Propositional Logic

In this chapter, we will begin the task of discovering what inferences are valid. The task is very complicated, however, and we will soon discover that the methods we employ in this chapter to show that certain inferences are valid cannot be used to show the validity of every valid inference. Therefore, we will have to supplement these methods in the next chapter.

6.1 *Some Valid Inferences and the Idea of Propositional Form*

Let us begin by considering the following inferences, all of which are obviously valid:

(I) If all men are mortal and Socrates is a man, then Socrates is mortal. All men are mortal and Socrates is a man.

Socrates is mortal.

(II) Either Socrates was a fool or he was a martyr. It is not the case that Socrates was a fool.

Socrates was a martyr.

(III) Either all politicians are fools or all politicians are clever actors. It is not the case that all politicians are fools.

All politicians are clever actors.

(IV) If all politicians are clever actors, then one cannot trust everything they say.
All politicians are clever actors.

One cannot trust everything they say.

These inferences resemble each other in certain ways and differ from each other in others. (I) and (II) are about Socrates, whereas (III) and (IV) are about politicians. The conclusions of (I) and (II) assert that something is the case about an individual, whereas the conclusions of (III) and (IV) do not.

There is, however, one important respect in which (I) and (IV) are alike and in which they differ from (II) and (III). The first premise of (I) and (IV) is a conditional statement whose antecedent is their second premise and whose consequent is their conclusion. This is not so in the case of (II) and (III). Pictorially, we can say that both (I) and (IV) have the following *form* (or structure):

If p, then q
p

q

Similarly, there is an important respect in which (II) and (III) are alike and in which they differ from (I) and (IV). Let us say that a statement is a *disjunctive statement* when it asserts that either one or the other simpler statement (one or the other of its *disjuncts*) is true. Thus, the first premise of (II) and (III) is a disjunctive statement, their second premise asserts that the first disjunct is false, and the conclusion is the second disjunct. This is not so in the case of (I) and (IV). Pictorially, we can say that both (II) and (III) have the following form (or structure):

Either p or q
It is not the case that p

q

To say that these inferences have the same form or structure is not to say that they are structurally alike in every respect. After all, the antecedent of the first premise of (I), which is also the second premise of (I), is the joint assertion of two statements (and is, therefore, a *conjunctive statement*), whereas this is not true of the antecedent of (IV). Similarly, the disjuncts of the first premise of (II) are statements attributing some property to some particular object, whereas the disjuncts of the first premise of (III) are statements attributing some property to a whole group of objects. So to say that these inferences are of the same form is to say only that there are some structural features that they share in common.

Why is it important that (I) and (IV) and (II) and (III) are of the same form? Because there is good reason to say that these inferences are valid since they are of the form that they are. After all, any inference of either of those forms will be valid.

Once we realize that this is so, we begin to suspect that there may be many other forms of inference such that any inference of that form is valid. Indeed, there are many. The following are additional examples of such forms:

$$\frac{p \text{ and } q}{p}$$

$$\frac{p \text{ if and only if } q}{p}$$

Thus, the inference:

$$\frac{\text{John went home and had dinner.}}{\text{John went home.}}$$

is valid, and it is valid simply because it is of the first of these new forms. Similarly, the inference:

$$\frac{\text{John went home if and only if Mary is at home.}}{\text{John went home.}}$$

is valid, and it is valid simply because it is of the second of these new forms.

Once logicians realized that many forms of inference are *valid forms of inference* (forms of inference such that every inference of that form is valid), they realized they had a method that would make their task of studying the validity of inferences much simpler. Instead of inquiring whether particular inferences were valid, they would inquire whether forms of inference were valid. Then, if they could show that a particular form were valid, they would also have shown that the many inferences of that form were valid. It is much easier to show that one form is valid than to show that all these inferences are valid. So logicians no longer study the validity of particular inferences; instead, they study the validity of forms of inference. For this reason logic is often called *formal logic*.

A second feature of the points we have just made has been noted by logicians. We can describe these different forms of inference in two different ways. The first one is to describe them in words. Thus, we can describe the form of (I) by saying that its first premise is a conditional statement whose antecedent is the second premise and whose consequent is the conclusion. Or we can describe its form by use of symbols. Thus, we can say that it is of the form:

if p, then q

p
_____

q

Even in these simple cases, it is far easier to understand the description of the form if we simply use symbols, such as p, q, r, to stand for statements. When we get to much more complicated inferences with many more symbols, we will find, as have all logicians, that the use of symbols to describe the forms of inference is indispensable. For this reason logic (or, at least, that part that so employs symbols) is often called *symbolic logic*.

One final point: So far, in our discussion of the structure of inferences, we have looked at the different premises and the conclusion to see whether they are composed of simpler statements. Thus, we said that the first premise of (II) is a disjunctive statement—that is, a statement that asserts the truth of one or another of two simpler statements. But when we got to these simpler statements, which are not themselves composed of still simpler statements, we did not try to look more carefully at their structure. In other words, we looked at the structure of the first premise of (II) only to the extent of breaking it down into constituent statements. We did not go on to say that the first disjunct says of some particular object that it has some property. We will continue to do this throughout this chapter. We will suppose that the basic building block out of which the premises and conclusions are composed is the statement; in analyzing their structure we will break them down at most to *simple statements* (statements not composed of any other statements), and not look at the structure of these more basic statements. For this reason we will be concerned only with the *statemental structure* of inferences (this is more commonly called, because of the mistaken view that it is propositions that are the bearers of truth-values, the *propositional structure*), and the system of logic we are developing here is called *statemental* (or, more commonly but incorrectly, *propositional*) *logic*. In Chapter 7, we shall see that this system is inadequate and that it has to be supplemented by a consideration of the structure of simple statements. But we shall see that this system of statemental logic is powerful enough.

6.2 Sentential Connectives:
Truth-Functional and Otherwise

In the last section we looked at four valid forms of inference:

If p, then q

p
_____

q

p or q

It is not the case that p
_____

q

p and q
_____

p

p if and only if q

q
_____

p

If we look at the symbols used for indicating these forms, we notice that, besides the line (which represents 'therefore') and the letters standing for statements (which are called the *statemental-* or *propositional-variables*), the only other symbols employed are 'it is not the case that', 'and', 'or', 'if and only if', and so on. In this section we will deal with the nature and function of these symbols.

Let us begin with 'it is not the case that'. How is this symbol used? Although it does not itself express any statement, when it is placed before a sentence that does, the resulting sentence expresses a new statement that is true (false) if the original statement was false (true). Thus, if the original statement expressed by 'John went home' was true (false), the statement expressed by 'it is not the case that John went home' is false (true).

Something similar can be said about 'and'. It, too, does not express a statement. However, when it is placed between two sentences that do, the resulting sentence expresses a new statement that is true if and only if the two original statements were true. Thus, if the statements expressed by 'John went home' and 'John had dinner' are true, the statement expressed by 'John went home and John had dinner' will also be true; otherwise, it will be false.

Let us call *sentential connectives* all those symbols which do not express statements but which, when combined with one or more symbols that do, produce a new symbol that expresses a new statement. Thus, 'it is not the case' and 'and' are sentential connectives. So is 'or'. It does not express any statement, but when it is placed between two sentences that do, the resulting sentence expresses a new statement that is false when both of the original statements were false. Thus, the statement expressed by 'John went home or John had dinner' is false when the statements expressed by both 'John went home' and 'John had dinner' are false. If one of those statements is true, then the new statement is also true. 'If and only if' is also a sentential connective. It, too, does not express a statement, but when it is placed between two sentences that do, the resulting sentence expresses a new statement that is true only in those cases in which the two original statements had the same truth-value. Thus, 'John went home if and only if John had dinner' expresses a true statement if both 'John went home' and 'John had dinner' express true statements or if both express false statements. Otherwise, the statement expressed by 'John went home if and only if John had dinner' will be false.

Our four symbols are not the only sentential connectives. There are many other types, such as the *epistemic connectives* ('I know that', 'I believe that', 'I suppose that', etc.), the *modal connectives* ('it must be the case that', 'it may be the case that', 'it cannot be the case that', etc.), the *deontic connectives* ('it ought to be the case that', 'it should not be the case that', etc.), the *causal connectives* ('because', 'since', etc.), and others. But there is one extremely important respect in which all our connectives differ from these other connectives; unlike the rest of them, our connectives are truth-functional connectives.

A *truth-functional* sentential connective is a sentential connective such that the truth-value of the new statement formed by use of the connective is completely determined by the truth-value(s) of the original statement(s) expressed by the original sentence(s). 'It is not the case' is obviously a truth-functional connective since the original statement's truth determines the falsehood of the new statement, whereas the original statement's falsehood would determine that the new statement is true. This relationship can be expressed in tabular form, called a *truth-table*:

p	It is not the case that p
T	F
F	T

Similarly, 'or' is obviously a truth-functional connective, since the new statement is false only if both original statements were false; otherwise, it is true.

The truth-table for 'or' is:

p	*q*	*p* or *q*
T	T	T
T	F	T
F	T	T
F	F	F

'And' is obviously a truth-functional connective since the new statement is true only if both original statements were true; otherwise, it is false. The truth-table for 'and' is:

p	*q*	*p* and *q*
T	T	T
T	F	F
F	T	F
F	F	F

Finally, 'if and only if' is also a truth-functional connective since the new statement is true only if both original statements had the same truth-value; if they did not, the new statement is false. The truth-table for 'if and only if' is:

p	*q*	*p* if and only if *q*
T	T	T
T	F	F
F	T	F
F	F	T

None of the other connectives are truth-functional connectives. Consider the statement expressed by 'I know that John went home'. Let us imagine that the statement expressed by 'John went home' is true. We cannot determine from that whether the statement expressed by 'I know that John went home' is also true. If John went home, I may know that he did or I may not. Therefore, the truth-table for 'I know that' would have to be:

p	I know that *p*
T	?
F	F

Consequently, 'I know that' is not a truth-functional connective. Nor is 'it may be the case that'. Consider, for instance, 'it may be the case that John went home'. Let us imagine that the statement expressed by 'John went home' is false. What, then, is the truth-value of the statement expressed by 'it may be the case that John went home'? We can't tell from our knowledge of the truth-value of the statement expressed by 'John went home'. So the truth-table for 'it may be the case that' would have to be:

p	It may be the case that p
T	T
F	?

It could similarly be shown that neither the deontic nor the causal connectives are truth-functional connectives.

Now, in our examination of propositional logic, we will only be concerned with the validity of forms of inference that can be expressed by truth-functional connectives. Thus, we will not treat the validity of forms of inference such as:

it must be the case that p
***
it may be the case that p or q

or:

I believe that p
p is true
***
I know that p

since these forms of inference involve non–truth-functional connectives. The type of propositional logic that we are developing here is known as *truth-functional propositional logic*.

Why are we confining our study? Partly because there is a very elegant and simple theory for truth-functional propositional logic that would have to be greatly complicated in order to deal with non–truth-functional propositional logic; partly because these other logics have not yet been adequately studied, and still contain many unresolved issues. Therefore, their study is inappropriate at an introductory level.

6.3 Negation, Conjunction, Disjunction, Conditional, and Biconditional

In this section we will introduce five simple truth-functional connectives and study the relations between these symbols and certain similar symbols used in ordinary language.

The first of these connectives is the symbol $\sim$, called the *tilde* or the *negation sign*. If the negation sign is placed before a sentence, the resulting sentence expresses a true (false) statement if and only if the original sentence expressed a false (true) statement. Moreover, the $\sim$ symbol can be placed before any sentence that expresses a statement, to convey the meaning 'it is not the case that'. Thus we may symbolize 'it is not the case that John went home' by '$\sim$ John went home'.

The negation sign can also be used to symbolize sentences that do not contain 'it is not the case that'. For example, 'John is not at home' may be written '$\sim$ John is at home'. We do this, obviously, because we suppose that 'John is not at home' expresses the same statement as 'it is not the case that John is at home'. The former sentence is an example of the *internal method of negating a sentence* (it is the *internal negation* of 'John is at home'), whereas the latter is an example of the *external method of negating a sentence* (it is the *external negation* of 'John is at home').

It is necessary to exercise great caution in this matter of internal negation. One might be tempted, for example, to symbolize 'each man is not mortal' as '$\sim$ each man is mortal'. This, however, would be a mistake, for 'each man is not mortal' does not assert the same statement as 'it is not the case that each man is mortal'. The former says that no man is mortal, that all are immortal, whereas the latter merely says that at least some men are mortal. In other words, 'each man is not mortal' cannot be symbolized as '$\sim$ each man is mortal', since the statement expressed by 'each man is not mortal' need not be true if the statement expressed by 'each man is mortal' is false. They would both be false if some men were mortal and some men were immortal. Hence, 'each man is not mortal' is not the internal negation of 'each man is mortal', and cannot be symbolized as '$\sim$ each man is mortal'.

Now let us consider 'John is unrealistic'. Can we symbolize that as '$\sim$John is realistic'? We can, provided that 'John is unrealistic' expresses the same statement as 'it is not the case that John is realistic'. But it is not clear whether it does. Let us imagine that John is somewhat aware of the facts when he decides upon a course of action, and that he does take them into account to some degree. But let us also imagine that he tends, somewhat, toward wishful thinking, and toward acting upon those wishful thoughts. It would not be correct to say that John is unrealistic (after all, he is to some degree a realist), but it might be correct to say that it is not the case that John is realistic. That is to say, there might be a shade of difference between 'John is unrealistic' and 'it is not the case that John is realistic'. If this difference does exist, then we cannot symbolize 'John is unrealistic' as '$\sim$John is realistic'. If, however, it does not exist, then that symbolization will be perfectly acceptable.

This same point can be made about most sentences containing words beginning with *un*, *in*, and so on—such as 'insensitive', 'intemperate',—in their predicates. Thus, we must be cautious about symbolizing 'Francis is insensitive' and '$\sim$Francis is sensitive'. And we must certainly not symbolize

'Fanny is ugly' as '∼Fanny is beautiful', since 'Fanny is ugly' surely does not express the same statement as does 'it is not the case that Fanny is beautiful'. Even if it is not the case that Fanny is beautiful, she may not be ugly.

There is only one safe rule in all these cases: Determine whether the sentence in question asserts the same statement as a sentence beginning with 'it is not the case that'. Then, and only then, can a tilde be used in symbolizing the sentence in question.

We turn now to the second of our connective symbols, the centered dot, which is called the *conjunction sign*. This symbol can be placed between any sentences expressing statements to form a new sentence that also expresses a statement, which is true if all the original statements were true; if one or more of the original statements were false, the new statement is also false.

In light of what we said about 'and' in the last section, it would appear that '·' is synonymous with 'and'. However, we shall soon see that that is not entirely correct, since our earlier account of the use of 'and' was an oversimplification. To begin with, 'and' cannot (or, at least, should not) be placed between just any sentences that express statements. There is something very queer about 'John went home and two plus two equals four'. In general, one places 'and' between sentences that express statements only if there is some connection between the statements expressed. This is not so in the case of '·'. It can be placed, without oddity, between any sentences that express statements.

This difference between 'and' and '·' does not, however, prevent us from using '·' in symbolizing sentences containing 'and'. For this difference means only that we cannot use 'and' in some cases in which we can use '·'; it does not mean that we cannot use '·' to symbolize 'and'. Therefore, we shall symbolize 'the Yankees won the American League pennant and the Mets won the National League pennant' as 'the Yankees won the American League pennant · the Mets won the National League pennant'.

Consider, now, 'John went home and had dinner'. We would certainly be tempted to symbolize this as 'John went home · John had dinner', but this is not entirely correct. After all, 'John went home and had dinner' also seems to express a third statement, namely, that John's having dinner followed his going home, but this is not expressed by 'John went home · John had dinner'. Intuitively, it is this temporal ordering of the events whose occurrence is expressed by the two sentences that provides the rationale for joining them by 'and'. But we need no rationale for joining them by the conjunction sign; so 'John went home · John had dinner' does not express that temporal ordering.

How, then, shall we symbolize 'John went home and had dinner'? We have two options. The first is to symbolize it as 'John went home · John had dinner · John's going home occurred before his having dinner'. This method has the advantage of truly symbolizing what is expressed in the original sentence. The second option is to disregard the temporal ordering aspect, claiming that it is somehow irrelevant, and simply symbolize it as 'John went home · John had dinner'. This method has the advantage of making symbolizations easier, but only at the price of making them inaccurate.

We can summarize this second point by stating that sentences of the form 'p and q' often express more than do the corresponding sentences of the form '$p \cdot q$'. We must add this additional content when we symbolize sentences of the former type if we want to make sure that our symbolizations are accurate. This is even more vital for sentences of the forms 'p but q', 'although p, q', 'p, despite the fact that q', and so on. Consider 'John went home but Francis was already there'. It certainly expresses all that is expressed by 'John went home · Francis was already there'. It would be a mistake, however, to symbolize the former by the latter, since the former expresses more than the latter. Moreover, given the notorious equivocity of 'but', it is not easy to say, in a given case, what this additional content is. The same point can be made about 'although John went home, Francis was already there' and 'John went home despite the fact that Francis was already there'.

Because of these difficulties, logicians are inclined to symbolize all these sentences as being of the form '$p \cdot q$', even though this symbolization omits something. Their line of reasoning is very simple: Our concern, after all, is with the validity of inferences from premises such as this or of conclusions such as this. Now, if we can show that the inference in question is valid if the premise is of the form '$p \cdot q$', then we will know that it is certainly valid for premises of the form 'p and q', 'p but q', 'although p, q', 'p despite the fact that q', and so on, since these premises say even more. And, if we can show that the inference is valid if the conclusion is of the form '$p \cdot q$', then it will also be valid if the conclusion is of the form 'p, but q', and so on. For even with the additional content of such conclusions, they can never be false (only inappropriate) when the corresponding conclusion of the former type is true. Since this is a well-taken point, we shall follow this procedure in our work.

One final point about what we can symbolize with '·'. Consider 'John and Francis got A's on their test' and 'John got an A in history and a B in literature'. In these sentences, 'and' is not a sentential connective and cannot be replaced by '·'. We can, however, use '·' in the symbolization of these sentences since the former expresses the same statement as does 'John got an A on his test and Francis got an A on her test', and can therefore be symbolized as 'John got an A on his test · Francis got an A on her test', while the latter expresses the same statement as 'John got an A in history and John got a B in literature', and can therefore be symbolized as 'John got an A in history · John got a B in literature'. However, one should be cautious about such examples. It won't do to symbolize 'John and Francis got married in the same way that we symbolized 'John and Francis got A's'. The former expresses the fact that they married each other, which would be omitted if we symbolized it as 'John got married · Francis got married'.

We turn now to the third of our connectives, the symbol ∨, called *vel* or the *disjunction sign*. The symbol ∨ can be placed between any sentences which express statements to form a new sentence which expresses a statement that is true if one or more of the original statements were true; if all original statements were false, the new statement is also false.

In light of what we said about 'or' in the last section, it would appear that ∨ is synonymous with 'or'. However, this would not be entirely correct. Like 'and', the connective 'or' cannot (or, at least, should not) be placed between just any sentences that express statements. However, this difference between 'or' and '∨' does not mean that we cannot use the symbol for sentences that contain 'or'; it means that we can use ∨ in some cases where we cannot use 'or'. Also, there are sentences such as 'John or Francis will get an A' and 'John will get an A in history or in literature', in which 'or' is not a sentential connective and cannot be symbolized by replacing 'or' with ∨. But we can use ∨ in the symbolization of these sentences since the former expresses the same statement as does 'John will get an A or Francis will get an A' and can therefore be symbolized as 'John will get an A ∨ Francis will get an A', while the latter expresses the same statement as 'John will get an A in history or John will get an A in literature' and can therefore be symbolized as 'John will get an A in history ∨ John will get an A in literature'.

We must discuss one more important distinction between 'or' and ∨, namely, 'or' is equivocal in a way that ∨ is not. Consider the following two sentences:

(1) Either we will go to the movies or we will go to the beach.
(2) John will get an A in history or John will get an A in literature.

Sentence (1) expresses the statement that we will go to the movies or to the beach but not to both, and that statement is false if we go to neither or to both. Sentence (2) expresses the statement that John will at least get an A in history or in literature and perhaps both, and that statement is false only if he gets an A in neither; it is not false if he gets an A in both. When 'or' is used in the former way, it is said to be used in the *exclusive sense;* it is used in the *inclusive sense* when it is used in the latter way. Since our truth-table for 'or' in section 6.2 had disjunctive statements as true when both the disjuncts were true, our account was true only of the inclusive sense of 'or', and ∨ corresponds to 'or' only when it is used inclusively.

Just as there is an important connection between the meaning of 'but', 'although', 'despite', and so on, on the one hand and 'and', on the other, so there is an important connection between 'unless' and 'except', on the one hand, and 'or', on the other. 'John will go home unless Mary is there', expresses something like what is expressed by 'John will go home or Mary is there'. But it would be a mistake to symbolize 'John will go home unless Mary is there as' 'John will go home ∨ Mary is there'. After all, 'John will go home unless Mary is there' expresses something like 'John will go home or Mary is there' only if 'or' is understood exclusively; but ∨ can be used only when 'or' is understood inclusively. The same point can be made about 'John will go home except when Mary is there'. So the connection between 'unless' and 'except' and 'or' is only a connection between those two connectives and exclusive disjunction, and therefore ∨ cannot be used in symbolizing those two connectives.

The fourth connective that we want to introduce is the symbol ≡, called the *biconditional* or the *material equivalence sign*. This symbol can be placed between any sentences expressing statements to form a new sentence which expresses a statement that is true if all the original statements had the same truth-value; if they did not, the new statement is false.

There is very little difference between ≡ and 'if and only if'. Whereas ≡ can be placed between any sentences that express statements (whether or not there is any connection between them), 'if and only if' should be placed between sentences only if there is some connection between the statements that they express.

Our fifth and last connective is the horseshoe symbol ⊃, called the *material conditional*. This symbol can be placed between any two sentences expressing statements to form a new sentence that expresses a false statement only when the statement expressed by the first sentence (the *antecedent*) is true and the statement expressed by the second sentence (the *consequent*) is false; in all other cases the statement expressed by the new sentence is true. The truth-table for this connective is shown below.

p	q	$p \supset q$
T	T	T
T	F	F
F	T	T
F	F	T

Unlike the four other connectives discussed in this section, ⊃ is not related to any particular English connective word. We use it, in doing truth-functional propositional logic, to convey a concept as close as we can get to the 'if–then' connective.

Consider the sentence 'If John goes home, then he will find that Mary is there'. When is the statement expressed by that sentence clearly false? It is clearly false if, when John goes home, he does not find Mary there. In other words, it would clearly be false if its antecedent were true and its consequent false. On the other hand, it would seem to be true if its antecedent

were true and its consequent true. So in at least this case, the truth-table of
⊃ corresponds, in its first two lines, to what is true about 'if–then'.

However, is 'If John goes home, then he will find that Mary is there'
true if John does *not* go home (i.e., if its antecedent is false)? The answer to
that is extremely unclear. One is often inclined even to say that there is no
answer—that such conditional statements are neither true nor false when their
antecedent is false. In this respect, 'if–then' differs markedly from ⊃ since
'John goes home ⊃ he will find that Mary is there'. is clearly true whenever
its antecedent is false.

This, then, is an important difference between 'if–then' and ⊃. Nevertheless, its importance should not be overrated. By itself it does not show that
'if–then' is not a truth-functional connective. That could be shown only if
one could show that there are cases in which an if–then statement has a
truth-value not determined by the truth-value of its constituent statements.
That has not yet been shown. More importantly, this difference does not
prevent us from symbolizing 'if–then' by ⊃. After all, whenever an if–then
statement is true (which occurs when both its antecedent and consequent are
true), the corresponding statement expressed by use of a material conditional
will also be true. Thus, whenever the statement S_3 expressed by 'if John goes
home, then he will find that Mary is there', is true, the statement S_2, expressed
by 'John goes home ⊃ he will find that Mary is there', will also be true. However, there will be cases in which the latter is true but the former has no truth-
value. Now let us imagine that we can validly infer some statement S_1
from the statement S_2, which means that whenever S_2 is true, S_1 must also be
true. If this is the case, we can also validly infer it from the statement S_3.
For whenever S_3 is true, S_2 is true, and whenever S_2 is true, S_1 must be true.
Thus, whenever S_3 is true, S_1 must be true; that is, the inference from the
statement S_3, expressed by 'if John goes home, then he will find that Mary is
there', is also valid. So we can study the validity of inferences whose premises
are expressed by sentences using material conditionals, knowing very well
that the corresponding inferences whose premises are expressed by the corresponding if–then sentences will also be valid. And if we can show that the
inference is valid when its conclusion is of the form '$p ⊃ q$', it will also be
valid if the conclusion is of the form 'if p, then q'. After all, the latter type of
conclusion cannot be false (only inappropriate) when the corresponding conclusion of the former type is true. So for the purpose of studying validity of
inferences, we can symbolize 'if–then' by ⊃.

We must consider, however, a second major difference between 'if–
then' and ⊃. Consider 'if $2 = 2$, then the earth is not flat'. Is the statement
it expresses true or false? One is again inclined to say that it is neither. But
the statement expressed by '$2 = 2 ⊃$ the earth is not flat' is clearly true. In
this case then, the truth-table of '⊃', even in its first line, does not correspond to what is true about 'if–then'. If–then sentences, in order to express

true statements, must not merely have true antecedents and true consequents; there must be a connection between them.

Although this is another important difference between 'if–then' and $\supset$; it, too, should not be overrated. For the same reasons advanced before, it shows neither that 'if–then' is not a truth-functional connective nor that (if we are studying the validity of inferences) we cannot symbolize 'if–then' by use of $\supset$.

The relationship between 'but' and the centered dot is analogous to the relationship between 'if–then' and $\supset$. In both cases, sentences containing the connective *word* express more than corresponding sentences containing the connective *symbol*. This does not mean, however, that statements expressed by the word can be false while statements expressed by the symbol are true. Consequently, when studying validity, we may use '·' to symbolize 'but' and $\supset$ to symbolize 'if–then'.

The two differences under discussion have given rise to the so-called *paradoxes of the material conditional:* (1) a statement expressed by any sentence of the form $p \supset q$ is true when its consequent is true; thus, '2 = 17 $\supset$ the earth is not flat' expresses a true statement. (2) A statement expressed by any sentence of the form $p \supset q$ is true when its antecedent is false; thus, '2 = 17 $\supset$ the moon is made out of blue cheese' expresses a true statement. However, there is nothing paradoxical about these two so-called paradoxes; on the contrary, they merely express aspects of the truth-table governing $\supset$. It only seems paradoxical when you read $\supset$ as 'if–then'. One should not. It may be safe to symbolize 'if–then' as $\supset$ for the sake of studying validity; however, they do not mean the same thing.

Statements of this form:	*Are normally symbolized:*
It is not the case that *p*	$\sim$p
a is not *P*	$\sim p$ (where *p* stands for '*a* is *P*')
a is un-*P*	$\sim p$ (where *p* stands for '*a* is *P*')
p and *q*	$p \cdot q$
p but *q*	$p \cdot q$
Although *p*, *q*	$p \cdot q$
p, despite *q*	$p \cdot q$
a did *A* and *B*	$p \cdot q$ (where *p* stands for '*a* did *A*' and *q* stands for '*a* did *B*')
p or *q*	$p \vee q$
p unless *q*	$(p \vee q) \cdot \sim(p \cdot q)$
p except if *q*	$(p \vee q) \cdot \sim(p \cdot q)$
p if and only if *q*	$p \equiv q$
If *p*, then *q*	$p \supset q$
q, if *p*	$p \supset q$
When *p*, then *q*	$p \supset q$

We have then our five connective symbols: $\sim$, $\cdot$, $\vee$, $\supset$, and $\equiv$. We know when and how to use them in symbolizing sentences to express the form of an inference. The results of our study are summarized in the table shown on page 98. We are now ready to begin studying the validity of inference-forms.

6.4 Introduction and Elimination Inferences

In this section, we will look at several valid inference-forms and show that they are valid. We have already encountered a few of them in section 6.1, and have said that they are valid. They intuitively were, but now we will show that they are. The rest of them are new. Of course, these are not the only valid inference forms, but for us they are basic, because in later sections we will use them as the basis for showing that other forms of inference are valid.

Let us begin with two inference-forms expressed by use of conjunction:

$$\frac{p \cdot q}{p} \quad \text{or} \quad \frac{p \cdot q}{q}$$

$$\frac{\begin{array}{c} p \\ q \end{array}}{p \cdot q}$$

The first inference-form, which we have already encountered in section 6.1, will be called the *and-elimination* form, whereas the other will be called the *and-introduction* form. The reason for these names is quite important, as we shall see later on. In the first case the sentence expressing the premise contains a '$\cdot$' that is not present in the sentence expressing the conclusion. In the second case the sentence expressing the conclusion contains a '$\cdot$' not present in the sentences expressing the premises.

It is easy to prove that any inference of either of these forms is valid. Let us first look at the and-elimination form. For an inference of that form to be invalid, it must have a true premise and a false conclusion. But that is impossible. If the conclusion is false, then the first (or second) of the two statements conjoined in the premise is false and the whole premise is false. This follows directly from the rules governing the use of '$\cdot$'. So no inference of this form can be invalid. Similarly, for an inference of the and-introduction form to be invalid, it must have true premises and a false conclusion. But it cannot. If the conclusion is false, it can only be because the statements represented by either p or q are false. But, then one of the premises is false; hence, no inference of this form can be invalid.

We will now look at two inference-forms expressed by use of disjunction:

$$\frac{p}{p \lor q} \quad \text{or} \quad \frac{q}{p \lor q}$$

$$\frac{\begin{array}{c} p \lor q \\ p \supset r \\ q \supset r \end{array}}{r}$$

The first of these will be called the *or-introduction form*, since its conclusion is expressed by a sentence containing a $\lor$ not present in the sentence expressing its premise; the second inference form will be called the *or-elimination form*, since one of the sentences expressing one of the premises contains a $\lor$ that does not occur in the sentence expressing the conclusion.

It is very easy to prove that any inference of the or-introduction form (abbreviated OI in our proofs) is valid. For an inference of the OI form to be *in*valid, it would have to have a true premise and a false conclusion. But that is impossible. For the conclusion to be false, both the statement represented by 'p' and the statement represented by 'q' would have to be false. But then the premise would not be true. So no inference of this form can be invalid. Now let us look at the more complicated or-elimination form. Could an inference of this form be invalid? For that to happen, the statement represented by 'r' would have to be false while all the premises are true. But then, since the statement represented by 'r' is false, the second and third premises—the statements represented by '$p \supset r$' and by '$q \supset r$'—will be true only if the statements represented by both 'p' and 'q' are false. But then the first premise cannot be true. Therefore, it cannot be the case that the conclusion is false and all the premises true; every inference of this form must therefore be valid.

Our next two inference-forms involve the biconditional. The *biconditional-introduction form* (BI) is:

$$\frac{\begin{array}{c} p \supset q \\ q \supset p \end{array}}{p \equiv q}$$

The *biconditional-elimination form* (BE) is:

$$\frac{p \equiv q}{p \supset q} \quad \text{or} \quad \frac{p \equiv q}{q \supset p}$$

It is easy to see that inferences of these forms are never invalid. Looking first at biconditional-introduction, such an inference could be invalid only if it were possible that the statement represented by '$p \equiv q$' were false while the statements represented by both '$p \supset q$' and '$q \supset p$' were true. But that is not possible, since the statement represented by $p \equiv q$ could be false only either if the statement represented by 'p' were true and the statement represented by 'q' were false (in which case the statement represented by '$p \supset q$' would not be true) or if the statement represented by 'q' were true and the statement represented by 'p' were false (in which case the statement represented by '$q \supset p$' would not be true).

Looking now at biconditional-elimination, we see essentially the same thing happening. Such an inference could be invalid only if it were possible that the statement represented by '$p \equiv q$' were true while the statement represented by '$p \supset q$' (or by '$q \supset p$') were false. But this is not possible. For the statement represented by '$p \supset q$' (or by '$q \supset p$') to be false, the statement represented by 'p' must be true while the statement represented by 'q' must be false (the statement represented by 'q' must be true while the statement represented by 'p' must be false); but then the statement represented by '$p \equiv q$' would not be true.

We come now to inferences involving negation. *Negation-introduction* (often known as *reductio ad absurdum*) is the following inference form:

$$\frac{p \supset (q \cdot \sim q)}{\sim p}$$

Such inferences must be valid because the statement represented by '$q \cdot \sim q$' cannot be true. So if the premise is true, it must be because the statement represented by 'p' is false. But then the statement represented by '$\sim p$' is true. So when the premise is true, the conclusion is also true, and the inference is valid.

Negation-elimination (sometimes known as *modus tollens*) is the following inference form:

$$\frac{\begin{array}{c} p \supset q \\ \sim q \end{array}}{\sim p}$$

This is also a valid form of inference. It would be invalid only if it were possible that the statement represented by '$\sim p$' were false while the statements represented by '$p \supset q$' and by '$\sim q$' were true. But this is not possible. If the statement represented by '$\sim p$' were false, then the statement represented by 'p' would be true. But if it were true, and if the statement represented by '$p \supset q$' were true, then the statement represented by 'q' must be true, and the statement represented by '$\sim q$' would be false.

The *double negation* form of inference is as follows:

$$\frac{\sim \sim p}{p} \quad \text{or} \quad \frac{p}{\sim \sim p}$$

The proof that this is a valid form of inference is not difficult. If these inferences were invalid, it would be possible for the statement represented by 'p' to be false while the statement represented by '$\sim\sim p$' was true, or for the statement represented by '$\sim\sim p$' to be false while the statement represented by 'p' was true. Neither is possible. If the statement represented by 'p' (by '$\sim\sim p$') is false, then the statement represented by '$\sim p$' is true, and the statement represented by '$\sim\sim p$' (by 'p') is false.

Finally, we come to some inference forms involving the material conditional. The first is *conditional-elimination* (usually known as *modus ponens*):

$$p \supset q$$
$$\underline{p}$$
$$q$$

This is obviously a valid inference form. For such an inference to be invalid, it would have to be possible that the statement represented by 'q' were false while the statements represented by 'p' and by '$p \supset q$' were true. But this is not possible. If the statement represented by 'p' were true while the statement represented by 'q' were false, then the statement represented by '$p \supset q$' could not be true.

Conditional-introduction is very different from the rest of our valid forms. It is the following mode of inference:

Given assumptions $A_1, \ldots, A_n$, q can be validly inferred from p.

Given assumptions $A_1, \ldots, A_n$, $p \supset q$.

What makes it different, of course, is that it involves the non–truth-functional-connective 'can be validly inferred from'. It is therefore the one exception to our claim that we would consider only truth-functional connectives.

Nevertheless, it is perfectly obvious that this is a valid mode of inference. For its conclusion to be false, it would have to be the case that, even though assumptions $A_1, \ldots, A_n$ are true, the statement represented by 'q' was false while the statement represented by 'p' was true. But then its premise would be false; the inference from the statement represented by 'p' to the statement represented by 'q' would not be valid. So the premise cannot be true when the conclusion is false, and any inference of the conditional-introduction form is valid.

Let us see where we stand now. So far we have shown, by fairly intuitive and informal methods, that eleven inference-forms are valid. We could, of course, continue in the preceding fashion, but as the inferences get more complicated, as they contain more premises, and as the premises and conclusion get longer, this mode of procedure will become less and less satisfactory. It will become increasingly difficult to follow our proofs, and we will have more and more doubts about our results. What we need is a much more carefully defined method, one in which we can check to see that we have made no mistakes.

The results and methods of this section serve as the basis for two such methods for showing that inferences are valid. The first, the *natural deduction technique*, starts from the results of this section and uses the validity of our eleven forms to show that other forms of inference are valid. We will spend the next three sections discussing this method. The second method, the *technique of semantic tableaux*, starts from the methods we employed in this section. It presents them much more carefully, in such a way that we can always check to see if they are being used properly, and then employs them to prove the validity of other modes of inference. We will discuss this method at the end of this chapter.

6.5 The Idea of a Proof

Let us imagine that we wanted to show that the following form of inference is valid:

$$p \supset q$$
$$q \supset r$$
$$\underline{\quad p \quad}$$
$$r$$

How could we do this? One way would be to argue as follows: Assume that two of the premises of such an inference, the statements represented by '$p \supset q$' and 'p', are true. Then, because of the validity of the conditional-elimination mode of inference, the statement represented by 'q' must be true. Now assume that the statement represented by '$q \supset r$' is true. Then, from it and from the statement represented by 'q', it follows, given the validity of the conditional-elimination mode of inference, that the statement represented by 'r' must be true. Putting all this together, we see that if all the premises of such an inference are true, then its conclusion must be true. Therefore, this form of inference is valid.

We can arrange this proof in a table as follows:

(1) $p \supset q$ An assumption
(2) $q \supset r$ An assumption
(3) p An assumption
(4) q Its truth follows from (1) and (3), given the validity of the conditional-elimination form of inference.
(5) r Its truth follows from (2) and (4), given the validity of the conditional-elimination form of inference.

We can use this same method to show that the following is a valid form of inference:

$$\frac{p \cdot q}{p \vee q}$$

We would argue as follows: Assume that the premise of such an inference, the statement represented by '$p \cdot q$', is true. Then, given the validity of the and-elimination form of inference, the statement represented by 'p' must be true. Consequently, given the validity of the or-introduction form of inference, the statement represented by '$p \vee q$' must be true. So, if the premise of such an inference is true, its conclusion must also be true, and this is a valid mode of inference. In our tabular method of presentation, we would have:

(1) $p \cdot q$ An assumption
(2) p Its truth follows from (1), given the validity
                of and-elimination inferences.
(3) $p \vee q$ Its truth follows from (2), given the validity of
                or-introduction inferences.

The justifications that we have been writing, on the right of each step, are quite cumbersome. A simpler way is to indicate the earlier steps from which the new step can be validly inferred, by giving their number, and to indicate the form of this inference by giving an abbreviation of its name. Thus to prove that:

$$\frac{\sim p \supset q}{\sim q}$$
$$p$$

is a valid mode of inference, we would show the proof as follows:

(1) $\sim p \supset q$ Assump.
(2) $\sim q$ Assump.
(3) $\sim \sim p$ (1)(2) NE
(4) p (3) DN

in which 'Assump.' stands for assumption, 'NE' stands for Negation Elimination, and 'DN' stands for Double Negation.

Thus far in our examples of this method for showing the validity of inference forms, we have not yet used the conditional-introduction inference form. Here is an example using the CI form. To show that

$$p \supset q$$
$$\frac{p \supset \sim q}{\sim p}$$

is a valid inference form, we would argue as follows (note the abbreviations used for Conditional Elimination, And-Introduction, and Negation Introduction):

(1) $p \supset q$	Assump.
(2) $p \supset \sim q$	Assump.
(3) p	Assump.
(4) q	(1)(3) CE
(5) $\sim q$	(2)(3) CE
(6) $q \cdot \sim q$	(4)(5) AI
(7) $p \supset (q \cdot \sim q)$	(6) CI
(8) $\sim p$	(7) NI

There is a very important difference between this proof and the preceding proofs. Until now, the only assumption we made in our proof is that the premises of the inference in question are true. In each case we tried to show that if this is so, the conclusion must also be true. Here, however, we made an additional assumption: In step (3) we assumed the truth of the statement represented by 'p'. Shouldn't this open the proof to challenge? After all, what we have shown is only that if the statements represented by '$p \supset q$', '$p \supset \sim q$', and 'p' are true, then the statement represented by '$\sim p$' is also true; what we have not shown and must show—is that if only the statements represented by '$p \supset q$' and '$p \supset \sim q$' are true, then the statement represented by '$\sim p$' is also true.

This objection, while perfectly understandable, misses the point of our argument. In step (3) we did make an additional assumption. And by the end of step (6), assuming that (1) and (2) are true, we had shown that we can validly infer the statement represented by '$q \cdot \sim q$', from the statement represented by 'p'. So, we concluded, assuming that (1) and (2) are true, that the statement represented by '$p \supset (q \cdot \sim q)$', and, therefore, the statement represented by '$\sim p$' are also true. By the use of CI in step (7), we got rid of our third assumption.

All this becomes much clearer if we amend our method as follows: Every time we introduce an assumption, we write the number of that step to the left of it. And when we infer, from previous steps, any new step, we write, to the left of its number, all numbers that appeared to the left of the number of the previous steps. The only time we drop one of these numbers is when we use CI, and then we drop only the number of the step in which we introduced the assumption that becomes the antecedent of the conditional in the new step. Finally, the proof is successful if, at the end, the only numbers remaining are the numbers of the steps in which we introduced as assumptions the premises of the inference of the form whose validity we are trying to prove.

According to this procedure, we would rewrite the preceding proof thus:

(1)	(1) $p \supset q$	Assump.
(2)	(2) $p \supset \sim q$	Assump.
(3)	(3) p	Assump.
(1)(3)	(4) q	(1)(3) CE
(2)(3)	(5) $\sim q$	(2)(3) CE
(1)(2)(3)	(6) $q \cdot \sim q$	(4)(5) AI
(1)(2)	(7) $p \supset (q \cdot \sim q)$	(6) CI
(1)(2)	(8) $\sim p$	(7) AI

Intuitively, the numbers at the right tell us upon what assumptions this new step is based.

Having looked at a few examples of this new method of showing that inference-forms are valid, let us say a few things about this method. We show that if the premises of some inference of this form are true, then its conclusion is also true. We do this by producing an ordered sequence of statements, all of which either are assumptions or are validly inferrable, by use of one of our eleven inference-forms, from earlier members of the sequence. The last member of the sequence must, of course, be the conclusion of the inference in question, and it must rest only upon assumptions that are premises of the inference in question. In such a case we say that the sequence is a *proof that if the premises of the inference are true, then its conclusion is also true, and a proof that any inference of the form in question is a valid inference.*

Applying this to our last example, we can say that steps (1) through (8) are a proof that if the statements represented by '$p \supset q$' and '$p \supset \sim q$' are true, then the statement represented by '$\sim p$' is also true. After all, (a) the last member of that sequence is the statement represented by '$\sim p$'; (b) it rested, as we can see by looking at the numbers on the left, only upon the statements represented by '$p \supset q$' and '$p \supset \sim q$', and (c) each member of the sequence either is an assumption [as are (1), (2), and (3)] or is derivable [as are (4) through (8)] from earlier members of the sequence by use of one of our eleven forms of inference. Consequently, that proof proves that any inference of the form in question is valid.

We now see how we can mechanically determine whether our proof is satisfactory. All we must do is to see (a) whether its last step is the conclusion of the inference in question, (b) whether the only assumptions that its last step depends upon are the premises of the inference in question, and (c) whether each step of the proof either is an assumption or is validly inferrable from an earlier step by use of one of our eleven valid forms of inference.

Let us now go back, for a moment, to our second proof, which was:

(1)	(1) $p \cdot q$	Assump.
(1)	(2) p	(1) AE
(1)	(3) $p \lor q$	(2) OI

We have therefore shown that one can validly infer the statement represented by '$p \vee q$', from the statement represented by '$p \cdot q$'. Therefore we could extend our proof as follows:

(4) $(p \cdot q) \supset (p \vee q)$ (3) CI

Notice that there are no assumptions upon which step (4) stands. Therefore, we have proved, not that the statement represented by '$(p \cdot q) \supset (p \vee q)$' is true if some other statements are true, but rather that it is simply true.

This point is extremely important. You will remember that we spoke, in Chapter 5, of two conceptions of logic. One conception is of logic as the study of the validity of inferences. The other is of logic as the study of what statements must be true. We said there that we would work with the first conception of logic, that we would be concerned primarily with the study of the validity of inferences. We also promised, however, that our methods for showing that certain inferences are valid (and that certain inference-forms are valid) could also be used to show that certain statements must be true (and that every statement of certain forms must be true). We have now fulfilled that promise. One of our sequences is a *proof that a certain statement must be true* (a) if that statement is the last member of the sequence, (b) if it rests upon no assumptions, and (c) if every member of the sequence either is an assumption or is derivable from the earlier members of the sequence by use of an inference which is of one of our eleven valid forms. Such a proof *proves that any statement of that form must be true*.

6.6 Some Proofs

In this section we will look at a variety of additional proofs, some of which prove that certain forms of inference are valid, whereas others prove that statements of certain forms must be true. Our purpose in looking at these proofs is twofold: first, it will give us some exercise in recognizing when proofs are satisfactory; second these inference-forms and statement-forms are outstanding ones that are worth knowing about; hence, a proof of the fact that they are valid forms of inference, or that any statement of that form must be true, is independently worthwhile.

Let us begin with some proofs that all statements of certain forms must be true. In particular, let us prove this about two of the following statement-forms:

(a) $p \vee (q \vee r) \equiv (p \vee q) \vee r$ Associative law for disjunction
(b) $p \cdot (q \cdot r) \equiv (p \cdot q) \cdot r$ Associative law for conjunction
(c) $p \vee q \equiv q \vee p$ Commutative law for disjunction
(d) $p \cdot q \equiv q \cdot p$ Commutative law for conjunction
(e) $p \cdot (q \vee r) \equiv (p \cdot q) \vee (p \cdot r)$ Distributive law for conjunction over disjunction
(f) $p \vee (q \cdot r) \equiv (p \vee q) \cdot (p \vee r)$ Distributive law for disjunction over conjunction

In effect, (a) and (b) tell us that brackets don't count when the sentence expressing the statement contains only one of these connectives; (c) and (d) tell us that the order of the two statements doesn't count; and (e) and (f) tell us what is expressed in a sentence containing both.

The proof of (a) is lengthy. (Note that OE stands for or-Elimination.)

PROOF OF (a)

(1)	(1) $p \lor (q \lor r)$	Assump.
(2)	(2) p	Assump.
(2)	(3) $p \lor q$	OI (2)
(2)	(4) $(p \lor q) \lor r$	OI (3)
	(5) $p \supset [(p \lor q) \lor r]$	CI (4)
(6)	(6) $q \lor r$	Assump.
(7)	(7) q	Assump.
(7)	(8) $p \lor q$	OI (7)
(7)	(9) $(p \lor q) \lor r$	OI (8)
	(10) $q \supset [(p \lor q) \lor r]$	CI (9)
(11)	(11) r	Assump.
(11)	(12) $(p \lor q) \lor r$	OI (11)
	(13) $r \supset [(p \lor q) \lor r]$	CI (12)
(6)	(14) $(p \lor q) \lor r$	OE (6)(10)(13)
	(15) $(q \lor r) \supset [(p \lor q) \lor r]$	CI (14)
(1)	(16) $(p \lor q) \lor r$	OE (1)(5)(15)
	(17) $[p \lor (q \lor r)] \supset [(p \lor q) \lor r]$	CI (16)
(18)	(18) $(p \lor q) \lor r$	Assump.
(19)	(19) $p \lor q$	Assump.
(20)	(20) p	Assump.
(20)	(21) $p \lor (q \lor r)$	OI (20)
	(22) $p \supset [p \lor (q \lor r)]$	CI (21)
(23)	(23) q	Assump.
(23)	(24) $q \lor r$	OI (23)
(23)	(25) $p \lor (q \lor r)$	OI (24)
	(26) $q \supset [p \lor (q \lor r)]$	CI (25)
(19)	(27) $p \lor (q \lor r)$	OE (19)(22)(26)
	(28) $p \lor q \supset [(p \lor (q \lor r)]$	CI (27)
(29)	(29) r	Assump.
(29)	(30) $q \lor r$	OI (29)
(29)	(31) $p \lor (q \lor r)$	OI (30)
	(32) $r \supset [p \lor (q \lor r)]$	CI (31)
(18)	(33) $p \lor (q \lor r)$	OE (18)(28)(32)
	(34) $[(p \lor q) \lor r)] \supset [p \lor (q \lor r)]$	CI (33)
	(35) $p \lor (q \lor r) \equiv (p \lor q) \lor r$	BI (17)(34)

As is clear from the last step, the proof divides into two parts, a proof of (17) and a proof of (34). Let us look at one of these parts, the proof of (17), since what we say about one part is equally applicable to the other. Obviously, as we look at (17), the idea was to prove (16) on the assumption that (1) is true. Since (1) is a disjunctive statement, we first assumed [in (2)] that its first disjunct was true and showed [in (5)] that, if this was true, then what (16) asserts would be true. We then assumed [in (6)] that the second disjunct of (1) is true, and showed [in (15)] that, if this was true, then what (16) asserts would be true. Given (5) and (15) we can infer by OE [as we did in (16)] that (16) is true on the assumption that (1) is true. Then (17) followed, as we had planned, by use of CI.

The proof of (d) is somewhat simpler:

PROOF OF (d)

(1)	(1) $p \cdot q$	Assump.
(1)	(2) q	AE (1)
(1)	(3) p	AE (1)
(1)	(4) $q \cdot p$	AI (2)(3)
	(5) $p \cdot q \supset q \cdot p$	CI (4)
(6)	(6) $q \cdot p$	Assump.
(6)	(7) p	AE (6)
(6)	(8) q	AE (6)
(6)	(9) $p \cdot q$	AI (7)(8)
	(10) $q \cdot p \supset p \cdot q$	CI (9)
	(11) $p \cdot q \equiv q \cdot p$	BI (5)(10)

Once more, as is clear from the last step, the proof divides itself into two parts, the proof of (5) and the proof of (10). To get (5), we assumed (1) and derived (4) from it. To get (10), we assumed (6) and derived (9) from it.

Although the proof of (a) is far longer than the proof of (d), they have the same essential structure. In both cases the conclusion, which is a bi-conditional statement, is inferred from two earlier steps in the proof, where these two earlier steps are conditional statements. And in both cases we get these two earlier steps by assuming the truth of their antecedents and deriving, upon that assumption, the proof of their consequents.

Both of these proofs also illustrate the central role of conditional-introduction. Because we can use this inference-form, we can make many assumptions, knowing that we can eliminate them later on (as we must do) by use of conditional-introduction.

There is another important group of statement-forms, such that every statement of that form must be true, which involves negation:

(g)	$\sim(p \lor q) \equiv \sim p \cdot \sim q$	De Morgan's law for disjunction
(h)	$\sim(p \cdot q) \equiv \sim p \lor \sim q$	De Morgan's law for conjunction
(i)	$p \supset q \equiv (\sim q \supset \sim p)$	Law of contraposition
(j)	$p \equiv p$	Law of identity
(k)	$p \lor \sim p$	Law of excluded middle
(l)	$\sim(p \cdot \sim p)$	Law of noncontradiction
(m)	$[\sim p \cdot (p \lor q)] \supset q$	Law of disjunctive syllogisms

Laws (j)–(l) are often called the *laws of thought* because, in certain more traditional systems of logic, they played a central role. From our perspective, however, there is nothing special about them.

We shall prove that two of these statement-forms are such that statements of that form must be true:

PROOF OF (i)

(1)	(1) $p \supset q$	Assump.
(2)	(2) $\sim q$	Assump.
(1)(2)	(3) $\sim p$	NE (1)(2)
(1)	(4) $\sim q \supset \sim p$	CI (3)
	(5) $p \supset q \supset (\sim q \supset \sim p)$	CI (4)
(6)	(6) $\sim q \supset \sim p$	Assump.
(7)	(7) p	Assump.
(7)	(8) $\sim \sim p$	DN (7)
(6)(7)	(9) $\sim \sim q$	NE (6)(8)
(6)(7)	(10) q	DN (9)
(6)	(11) $p \supset q$	CI (10)
	(12) $\sim q \supset \sim p \supset (p \supset q)$	CI (11)
	(13) $p \supset q \equiv \sim q \supset \sim p$	BI (5)(12)

The general structure of this proof is the same as the structure of the last two proofs; so we will say nothing more about it. However, two points in this proof are worth elaborating upon. The first concerns (7) through (9). Many people would go directly from (7) to (9). This is a mistake. The statement represented by 'p' is not the denial of the consequent of the statement represented by '$\sim q \supset \sim p$'. Its denial is the statement represented by '$\sim\sim p$', which is why we needed step (8) as an intermediary step. Second, you will notice how, in step (4), we first eliminated one assumpton and then, in step (5), we eliminated the other assumption. This will always be so. The inference-form—conditional-introduction—involves dropping only one assumption; if we want to drop more than one, we must use it more than once.

PROOF OF (k)

(1)	(1) $\sim(p \vee \sim p)$	Assump.
(2)	(2) p	Assump.
(2)	(3) $p \vee \sim p$	OI (2)
(1)(2)	(4) $p \vee \sim p \cdot \sim(p \vee \sim p)$	AI (1)(3)
(1)	(5) $p \supset [p \vee \sim p \cdot \sim(p \vee \sim p)]$	CI (4)
(1)	(6) $\sim p$	NI (5)
(1)	(7) $p \vee \sim p$	OI (6)
(1)	(8) $p \vee \sim p \cdot \sim(p \vee \sim p)$	AI (1)(7)
	(9) $\sim(p \vee \sim p) \supset [(p \vee \sim p) \cdot \sim(p \vee \sim p)]$	CI (8)
	(10) $\sim \sim(p \vee \sim p)$	NI (9)
	(11) $p \vee \sim p$	DN (10)

The structure of this proof is very different from the structure of the three other proofs that we have examined in this section. There is a very simple reason for this. They were all proofs of some biconditional statement; so they consisted of two main parts, each of which was a proof of a conditional statement. In this case the statement of which this is supposed to be a proof is not a biconditional statement; so our proof has a different structure. What we do is assume [as we did in (1)] the denial of the statement for which we want to offer a proof, derive, on that assumption, a contradiction [as we did in (8)], and then by use of CI, NI, and DN, infer the truth of the statement of which this is a proof. This is a famous type of proof, resorted to when nothing else seems to work; such proofs are called *indirect proofs*.

Let us now look at some more inference-forms and prove them valid :

$$
\begin{array}{l}
p \vee q \\
\underline{\sim p} \\
q
\end{array}
\qquad \text{Disjunctive Syllogism}
$$

$$
\begin{array}{l}
p \supset q \\
\underline{q \supset r} \\
p \supset r
\end{array}
\qquad \text{Hypothetical syllogism}
$$

$$
\begin{array}{l}
p \supset q \\
r \supset s \\
\underline{p \vee r} \\
q \vee s
\end{array}
\qquad \text{Constructive dilemma}
$$

$$
\begin{array}{l}
p \supset q \\
r \supset s \\
\underline{\sim q \vee \sim s} \\
\sim p \vee \sim r
\end{array}
\qquad \text{Destructive dilemma}
$$

First let us prove that the dilemmas are valid forms of inference:

PROOF OF THE CONSTRUCTIVE DILEMMA

(1)	(1) $p \supset q$	Assump.
(2)	(2) $r \supset s$	Assump.
(3)	(3) $p \vee r$	Assump.
(4)	(4) p	Assump.
(1)(4)	(5) q	CE (1)(4)
(1)(4)	(6) $q \vee s$	OI (5)
(1)	(7) $p \supset (q \vee s)$	CI (6)
(8)	(8) r	Assump.
(2)(8)	(9) s	CE (2)(8)
(2)(8)	(10) $q \vee s$	OI (9)
(2)	(11) $r \supset (q \vee s)$	CI (10)
(1)(2)(3)	(12) $q \vee s$	OE (3)(7)(11)

The structure of this proof is very simple. We first assume all the premises. Since the last of them [(3)] is a disjunctive statement, we decide to use OE to get the conclusion. So we assume [in (4)] the first disjunct and show [in (7)] that if it is true, then the conclusion is true; we than assume [in (8)] the second disjunct and show [in (11)] that if it is true, then the conclusion is true. The conclusion then follows, as we planned, by OE. Notice that we already had the conclusion in steps (6) and (10), but we could not stop the proof at that point; in (6), we only had it on an extra assumption [(4)], and in (10) we only had it on an extra assumption [(8)].

PROOF OF THE DESTRUCTIVE DILEMMA

(1)	(1) $p \supset q$	Assump.
(2)	(2) $r \supset s$	Assump.
(3)	(3) $\sim q \vee \sim s$	Assump.
(4)	(4) $\sim q$	Assump.
(1)(4)	(5) $\sim p$	NE (1)(4)
(1)(4)	(6) $\sim p \vee \sim r$	OI (5)
(1)	(7) $\sim q \supset (\sim p \vee \sim r)$	CI (6)
(8)	(8) $\sim s$	Assump.
(2)(8)	(9) $\sim r$	NE (2)(8)
(2)(8)	(10) $\sim p \vee \sim r$	OI (9)
(2)	(11) $\sim s \supset (\sim p \vee \sim r)$	CI (10)
(1)(2)(3)	(12) $\sim p \vee \sim r$	OE (3)(7)(11)

The structure of this proof is exactly the same as the structure of the previous proof, except that here, in steps (5) and (9), we use NE instead of CE.

Notice that in these two proofs, unlike in the proofs of the truth of statements, the last step rests upon assumptions. This is to be expected. When we offer a proof that an inference is valid, we are trying to show that if certain assumptions are correct (viz., the truth of the premises of the inference), something else must be true. But when we are trying to offer a proof that some statement is true, we are trying to show that, no matter what else is true, this statement must be true. Consequently, the first type of proof will have a conclusion that rests upon assumptions, whereas the second type will not.

We turn now to the syllogisms:

PROOF OF THE HYPOTHETICAL SYLLOGISM

(1)	(1) $p \supset q$	Assump.
(2)	(2) $q \supset r$	Assump.
(3)	(3) p	Assump.
(1)(3)	(4) q	CE (1)(3)
(1)(2)(3)	(5) r	CE (2)(4)
(1)(2)	(6) $p \supset r$	CI (5)

This proof has a structure different from the last two proofs. We naturally begin by assuming [in (1) and (2)] the truth of the premises of the inference in question. But then, since the conclusion is a conditional statement, we add [in (3)] as an additional assumption that its antecedent is true, and show [in (5)] that we can validly infer from this that its consequent is true. Consequently, we may infer [as we do in (6)], by use of CI, that the conclusion is true.

PROOF OF THE DISJUNCTIVE SYLLOGISM

(1)	(1) $p \lor q$	Assump.
(2)	(2) $\sim p \cdot \sim q$	Assump.
(3)	(3) p	Assump.
(2)	(4) $\sim p$	AE (2)
(2)(3)	(5) $p \cdot \sim p$	AI (3)(4)
(3)	(6) $\sim p \cdot \sim q \supset (p \cdot \sim p)$	CI (5)
(3)	(7) $\sim(\sim p \cdot \sim q)$	NI (6)
	(8) $p \supset \sim(\sim p \cdot \sim q)$	CI (7)
(9)	(9) q	Assump.
(2)	(10) $\sim q$	AE (2)
(9)(2)	(11) $q \cdot \sim q$	AI (9)(10)
(9)	(12) $\sim p \cdot \sim q \supset (q \cdot \sim q)$	CI (11)
(9)	(13) $\sim(\sim p \cdot \sim q)$	NI (12)
	(14) $q \supset \sim(\sim p \cdot \sim q)$	CI (13)
(1)	(15) $\sim(\sim p \cdot \sim q)$	OE (1)(8)(14)
(16)	(16) $\sim p$	Assump.
(17)	(17) $\sim q$	Assump.
(16)(17)	(18) $\sim p \cdot \sim q$	AI (16)(17)
(1)(16)(17)	(19) $(\sim p \cdot \sim q) \cdot \sim(\sim p \cdot \sim q)$	AI (15)(18)
(1)(16)	(20) $\sim q \supset [(\sim p \cdot \sim q) \cdot \sim(\sim p \cdot \sim q)]$	CI (19)
(1)(16)	(21) $\sim \sim q$	NI (20)
(1)(16)	(22) q	DN (21)

This proof is a bit devious. In steps (1) through (15) we show that if the statement represented by '$p \lor q$' is true, then the statement represented by '$\sim(\sim p \cdot \sim q)$' will also be true. But then, one of our premises is that the statement represented by '$\sim p$' is true; thus, we assume so in step (16). The rest is easy: we show, in steps (17) through (20), that the assumption that the statement represented by '$\sim q$' is true will lead to a contradiction; therefore, by use of NI and DN, we conclude that the statement represented by 'q' must be true.

Intuitively, there is a way that we could greatly simplify this proof. We would replace (1) through (15) with the following:

(1)	(1) $p \lor q$	Assump.
	(2) $(p \lor q) \equiv \sim(\sim p \cdot \sim q)$	An instance of De Morgan's law
	(3) $(p \lor q) \supset \sim(\sim p \cdot \sim q)$	BE (2)
(1)	(4) $\sim(\sim p \cdot \sim q)$	CE (1)(3)

After that, the rest of the proof would follow exactly as previously. In other words, we could intuitively simplify this proof immensely if we could make use of De Morgan's law. But isn't this cheating? This isn't part of our method, is it? Well, it isn't part of our method, but it isn't really cheating. After all, instead of simply using [as step (2)] an instance of De Morgan's law, we could have written the whole proof of De Morgan's law for that instance of it, and then continued as we wanted. Thus, simply writing steps (1) through (4) can be viewed as a shorthand for a longer first part of the proof that included, between steps (1) and (2), a full proof of that instance of De Morgan's law.

Let us generalize on this point. Let us call any statement-form about which we can prove by our methods that every statement of that form must be true a *theorem*. For example, forms (a) through (m) are theorems. Then, any time we wish, we can introduce an instance of one of these theorems—a statement which is of one of these forms—into one of our proofs. This step will rest upon no assumptions, and its justification will be written TI (standing for Theorem-Introduction) followed by one of the letters *a* through *m*, indicating which theorem it is an instance of. The justification for doing this is simply that we could have put in the proof of that statement from no assumptions. By allowing ourselves this method, which we shall call the method of *theorem-introduction*, we can considerably shorten our proofs while remaining confident that we have not gone beyond what our method allows us. In the next section, we will see more examples of how helpful it is to have the method of theorem-introduction available.

6.7 Strategies for Inventing Proofs

In most of the proofs we have looked at so far, it has not been too difficult to see that it has been a successful proof with a clearcut organization and structure. But this neither helps us see how these proofs were thought up nor helps us learn how to think up new proofs. In this section we will try to learn how one goes about inventing a proof.

This does not mean that we will be looking for a mechanical procedure that churns out proofs whenever there is one. Indeed, it can be proved (by methods far more powerful than we can discuss in this introductory text) that there can be no mechanical procedure which, when presented with a valid inference, gives a proof (using our methods) of the validity of the inference. Instead, what we will be looking for is a series of hints for constructing proofs—in short, strategies for inventing proofs.

Let us begin by trying to find some proofs that some inferences are valid. For example, let us try to invent a proof of the validity of the following form of inference:

$$p \supset q$$
$$\underline{p}$$
$$p \cdot q$$

We know that the last step in our proof will be the statement represented by '$p \cdot q$'. Now we have an inference form that we can use to introduce statements of that form into our proofs. It is the and-introduction form of inference (hence, its name; it is the only form whose use necessarily introduces into a proof a conjunctive statement). So we can get our conclusion if, earlier in the proof, we have the statements represented by 'p' and 'q'. Now, one of these is a premise of our inference; so it can be introduced into our proof as an assumption. The other is not; however, it follows easily from our two premises. So our proof is very simple:

(1)	(1) $p \supset q$	Assump.
(2)	(2) p	Assump.
(1)(2)	(3) q	CE (1)(2)
(1)(2)	(4) $p \cdot q$	AI (2)(3)

A very similar mode of reasoning leads us to a proof of the validity of the following inference-form:

$$p \equiv q$$
$$\sim\,\sim p$$
$$\overline{p \cdot q}$$

Once more, we know that the last statement in our proof must be the statement represented by '$p \cdot q$', and we know that we can get that, by use of and-introduction, if earlier in our proof we have the statements represented by 'p' and by 'q'. Neither of these statements is a premise of our inference, but one—the statement represented by 'p'—follows directly, by use of an inference of the double-negation form, from one of our premises—the statement represented by '$\sim\sim p$'. So far, therefore, we suspect that our proof will look like this:

(1)	(1) $p \equiv q$	Assump.
(2)	(2) $\sim\,\sim p$	Assump.
(2)	(3) p	DN (2)

$$q$$
$$p \cdot q \qquad \text{AI}$$

The only remaining question is how to get the statement represented by 'q'. We haven't yet done anything with our first assumption (which is the first premise of our inference); so let us see what we can infer from it. It is a biconditional statement, and we have only one form of inference—the biconditional elimination-form of inference—which can always be used to infer something from a biconditional statement (hence, its name). We can thereby infer the statement represented by '$p \supset q$' from the statement represented by '$p \equiv q$'. Now we are done, since from that statement, and from (3), we can infer the statement represented by 'q' by a conditional-elimination inference. So our total proof will be as follows:

(1)	(1) $p \equiv q$	Assump.
(2)	(2) $\sim \sim p$	Assump.
(2)	(3) p	DN (2)
(1)	(4) $p \supset q$	BE (1)
(1)(2)	(5) q	CE (3)(4)
(1)(2)	(6) $p \cdot q$	AI (3)(5)

A slightly more complicated version of this mode of reasoning leads us to a proof of the validity of the following form of inference:

$$\frac{q \supset r}{(p \lor q) \supset (p \lor r)}$$

Once more, we know that the last statement in our proof must be the conditional statement represented by '$(p \lor q) \supset (p \lor r)$' and that we can get it, by use of an inference of the conditional-introduction form, if we have as our previous step in the proof the statement represented by '$p \lor r$' proved on the assumption that the statement represented by '$p \lor q$' is true. So far, we suspect that our proof will look like this:

(1)	(1) $q \supset r$	Assump.
(2)	(2) $p \lor q$	Assump.
(1)(2)	$p \lor r$	
(1)	$(p \lor q) \supset (p \lor r)$	CI

The only remaining question is how to fill in the step between the end and the beginning of the proof. We have two assumptions, a conditional assumption and a disjunctive assumption; a good guess is that we will use either a conditional-elimination inference or a disjunctive-elimination inference. We cannot use the former straight off, because we don't have the statement represented by 'q'; so we will try a disjunctive-elimination inference. This means that we now suspect that our proof will look like this:

(1)	(1) $q \supset r$	Assump.
(2)	(2) $p \vee q$	Assump.
(3)	(3) p	Assump.

$$p \vee r$$
$$p \supset (p \vee r)$$
$$q$$

$$p \vee r$$
$$q \supset (p \vee r)$$

(1)(2)	$p \vee r$	OE
(1)	$(p \vee q) \supset (p \vee r)$	CI

Filling in the remaining steps is simple, and our final proof becomes:

(1)	(1) $q \supset r$	Assump.
(2)	(2) $p \vee q$	Assump.
(3)	(3) p	Assump.
(3)	(4) $p \vee r$	OI (3)
	(5) $p \supset (p \vee r)$	CI (4)
(6)	(6) q	Assump.
(1)(6)	(7) r	CE (1)(6)
(1)(6)	(8) $p \vee r$	OI (7)
(1)	(9) $q \supset (p \vee r)$	CI (8)
(1)(2)	(10) $p \vee r$	OE (2)(5)(9)
(1)	(11) $(p \vee q) \supset (p \vee r)$	CI (10)

What were the strategies we used in inventing these proofs? They seem to come down to the following procedures:

(a) Assume that the last step will be inferred by use of the corresponding introduction inference and try to get, earlier in the proof, the necessary premises for such an inference. Thus, if the conclusion is a conjunctive statement, assume that it will be inferred by a conjunction-introduction inference, and try to get, earlier in the proof, its two conjuncts. If the conclusion is a conditional statement, assume that it will be inferred by a conditional-introduction inference, and try to get, earlier in the proof, a proof of its consequent on the assumption of the truth of its antecedent. Similarly, although we have not yet had examples of this, if the conclusion is a disjunctive statement (negative statement, biconditional statement), assume that it will be inferred by a disjunction-(negation-, biconditional-) introduction inference, and try to get, earlier in the proof, a proof of one of its disjuncts (a proof that if the statement of which it is the denial is true, then some contradiction is also true,—a proof of two statements, one of which says that if the first statement in the biconditional statement is true, then so is the second statement in it, and the other of which says that if the second statement is true, then so is the first).

(b) Assume, immediately, the truth of all premises of the inference, and then assume that you will be using, if possible, the corresponding elimination inferences. Thus, if one of the premises is a conjunctive statement, assume that you will be inferring the truth of one or both of its conjuncts; if one of the premises is a conditional statement and another premise (or some other later step in the proof) is the antecedent of that statement, assume that you will be inferring the truth of its consequent. And so on for negative, disjunctive, and biconditional statements.

(c) Fill in the steps between what you assume, by using (a), the end of the proof will be, and what you guess, by using (b), the beginning of the proof will be.

Much as these strategies can be used (as we have used them before) to find a proof of the validity of certain inference-forms, we can also use them to help us find proofs that certain statement-forms are theorems. Thus, let us now use them to find a proof of De Morgan's law for disjunction, for the statement-form '$\sim(p \lor q) \equiv (\sim p \cdot \sim q)$'. The statement that we will prove true is biconditional and is represented by '$\sim(p \lor q) \equiv (\sim p \cdot \sim q)$'. So, earlier in the proof, we should have the statements represented by '$\sim(p \lor q) \supset (\sim p \cdot \sim q)$' and by '$(\sim p \cdot \sim q) \supset \sim(p \lor q)$'. Since each of these statements is conditional, we should have, before each of them, a proof of their consequent on the assumption that their antecedent is true. So far, then, the proof should look like this:

(1)	(1) $\sim(p \lor q)$	Assump.
(1)	$\sim p \cdot \sim q$	
	$\sim(p \lor q) \supset (\sim p \cdot \sim q)$	CI
	$\sim p \cdot \sim q$	Assump.
	$\sim(p \lor q)$	
	$(\sim p \cdot \sim q) \supset \sim(p \lor q)$	CI
	$\sim(p \lor q) \equiv \sim p \cdot \sim q$	BI

And all we need do is fill in the missing steps. Let us first concentrate on filling in the steps between the statements represented by '$\sim(p \lor q)$' and by '$\sim p \cdot \sim q$'. Since we want to get a conjunctive statement, we must first prove each conjunct; and since each conjunct is a negative statement, we will assume the statement of which it is a denial and try to get a contradiction.

So the first gap is going to look like this:

(1)	(1) ~(p ∨ q)	Assump.
(2)	(2) p	Assump.
(1)	~p	
	q	Assump.
	~q	
	~p · ~q	AI

We can fill it in so that it becomes:

(1)	(1) ~(p ∨ q)	Assump.
(2)	(2) p	Assump.
(2)	(3) p ∨ q	OI (2)
(1)(2)	(4) p ∨ q · ~(p ∨ q)	AI (1)(3)
(1)	(5) p ⊃ [p ∨ q · ~(p ∨ q)]	CI (4)
(1)	(6) ~p	NI (5)
(7)	(7) q	Assump.
(7)	(8) p ∨ q	OI (7)
(1)(7)	(9) p ∨ q · ~(p ∨ q)	AI (1)(8)
(1)	(10) q ⊃ [p ∨ q · ~(p ∨ q)]	CI (9)
(1)	(11) ~q	NI (10)
(1)	(12) ~p · ~q	AI (6)(11)
	(13) ~(p ∨ q) ⊃ (~p · ~q)	CI (12)

Let us now turn to filling in the second gap in the original outline, that between the statements represented by '~p · ~q' and by '~(p ∨ q)'. Since we want to get a negative statement, we will probably assume the statement of which it is a denial (in this case, the statement represented by 'p ∨ q'), show that if it is true, a contradiction is also true, infer that our negative statement is true, and be done. Thus, the second gap will look like this:

(14)	(14) ~p · ~q	Assump.
(15)	(15) p ∨ q	Assump.
(14)	~(p ∨ q)	NI

What we must do now is get a contradiction from the assumption that the statement represented by 'p ∨ q' is true. Since that is a disjunctive statement, we will try to get the *same* contradiction from each of the disjuncts and therefore, by a disjunction-elimination inference, from the whole disjunction.

This is easy, and we get the following as the second part of the proof:

(14)	(14) $\sim p \cdot \sim q$	Assump.
(15)	(15) $p \vee q$	Assump.
(16)	(16) p	Assump.
(14)	(17) $\sim p$	AE (14)
(14)(16)	(18) $p \cdot \sim p$	AI (16)(17)
(16)	(19) $\sim p \cdot \sim q \supset (p \cdot \sim p)$	CI (18)
(16)	(20) $\sim(\sim p \cdot \sim q)$	NI (19)
(14)(16)	(21) $(\sim p \cdot \sim q) \cdot \sim(\sim p \cdot \sim q)$	AI (14)(20)
(14)	(22) $p \supset [(\sim p \cdot \sim q) \cdot \sim(\sim p \cdot \sim q)]$	CI (21)
(23)	(23) q	Assump.
(14)	(24) $\sim q$	AE (14)
(14)(23)	(25) $q \cdot \sim q$	AI (23)(24)
(23)	(26) $(\sim p \cdot \sim q) \supset (q \cdot \sim q)$	CI (25)
(23)	(27) $\sim(\sim p \cdot \sim q)$	NI (26)
(14)(23)	(28) $(\sim p \cdot \sim q) \cdot \sim(\sim p \cdot \sim q)$	AI (14)(27)
(14)	(29) $q \supset [(\sim p \cdot \sim q) \cdot \sim(\sim p \cdot \sim q)]$	CI (28)
(14)(15)	(30) $(\sim p \cdot \sim q) \cdot \sim(\sim p \cdot \sim q)$	OE (15)(22)(29)
(14)	(31) $p \vee q \supset [(\sim p \cdot \sim q) \cdot \sim(\sim p \cdot \sim q)]$	CI (30)
(14)	(32) $\sim(p \vee q)$	NI (31)
	(33) $(\sim p \cdot \sim q) \supset \sim(p \vee q)$	CI (32)
	(34) $\sim(p \vee q) \equiv (\sim p \cdot \sim q)$	BI (13)(33)

Steps (1) through (34) form a difficult proof of De Morgan's law for disjunction, but even it is manageable as long as we follow our strategy considerations.

Although our strategies often work, there will be cases in which they will not help us. A good example of this occurs when we attempt to find a proof that every statement of the form '$(p \supset q) \equiv (\sim p \vee q)$' must be true. Since our conclusion will be a biconditional statement, we immediately suspect that we will first get the two conditional statements and then infer our conclusion by using the biconditional-introduction form. To prove the two conditional statements, we will probably assume the truth of their antecedent and then show, on that assumption, that their consequent must be true. We suspect, on the basis of our normal strategy considerations, that our proof will look like this:

(1)	(1) $p \supset q$	Assump.
(1)	$\sim p \vee q$	
	$(p \supset q) \supset (\sim p \vee q)$	CI
	$\sim p \vee q$	Assump.
	$p \supset q$	
	$(\sim p \vee q) \supset (p \supset q)$	CI
	$(p \supset q) \equiv (\sim p \vee q)$	BI

All we must do is fill in the two gaps. Let us first try to fill in the gap between the statement represented by '$p \supset q$' and the statement represented by '$\sim p \vee q$'. Our conclusion is a disjunctive statement; so all that we have to get is one disjunct. But how can we do that? Nothing suggests itself.

It is on just such occasions that we use a second strategy, the *strategy of indirect proof*. We assume the denial of what we want to prove, get a contradiction on that assumption, and then, by use of CI, NI, and DN inferences, get our original conclusion. It was this same strategy that we used in section 6.6 to invent our proof for the law of the excluded middle. Following it here, we have little trouble filling the gap:

(1)	(1) $p \supset q$	Assump.
(2)	(2) $\sim(\sim p \vee q)$	Assump.
	(3) $\sim(\sim p \vee q) \equiv \; \sim \sim p \cdot \sim q$	TI (g)
	(4) $\sim(\sim p \vee q) \supset \; \sim \sim p \cdot \sim q$	BE (3)
(2)	(5) $\sim \sim p \cdot \sim q$	CE (2)(4)
(2)	(6) $\sim \sim p$	AE (5)
(2)	(7) p	DN (6)
(1)(2)	(8) q	CE (1)(7)
(2)	(9) $\sim q$	AE (5)
(1)(2)	(10) $q \cdot \sim q$	AI (8)(9)
(1)	(11) $[\sim(\sim p \vee q)] \supset (q \cdot \sim q)$	CI (10)
(1)	(12) $\sim \sim(\sim p \vee q)$	NI (11)
(1)	(13) $\sim p \vee q$	DN (12)
	(14) $(p \supset q) \supset (\sim p \vee q)$	CI (13)

Notice, of course, how we used theorem (g), De Morgan's law for disjunction, to come up with step (4). Otherwise, we would have had to run through half the proof of De Morgan's law for the special case of the statement represented by '$\sim(\sim p \vee q)$'. A similar shortcut makes the second half of the proof proceed quickly. We are trying to bridge the gap between the statement represented by '$\sim p \vee q$' and that represented by '$p \supset q$'. Here we can employ our ordinary strategy. Since we want to prove a conditional statement, we assume the antecedent and try to show, on the assumption that the antecedent is true, that the consequent is also true. The proof goes through very simply:

(15)	(15) $\sim p \vee q$	Assump.
(16)	(16) p	Assump.
(16)	(17) $\sim \sim p$	DN (16)
	(18) $[\sim \sim p \cdot (\sim p \vee q)] \supset q$	TI (m)
(15)(16)	(19) $\sim \sim p \cdot \sim p \vee q$	AI (15)(17)
(15)(16)	(20) q	CE (18)(19)
(15)	(21) $p \supset q$	CI (20)
	(22) $(\sim p \vee q) \supset (p \supset q)$	CI (21)
	(23) $(p \supset q) \equiv (\sim p \vee q)$	BI (14)(22)

This final example of inventing proofs illustrates, therefore, two important points. First, when our ordinary strategies do not work, we should try to use an indirect proof. Second, we must always be alert, whichever strategy we are using, to the possibility that we can save ourselves considerable trouble by using the method of theorem-introduction.

6.8 Semantical Tableaux: A Second Method of Proof

In the last three sections we have developed a method, based upon the results of section 6.4, for showing that certain inference-forms are valid and that certain statement-forms are theorems. In this section we will, as promised earlier, develop an alternative method for doing this, based upon the intuitive methods developed in section 6.4. But before doing this, we should first look at the motivations for finding an alternative method to the one we have already developed.

There are two major shortcomings to the proof-method previously developed in this chapter. First, even with our strategy considerations it is often not so easy to construct a proof. It would make our task far easier if we had a mechanical method for proving validity and theoremhood. Second, with our proof-method we know that if we cannot find a proof, there are two explanations possible: there is a proof but we haven't found it yet, or there is no proof because the inference-form is not valid or because the statement-form is not a theorem. Because we are never in a position to rule out the first possibility, we can never (by use of that method) conclude that an inference-form is not a valid form or that a statement-form is not a theorem. It would therefore be much better if we had a method that enabled us to come to such conclusions. The method we will introduce in this section, the *method of semantic tableaux*, will have both these advantages.

How did we intuitively show, in section 6.4, that our 11 basic forms of inference are valid? We assumed that the premises of such an inference were true and its conclusion false, and showed that that assumption led to a contradiction; thus, we concluded that the assumption could not be the case for any inference of that form, and that all such inferences are valid. Thus, in the case of the and-elimination form, we argued that if the conclusion were false, the premise must be false (since the conclusion is one of the conjuncts of the premise), which contradicts the assumption that the premise is true.

This, then, is the basic idea behind our method. We will construct a table with two sides, one for true statements and the other for false statements. We will put the symbols representing the premises on the true side and the

symbols representing the conclusion on the false side. We shall then see what else, given our initial assumptions, must be true (and put the symbols for those statements on the true side) and what else must be false (and put the symbols for those statements on the false side). If it turns out that some statement must be both true and false (i.e., if the same symbol appears on both sides of the table), then our initial assumption has led to a contradiction. We can conclude, then, that the conclusion cannot be false when the premises are true, and that the inference-form in question is therefore valid. But if, at the end, there is no contradiction, then we will conclude that the premises can be true and the conclusion false, and that the inference-form in question is not valid.

A few examples will help make all this clear. Let us use our new method to show that the following is a valid form of inference:

$$\frac{\sim p}{p \supset q}$$

The table showing this is the following:

	True	False
(1)	$\sim p$	
(2)		$p \supset q$
(3)	p	q
(4)		p

In step (1) we put the symbol representing the premise in the true column, and in step (2) we put the symbol representing the conclusion in the false column. Given the meaning of '$\supset$', the statement represented by '$p \supset q$' can be false only when its antecedent is true and its consequent false. So in step (3) we put the symbol representing its antecedent in the true column and the symbol representing its consequent in the false column. Finally, given the meaning of '$\sim$', the statement represented by '$\sim p$' can be true only when the statement represented by 'p' is false. So we put 'p' in the false column. Now 'p' appears in both columns; so in order for our premise to be true while our conclusion is false, the statement represented by 'p' would have to be true and false. Since that is impossible, the premise cannot be true and the conclusion false; hence, any inference of this form is valid.

As a second simple example, let us use our new method to show that the following is a valid inference-form:

$$\frac{p \cdot q}{p \vee q}$$

The following table shows that it is valid:

	True	False
(1)	$p \cdot q$	
(2)		$p \vee q$
(3)	p	
	q	
(4)		p
		q

In step (1), we put the symbol representing the premise in the true column, and in step (2) we put the symbol representing the conclusion in the false column. The premise is a conjunctive statement, that is true only when both its conjuncts are true. So in step (3) we put the symbols standing for them in the true column. Furthermore, the conclusion is a disjunctive statement that is false only when both its disjuncts are false. So in step (4) we put the symbols standing for them in the false column. At this point both 'p' and 'q' appear in both columns, meaning that our premise can be true while our conclusion is false only if the statements represented by both of these symbols are both true and false. Since this is impossible, the premise cannot be true while the conclusion is false; hence, any inference of this form is valid.

The same method enables us to show that the following is not a valid form of inference:

$$\frac{\sim p \cdot \supset q}{\sim p \supset q}$$

The following table shows this:

	True	False
(1)	$\sim p \cdot \sim q$	
(2)		$\sim p \supset q$
(3)	$\sim p$	
	$\sim q$	
(4)		p
		q
(5)	$\sim p$	q
(6)		p

In step (1) we put the symbol representing the premise in the true column, and in step (2) we put the symbol representing the conclusion in the false column. Now, the premise is a conjunctive statement true only when both its conjuncts are true; so in step (3) we put the symbols representing them in the true column. Since they both are negative statements, that are true only when the statements of which they are the negation are false, we put the symbols for those statements in the false column in step (4). Our conclusion is a hypothetical statement that is false only when its antecedent is true and its consequent false. So in step (5) we put the symbol for the antecedent in the true column and the symbol for the consequent in the false column. Finally, since the antecedent is a negative statement that is true only when the statement of which it is the negation is false, we put the symbol for that statement in the false column in step (6). There is now nothing more that we can do, and no symbol has turned up on both sides. So if the statements represented by both '*p*' and '*q*' are false, our premise will be true while our conclusion is false. Thus, inferences of this form can be invalid, and this is not a valid form of inference.

Much as we use this method to prove that inference-forms are valid, we can also use it to show that statement-forms are theorems. The only difference is that we begin by assuming that a statement of that form is false. If we can get our contradiction from that assumption (i.e., if the same symbol appears on both sides of the table), then statements of that form must be true, and that statement-form is a theorem. If, however, we end up with no contradiction, then that statement can be false; hence, that statement-form is not a theorem.

All this leads us to a very simple proof of the law of the excluded middle:

	True	False
(1)		$p \lor \sim p$
(2)		p
		$\sim p$
(3)	p	

In step (1) we put the symbol representing the statement in question in the false column. Since it is a disjunctive statement, it is false only if both its disjuncts are false. So in step (2) we write the symbols for both those statements in the false column. Since '$\sim p$' appears in the false column, the statement it represents is false; since it is a negative statement, the statement of which it is the negation is true. So we can write '*p*' in the true column in step (3). We now have a contradiction since '*p*' appears in both columns. Therefore, the statement cannot be false, and the law of contradiction is a theorem. Note, by the way, that this is a much simpler proof of the law of the excluded middle than the one in section 6.6 using the old method. We shall see, as we go along, that this is characteristic of most proofs using tableaux.

There is only one minor complication with our new method. Let us look at the table to prove the validity of the disjunctive-syllogism form, the form of inference:

$$p \lor q$$
$$\sim p$$
$$\overline{}$$
$$q$$

to see how this complication arises. We begin the table quite normally:

	True	False
(1)		q
(2)	$\sim p$	
(3)	$p \lor q$	
(4)		p

In step (1) we put the symbol for the conclusion in the false column, whereas in steps (2) and (3) we put the symbols for the premises in the true column. Since the first premise is a negative statement, we put, in step (4), the symbol representing the statement of which it is the negation in the false column. So far, no contradiction has appeared. But we must still work on the '$p \lor q$' occurring in the true column. We want to indicate that either the statement represented by 'p' or the one represented by 'q' must be true, but how do we accomplish this?

The solution for that problem is to construct a subcolumn so that our table will now look like this:

	True	False
(1)		q
(2)	$\sim p$	
(3)	$p \lor q$	
(4)		p
(5)	p | q	

We now have our contradiction because, for each of the two subcolumns in the true column, there is a symbol that appears in them that also appears in the false column. Intuitively, if the statement represented by '$p \lor q$' is to be true, either the statement represented by 'p' must be true [but it cannot, as we see from step (4)], or the statement represented by 'q' must be true [but it cannot, as we see from step (1)]. Both these possibilities lead to a contradiction; so the original assumption that the statement represented by 'q' is false while the statements represented by '$p \lor q$' and '$\sim p$' are true also leads to a contradiction. Therefore, the premises of our inference cannot be true while the conclusion is false; hence, any inference of this form is valid.

Notice, however, that even though we must construct subcolumns, this proof is still far simpler than the 22-step proof of the validity of this form of inference, constructed in section 6.6. Tableaux, even with subcolumns, are rarely very long.

Before we look at a few final examples of more complicated tableaux, let us state the formal rules for operating with them.

(1) If one wants to prove that an inference is valid, one puts the symbols representing the premises in the true column and the symbol representing the conclusion in the false column. If one is trying to prove that a statement must be true, one puts the symbols representing it in the false column.

(2)

If the line in the table on which you want to operate is of the form:		*Then you add to the table the corresponding symbol(s) of this form:*	
True	False	True	False
~A			A
True	False	True	False
	~A	A	
True	False	True	False
A · B		A	
		B	
True	False	True	False
	A · B		A | B
True	False	True	False
A ∨ B		A | B	
True	False	True	False
	A ∨ B		A
			B
True	False	True	False
A ⊃ B		~A | B	
True	False	True	False
	A ⊃ B	A	B
True	False	True	False
A ≡ B		A | ~A	
		B | ~B	
True	False	True	False
	A ≡ B		A | ~A
			~B | B

(3) A contradiction is reached if (a) there are no subcolumns, but a symbol appears on both sides of the table, or if (b) there are subcolumns, and for each subcolumn on one side of the table there are symbols occurring in it such that at least one of them occurs in every corresponding subcolumn on the other side of the table.

(4) If a contradiction is reached, then the inference in question is valid, or the statement in question is true; if none is reached, even after all the operations listed under (2) are applied to all the applicable symbols, then the inference in question is not valid, and the statement in question may be false.

Here are a few examples of the use of this method. To make these examples more informative, we will look at inference-forms that we have already proved valid by our old methods and statement-forms that we have already proved to be theorems by our old methods. By doing this, we shall see even more clearly how simple this new method is.

The following table proves that the associative law for disjunction is a theorem:

	True		False	
(1)			$p \lor (q \lor r) \equiv (p \lor q) \lor r$	
(2)			$p \lor (q \lor r)$ $\sim[(p \lor q) \lor r]$	$(p \lor q) \lor r$ $\sim[p \lor (q \lor r)]$
(3)			p $q \lor r$	$p \lor q$ r
(4)			q r	p q
(5)	$(p \lor q) \lor r$	$p \lor (q \lor r)$		
(6)	$p \lor q$ | r	p | $q \lor r$		
(7)	p | q	q | r		

In step (1) we suppose that our statement is false and write, in the false column, a symbol representing it. Since the symbol is of the form '$A \equiv B$', we begin two subcolumns in step (2), one headed by the symbol of the form 'A' and the symbol of the form '$\sim B$', and the other by the symbol of the form '$\sim A$' and of the form 'B'. Since the first symbol in each of these subcolumns is of the form '$A \lor B$', we write down, in step (3), the symbols of the form 'A' and of the form 'B'. Since one of these is still of the form '$A \lor B$,' we do the same thing again in step (4). We turn now to the second symbol introduced in the subcolumns in step (2). Both these symbols are of the form '$\sim A$'; so we should write down the symbol of the form 'A' in the true column. We do that in step (5), making two subcolumns in the true column to correspond to the two subcolumns in the false column. Since the symbols introduced in step (5) are of the form '$A \lor B$', we make two more subcolumns for each one that we already have, one headed, as in step (6), with the symbol of the form '*A*' and the other with the symbol of the form '*B*'. Since we are still left with some symbols of that form, we repeat it in step (7). Having done all that, we reach a contradiction. After all, in each of the six subcolumns on the true side, there is a symbol occurring in it (either '*p*' or '*q*' or '*r*') which occurs in both of the subcolumns on the other side of the table. Consequently, the statement in question must be true, and the associative law for disjunction is a theorem.

As another example, let us look at the following table, which proves that the commutative law for conjunction is a theorem:

	True		False	
(1)			$p \cdot q \equiv q \cdot p$	
(2)			$p \cdot q$	$q \cdot p$
			$\sim(q \cdot p)$	$\sim(p \cdot q)$
(3)			p | q	q | p
(4)	$q \cdot p$	$p \cdot q$		
(5)	q	p		
	p	q		

In step (1) we suppose that our statement is false and write, in the false column, a symbol representing it. Since the symbol is of the form '*A* $\equiv$ *B*', we begin two subcolumns in step (2), one headed by the symbol of the form '*A*' and the symbol of the form '$\sim$*B*', and the other by the symbol of the form '$\sim$*A*' and the symbol of the form '*B*'. Since the first symbol in each of these subcolumns is of the form '*A* $\cdot$ *B*', we begin, in step (3), two new subcolumns for each of the previous columns, starting one with the appropriate symbol of the form '*A*' and the other with the appropriate symbol of the form '*B*'. We turn now to the second symbol introduced in the subcolumns in step (2). Both of those symbols are of the form '$\sim$*A*' so we should write down the symbol of the form '*A*' in the true column. We do that in step (4), starting two subcolumns in the true column to correspond to the two subcolumns we had in the false column in step (2). Then, in step (5), since we have a symbol of the form '*A* $\cdot$ *B*', we write down the symbols of the form '*A*' and of the form '*B*'. Having done so, we reach a contradiction. After all, in each of the two subcolumns on the true side, there occur some symbols ('*p*' and '*q*') such that at least one of them occurs in every subcolumn on the other side of the table. Consequently, the statement in question must be true, and the commutative law for conjunction is a theorem.

Let us look at one final example. We want to show that the following is a valid inference-form:

$$\frac{q \supset r}{(p \lor q) \supset (p \lor r)}$$

The following table shows this:

	True		False	
(1)	$q \supset r$			
(2)			$(p \lor q) \supset (p \lor r)$	
(3)	$\sim q$	r		
(4)			q	
(5)	$p \lor q$	$p \lor q$	$p \lor r$	$p \lor r$
(6)			p	p
			r	r
(7)	p | q	p | q		

In step (1) we write in the true column a symbol representing the premise, and in step (2) we write in the false column a symbol representing the conclusion. Since the symbol in the true column is of the form '$A \supset B$', we begin, in step (3), two subcolumns, one headed by the symbol of the form '$\sim A$' and the other by the symbol of the form 'B'. Since one of these is of the form '$\sim A$', we start, in step (4), two subcolumns in the false column, and write the symbol of the form 'A' in the left subcolumn (which corresponds to the left-hand one on the true side) and nothing in the right subcolumn (which corresponds to the right-hand one on the true side). Now, since the symbol we wrote in step (2) is of the form '$A \supset B$', we put, in step (5), the symbol of the form 'A' in every subcolumn in the true column and the symbol of form 'B' in every subcolumn in the false column. Since the symbol put in the false subcolumns in step (5) is of the form '$A \lor B$', we put, in each of those columns in step (6), the symbols of both form 'A' and form 'B'. Turning back, finally, to the symbol we introduced in every subcolumn on the true side in step (5), we note that it is of the form '$A \lor B$'; so in step (7) we start for each of those subcolumns, two new subcolumns, one headed with the symbol of the form 'A' and the other with the symbol of the form 'B'. Having done so, we reach a contradiction. After all, for each of the subcolumns on the true side, there occur symbols (either 'p' or 'q') such that at least one of them occurs in every corresponding subcolumn on the other side of the table. Consequently, the premise cannot be true while the conclusion is false; hence, the inference in question is valid.

As you will probably have noticed, there is one subtle difference between this case and the previous two cases. It is not true in this case that each of the subcolumns on the true side contains some symbols such that at least one of them occurs in every subcolumn on the other side. After all, there is no symbol in the second subcolumn (containing, all together, '$q \supset r$', '$\sim q$', '$p \lor q$', and 'q') on the true side that occurs in the second subcolumn on the false side. Still, that does not count, since only the first subcolumn on the false side corresponds to the first two subcolumns on the true side. Only the first subcolumn on the false side contains the symbol '*q*', which was put there, in step (4), because of the occurrence of '∼*q*' in the first subcolumn of the true side in step (3).

As all the previous examples indicate, the proofs using semantical tableaux are much shorter than the corresponding proofs by our first method. More importantly, they have the two important features mentioned in the beginning of this section. There is a mechanical method of inventing proofs (you simply follow the rules for the tableaux), and the method tells you (if you end with no contradiction) when something is not a theorem or when an inference-form is not valid. For all these reasons this method has become very popular in recent years.

EXERCISES FOR CHAPTER 6

Part I

A. Indicate whether each of the following sentences expresses a disjunctive, conjunctive, negative, or conditional statement. State its disjuncts or conjuncts, what the statement negates, or its antecedent and consequent:
1. It is not the case that $2 + 2 = 7$.
2. Either $2 + 2 = 4$ or I am crazy.
3. If $2 + 2$ does not equal 4, then the world is crazy.
4. $2 + 2 = 4$ and $2 + 3 = 5$.
5. $2 + 2$ does not equal 7.
6. $2 + 2$ and $3 + 1$ both equal 4.
7. Unless $2 + 2 = 4$, I am crazy.
8. The world is crazy since $2 + 2$ does not equal 4.
9. $2 + 2 = 4$, and either a number is odd or it is even.
10. If the world is crazy and I am sane, then $2 + 2 = 7$ or $2 + 2 = 6$.
11. It is not the case that the whole world is sane, and yet $2 + 2 = 6$ or $2 + 2 = 7$.
12. If $2 + 2 = 4$, then either it does not also equal 5 or $4 = 5$.

B. Which of the following sentences express simple statements?
1. John loves Mary.
2. John does not love Mary.
3. John loves someone who is loved by all men.
4. John loves someone who believes that the world lives by love.
5. There is someone besides Mary whom John loves.
6. John loves Mary but not Cynthia.
7. John loves someone who believes in the power of love.
8. There is someone whom John loves and that someone is Mary.

C. For each of the following inferences, indicate some statemental inference-form of which it is an instance.

(1) This book is long.
This book is a logic text.
───────────────────────
This book is a long logic text.

(2) Either this book is long or it is short.
It is not short.
───────────────────────
It is long.

(3) This book is long if and only if its author wrote a long book.
This book is long.
───────────────────────
Its author wrote a long book.

(4) If this book is a logic book, it is long.
This book is long.
───────────────────────
This book is a logic book.

(5) This book is long or it is a logic text.
This book is long.
───────────────────────
It is not a logic text.

(6) This book is long if and only if it is not a logic text.
It is a logic text.
───────────────────────
It is a long book.

(7) Either this book is long, or it is a logic text and it is inadequate.
This book is not long.
───────────────────────
It is a logic text and it is inadequate.

(8) If this book is long, then either it covers a lot of material or else it is poorly written.
It is long and it is not poorly written.
───────────────────────
It covers a lot of material.

(9) This book is long, and either it is a logic text or it is inadequate.
This book is not a logic text.
───────────────────────
This book is adequate.

(10) If this book is either long or a logic text, then it is a book to read slowly.
It is not a book to read slowly.
───────────────────────
This book is both long and a logic text.

D. Which of the following are sentential connectives, which are truth-functional sentential connectives, and which are neither? Defend your answer.
1. all
2. until
3. since
4. or (understood exclusively)
5. perhaps

E. Using our symbolism, symbolize each of the following statements:
1. Every number is odd or every number is even.
2. Some numbers are odd and some numbers are even.
3. Not every number is odd.
4. If every number is either odd or even, then no number is neither.
5. Every number is either odd or even.
6. No number is both odd and even.
7. If not all numbers are odd, then some numbers are even.
8. When a number is odd, then either the number before it or the number after it is even.
9. Unless the number you're thinking of is odd, it is even.
10. The number you're thinking of is odd only when it follows or is followed by an even number.

F. Symbolize each of the following inferences and determine, for each one, whether it is of one of our eleven basic forms. If so, which one?

(1) Either all men are mortal or all men are immortal.
Not all men are immortal.

All men are mortal.

(2) If all men are mortal, then no man lived forever.
No man lived forever.

All men are mortal.

(3) If all men are mortal, then no man lived forever.
It is not true that no man lived forever.

Not all men are mortal.

(4) If all men are immortal, then Socrates is both mortal and immortal.

All men are not immortal.

(5) Either all men are immortal or most men are.
If all men are mortal, then so will I be mortal.
If most men are mortal, then so will I be mortal.

I will not be immortal.

(6) All men are immortal.

Not all men are mortal or not all men are mortal.

(7) All men are mortal if and only if the gods so desire it.
The gods so desire it.

All men are mortal.

(8) All men are mortal and some men like it that way.

All men are mortal.

G. Prove that each of the following inferences is valid:

(1) If Frances is beautiful, John will love her.
If John will love her, then he will marry her.
John will not marry her.

Frances is not beautiful.

(2) Frances is beautiful and John loves her.
If Frances is beautiful, John will pursue her.
If John loves her, he will marry her.

John will pursue and marry Frances.

(3) John will not both pursue and marry Frances.
But he will pursue her.

John will not marry her.

(4) Since Frances is beautiful, John will marry her.
If John will marry her, then he doesn't love her if and only if she isn't beautiful.

John loves Frances if she is beautiful.

(5) Unless Frances is beautiful, John must love her.
If John loves her, then he will marry her.
If Frances is beautiful, it is not the case that he won't marry her.

John will marry her.

(6) Even though Frances is beautiful, John loves her.
John will marry her if he loves her.

Frances is beautiful and John will marry her.

H. Prove that each of the following statements must be true:

1. If $2 + 2 = 4$, then if $2 + 3 = 5$, $2 + 2$ will equal 4 and $2 + 3$ will equal 5.
2. Either $2 + 2 = 4$ or $2 + 3 = 5$ when $2 + 2 = 4$.
3. If $2 + 2$ does not equal 5, it is not the case that both $2 + 2 = 5$ and $2 + 3 = 6$.
4. That $2 + 2$ does not equal 5 means that it equals 4, if either it equals 4 or it equals 5.
5. If, whether or not 4 is my favorite number, $2 + 2 = 4$, it must be the case that $2 + 2 = 4$.

I. Prove that each of the following inference-forms is valid (do not use TI):

(1) $p \cdot (q \cdot r)$
$\overline{(p \cdot q) \cdot r}$

(2) $p \lor q$
$\overline{q \lor p}$

(3) $p \cdot (q \lor r)$
$\overline{(p \cdot q) \lor (p \cdot r)}$

(4) $\dfrac{\sim(p \lor q)}{\sim p \cdot \sim q}$

◆ (5) $p \lor q$
$p \supset r$
$\dfrac{q \supset \sim \sim r}{r}$

(6) $p \cdot q$
$\dfrac{q \supset r}{p \cdot r}$

(7) $(p \lor q) \supset r$
$\dfrac{\sim r}{\sim p \lor q}$

(8) $p \cdot \sim r$
$\dfrac{q \supset r}{\sim(p \equiv q)}$

(9) $p \cdot (q \supset \sim r)$
$\dfrac{r \cdot (p \equiv s)}{\sim q \cdot s}$

◆ (10) $p \supset q$
$q \supset (r \equiv s)$
$\dfrac{\sim r \cdot s}{\sim p}$

J. Prove that each of the following statement-forms is a theorem. Use only the theorems indicated.
   (1) $p \equiv p$
   (2) $\sim(p \cdot \sim p)$
   (3) $[\sim p \cdot (p \lor q)] \supset q$ Use theorem (g).
   (4) $p \cdot q \equiv q \cdot p$
   (5) $p \lor (q \cdot r) \equiv (p \lor q) \cdot (p \lor r)$
   (6) $\sim(p \cdot q) \equiv \sim p \lor \sim q$ Use theorem (g).

K. Each of the following statements is true because it is an instance of one of the thirteen theorems discussed in this chapter. In each case indicate which theorem.
   1. You smoke heavily if and only if you do.
   2. You smoke heavily and you're overweight if and only if you're overweight and smoke heavily.
   3. It is not the case that you either are overweight or smoke heavily if and only if you neither smoke heavily nor are overweight.
   4. Either you smoke heavily or you do not.

5. You smoke heavily or you're overweight and work too hard if and only if you smoke heavily or you're overweight and you smoke heavily or you work too hard.
6. You're not both a heavy smoker and overweight if and only if you're not a heavy smoker or you're not overweight.
7. You're not both a heavy smoker and not a heavy smoker.
8. You're overweight if you're not a heavy smoker but are either a heavy smoker or overweight.

L. For each of the following inferences, indicate whether it is a disjunctive syllogism, a hypothetical syllogism, a constructive dilemma, or a destructive dilemma:

(1) If you smoke heavily, you work too hard.
Your working too hard means that you're overweight.

You're overweight if you smoke heavily.

(2) If you smoke heavily, you will get lung cancer.
If you are overweight, you will get a heart attack.
You smoke heavily or you are overweight.

You will get lung cancer or a heart attack.

(3) Either you smoke heavily or you're overweight.
You don't smoke heavily.

You're overweight.

(4) You will get lung cancer if you smoke heavily.
Since you're overweight, you will get a heart attack.
You won't get lung cancer or you won't get a heart attack.

You don't smoke heavily or you're not overweight.

M. For each of the inference-forms in Exercise I and statement-forms in Exercise J, show that it is valid or that it is a theorem by use of the method of semantic tableaux.

N. By use of the method of semantic tableaux, show that the following (if inference-forms) are not valid or (if statement-forms) are not theorems:

(1) $p \supset q$
q
p

(2) $p \lor q$
p
$\sim q$

(3) $p \equiv q$
$p \cdot q$

(4)　$p \vee q$
　　$\dfrac{\sim p}{\sim q}$

(5)　$(p \cdot q) \equiv (p \vee q)$

(6)　$(p \supset q) \equiv (q \supset p)$

(7)　$(p \supset q) \supset \sim p$

(8)　$(p \vee q) \supset (p \vee r)$

Part II

1. Explain why it makes no sense to talk of *the* statement-form of an inference.
2. Critically evaluate the following argument: The trouble with formal logic is that it pays no attention to the content of the statements in an inference, just to their structure; therefore, it is doomed to failure.
3. Why is 'and' a sentential connective and not a statemental connective (a symbol that is placed between two statements to form a new statement)?
4. Why is it easier to develop a theory for the validity of inferences involving truth-functional connectives than for those involving non–truth-functional connectives?
5. We have assumed that if the statement symbolized by 'p and q' is true, then the statement symbolized by 'p, but q' cannot be false, only inappropriate. We have also assumed that if the statement symbolized by '$p \supset q$' is true, then the corresponding statement symbolized by 'if p, then q' cannot be false, only inappropriate. Are these assumptions correct?
6. Construct a symbolization for statements of the form '$p \vee q$' that uses only '$\cdot$' and '$\sim$'. Similarly, construct a symbolization for statements of the form '$p \cdot q$' that uses only '$\vee$' and '$\sim$'.
7. Is 'given assumptions — — —, ——— can be validly inferred from – – –' a sentential connective? Is it a truth-functional connective? Given your answer to these questions, would you in any way modify our description of the system constructed in this chapter?
8. What assumptions were made in our arguments to prove that our eleven basic forms are valid? How would you defend these assumptions?
9. Our method of natural-deduction proofs obviously assumes the validity of our basic forms. What else does it assume? Justify each of these additional assumptions.
10. Why are we allowed to eliminate assumptions when we use an inference of the CI form? Why can't we eliminate them when we use some other type of inference?
11. Prove that there are an infinite number of theorems and an infinite number of valid inference-forms.

12. Many people are suspicious of indirect proofs. Because the validity of these proofs depends only upon the validity of three inference-forms, CI, NI, and DN, they must therefore be suspicious about one of these forms. Can you think of any reasons for doubting the validity of one of these forms?

13. In light of our strategy considerations, explain why we found it useful to have so many basic forms of inference. Can you think of any way in which we could cut down the number of basic valid inference-forms?

14. Critically evaluate this argument: Since we already have a method for proving things—our system of natural deduction—the strategy rules are superfluous.

15. It is often said that a natural-deduction approach to logic is purely syntactical, whereas a semantic tableaux (as its name suggests) is not. Explain what is meant by such a claim.

16. Explain why semantical tableaux of the type discussed in this chapter must, no matter how complicated the formulas we start with, end after a finite number of steps with a contradiction or with nothing more to do.

CHAPTER

7

Quantification Theory

In Chapter 6 we developed some very powerful methods for proving that certain inference-forms are valid and that certain statement-forms are theorems. They are not, however, powerful enough, for we shall soon see that the validity of many valid forms of inference cannot be proved by those methods. This chapter will be devoted to supplementing the methods of the last chapter so that they can handle these additional inferences.

7.1 Some Valid Inferences
and the Idea of Quantificational Form

Let us begin by considering the following two inferences, both of which are obviously valid:

All men are mortal.
Socrates is a man.

Socrates is mortal.

All horses are animals.

Every head of a horse is a head of an animal.

What are their propositional forms? Well, the first seems to be of the form:

p
q
r

whereas the second seems to be of the form:

$$\frac{p}{q}$$

and neither of these forms is a valid form of inference. Of course, this in no way interferes with the validity of these inferences; there can be valid inferences that are not of a valid form. But it does mean that from the point of view of propositional form, these inferences are not formally valid inferences and their study lies beyond the scope of formal logic.

This situation is unsatisfactory, partly because we want our system of formal logic to cover as many valid inferences as possible, and partly because there is good reason to believe that these inferences are valid because of their structure or form. After all, there seem to be many inferences such as:

> All politicians are crafty.
> Senator Jones is a politician.
> _____
> Senator Jones is crafty.

which are valid and which seem to have the same structure as our inference involving Socrates. Thus, one is inclined to suppose that they are formally valid, even though from the point of view of their propositional form they are not. Similarly, there seem to be many inferences such as:

> All men are lovers.
> _____
> All deaths of men are deaths of lovers.

which are valid and which seem to have the same structure as our inference involving horses. Thus, one is inclined to suppose that they are formally valid, even though from the point of view of their propositional form they are not.

All this leads us to suspect that there must be more structure to statements and inferences than is revealed by an examination of their propositional structure. In particular, one must conclude that if we are going to develop a fully adequate formal logic, we must look at the structure of the simple statements that are constituents of our premises and conclusion.

What, from the new point of view, is the structure of our first and third inferences? They both seem to have the following structure:

> For all x, if x is a P, then x is a Q.
> a is a P.
> _____
> a is a Q.

In the first inference 'a' will stand for Socrates, 'P' will stand for the property of being a man, and 'Q' for the property of being mortal. For the third inference 'a' stands for Senator Jones, 'P' for the property of being a politician, and 'Q' for the property of being a crafty person.

From this new point of view, the structure of the second and fourth inferences is:

For all x, if x is a P, then x is a Q.
___
For all y, if there is a z which is a P and y is the R of z, then there is a w such that w is a Q and y is the R of w.

In the first inference 'P' stands for the property of being a horse, 'Q' for the property of being an animal, and 'R' for the property of being a head. In the second inference 'P' stands for the property of being a man, 'Q' for the property of being a lover, and 'R' for the property of being a death.

The symbols 'there is a' and 'for all' are known as *quantifiers* (the former is the *existential quantifier* and the latter is the *universal quantifier*). Since these two symbols play a central role in expressing the forms of statements and inferences from this new perspective, the system of logic that considers these new inference-forms and statement-forms is known as *quantification theory*.

Let us look at one more example of the difference between the propositional structure of an inference and its quantificational structure. Consider the following inference:

Either all men are brave or all men are crazy.
Joe is a man and Joe is not crazy.
___
All men are brave.

The propositional form of this inference is:

$p \lor q$
$r \cdot s$
___
t

whereas its quantificational form is:

Either for all x, if x is a P, then x is a Q, or
      for all x, if x is a P, then x is an R.
a is a P and it is not the case that a is an R.
___
For all x, if x is a P then x is a Q.

We note two important points here. First, the propositional form of this inference is not a valid form of inference; so from the point of view of propositional form and propositional logic, this inference is not formally valid. However, the quantificational form of this inference is a valid one; so from the point of view of quantificational form and quantification theory, this inference is formally valid. Second, any information that we are given by being told the propositional form of this inference is also given to us when we are told the quantificational form of the inference. For when we are told the quantificational form, we are told that the first premise of this inference is a disjunctive statement, that the second premise is a conjunctive statement, and that the conclusion is not identical with either of the premises or with their disjuncts or conjuncts; and this is all the information conveyed to us when we are given the propositional structure of this inference. On the other hand, we are given information when we are told the quantificational form of this inference, which we are not given when we are told its propositional form. Thus, only when we are told its quantificational form do we learn that the first premise asserts either that all objects of a given type have one property or that they all have some other property. So, the quantificational form of an inference contains more than the propositional form of that inference. In some sense this is why quantification theory is a more powerful system than propositional logic.

Before ending this section, let us see what this tells us about the notion of structure or form. We have an intuitive idea that there is such a thing as *the* structure or form of a statement or inference. It is not easy to see, however, exactly what this means, for we have just seen that for any statement or inference there exist its propositional form and quantificational form. Which of these, or what other form, is *the* form of the inference? Doesn't it seem more plausible to say that any inference or statement is of many different forms—some containing more, and some less, of the structural features of the inference or statement?

If we say this, however, then we must stop asking whether a given valid inference is formally valid. For to ask that is to ask whether its form is a valid form of inference, and we have just agreed to stop talking about determining its form. What we must ask, instead, is whether this given inference is, from the point of view of either propositional logic or quantification theory, a formally valid inference. This question is legitimate, since it does not presuppose that there is some form which is the form of the inference. All that we are asking is whether certain forms of this inference—in particular, its propositional and/or its quantificational forms—are valid forms of inference. And, of course, as we have already seen, the answers to these questions about these different forms may not be the same.

7.2 The Symbols of Quantification Theory

If we examine the symbols used to indicate the quantificational forms that we were looking at in section 7.1, we notice that they divide themselves into several groups. First, we have symbols such as '*a*', '*b*', and '*c*', which represent particular objects. We shall call them our *individual constants*. Then there are symbols such as 'x', 'y', and 'z', which range over all particular objects. These are our *individual variables*. Then there are our *quantifiers*, 'for all' and 'there exists a (n)'. We also used our familiar sentential connectives, such as 'if–then', 'either–or', and others. Finally, we had symbols that are *predicates*, which represent properties or relations, such as 'P', 'Q', 'R', 'F', 'G', and 'H'.

Now, to simplify our symbols for the forms of inference, let us (1) replace all occurrences of symbols of the form 'there exists a (n)' with symbols of the form '(∃)' and all occurrences of symbols of the form 'for all' with symbols of the form '( )'. In both of these cases, the variable following the English symbol is to be placed in the parentheses in our new symbol. So 'for all x' will be rewritten as '(x)', and 'there exists a y' will be rewritten as '(∃y)'; (2) rewrite symbols such as 'a is a P' or 'x is the P of y' as 'Pa' and 'Pxy'. Note that by following this process, we use a variable in symbolizing a formula only when that variable is also in one of the quantifiers. Variables cannot occur otherwise.

To see how much simpler this makes things, and also to get some experience in the use of our new symbols, let us now rewrite the three forms of inference that we examined in section 7.1. Instead of writing:

> For all x, if x is a P, then x is a Q.
> a is a P.
> _____
> a is a Q.

we will write:

> $(x)(Px \supset Qx)$
> Pa
> _____
> Qa

Instead of writing:

> For all x, if x is a P, then x is a Q.
> _____
> For all y, if there is a z which is a P and y is the R of z, then there is a w such that w is a Q and y is the R of w.

we will write:

> $(x)(Px \supset Qx)$
> _____
> $(y)[(\exists z)(Pz \cdot Ryz) \supset (\exists w)(Qw \cdot Ryw)]$

And we will write:

$$(x)(Px \supset Qx) \vee (x)(Px \supset Rx)$$
$$Pa \cdot \sim Ra$$

$$(x)(Px \supset Qx)$$

instead of writing:

> Either for all x, if x is a P, then x is a Q, or for all x, if x is a P, then x is an R.
> a is a P and it is not the case that a is an R.
>
> ---
>
> For all x, if x is a P, then x is a Q.

Four statement-forms are quite widely known because they serve as the basis for the traditional Aristotelian syllogisms, the traditional partial system of quantification theory (partial because it deals only with the validity of inferences involving statements of these four forms). The four forms are:

> All P's are Q's.
> Some P's are Q's.
> No P's are Q's.
> Some P's are not Q's.

All sentences of the first of these forms can be symbolized, in our system, by symbols of the form '$(x)(Px \supset Qx)$'. Thus, we symbolize the statement expressed by 'all men are mortal' by '$(x) (Px \supset Qx)$'; in which 'P' represents the property of being a man and 'Q' the property of being mortal. All statements of the second of these forms can be symbolized by symbols of the form '$(\exists x)(Px \cdot Qx)$'. Thus, the statement expressed by 'some men are mortal' can be symbolized by '$(\exists x)(Px \cdot Qx)$', in which 'P' represents the property of being a man and 'Q' the property of being mortal. All statements of the third of these forms can be symbolized by symbols of the form '$(x)(Px \supset \sim Qx)$'. Thus, we symbolize the statement expressed by 'no men are mortal' by '$(x)(Px \supset \sim Qx)$', in which 'P' once more represents the property of being a man and 'Q' once more represents the property of being mortal. Finally, all symbols of the fourth of these forms can be symbolized by symbols of the form '$(\exists x)(Px \cdot \sim Qx)$'. Thus, we symbolize the statement expressed by 'some men are not mortal' by '$(\exists x)(Px \cdot \sim Qx)$', in which '$P$' represents the property of being a man and 'Q' the property of being mortal.

Although we shall follow this procedure in this book, it is worthwhile to note that these symbolizations may not be entirely adequate. First, there may be a difference between a statement expressed by a symbol of the form 'some *P*'s are *Q*'s' and the statement expressed by the corresponding symbol of the form 'there is an *x* which is a *P* and is a *Q*'. Statements of the latter form are clearly true as long as there is one object that has both of the properties in question. But in at least some cases, statements of the former form seem to be true only when there are at least a few objects (and not merely one) having both these properties. Second, if all objects which are *P*'s are also *Q*'s, then the statement that there is a *P* which is a *Q* is clearly true, but the statement that some *P*'s are *Q*'s may not be true. 'Some *P*'s are *Q*'s' seems to carry with it the implication that only some *P*'s, and not all *P*'s, are *Q*'s. So when we symbolize the statement expressed by 'some men are mortal' by '$(\exists x)(Px \cdot Qx)$', we are interpreting the first sentence to mean the same thing as 'there is at least one man (and maybe more, maybe even all) that is mortal'. (If the user does not so intend it, then our symbolization will not be correct.)

Let us now look at the symbolization of statements of the form 'all *P*'s are *Q*'s' by symbols of the form '$(x)(Px \supset Qx)$'. Let us imagine that no objects have the property *P*. Then the statement expressed by '(x) $(Px \supset Qx)$' will certainly be true. It will, after all, be true of every object that if it is a *P*, then it is a *Q*, since a conditional statement is always true if its antecedent is false. But in such a case, will it be true that all *P*'s are *Q*'s? The answer to that question is unclear. Sometimes the statement expressed by 'all *P*'s are *Q*'s' implies that there are *P*'s, and sometimes it does not. If it does (in which case it is said to have *existential import*), then the statement expressed by 'all *P*'s are *Q*'s' will not be true. If it does not (in which case it is said to lack existential import), then the statement expressed by 'all *P*'s are *Q*'s' will be true. So we can symbolize statements expressed by symbols of the form 'all *P*'s are *Q*'s' by symbols of the form '$(x)(Px \supset Qx)$' only if those statements do not have existential import.

To summarize, then, we realize that our symbolizations of the Aristotelian forms are adequate only if we understand the statements expressed by symbols of the form 'All *P*'s are *Q*'s' as lacking existential import, and only if we suppose that the statements expressed by symbols of the form 'some *P*'s are *Q*'s' are the same statements as those expressed by the corresponding symbols of the form 'there is at least one *P* (and maybe more, maybe even all) that is a *Q*'. This is how we shall understand these symbols in this book, which is why we shall continue to so symbolize statements of the four Aristotelian forms.

Not all statements of the four Aristotelian forms are quite as simple as the ones we have examined so far. Thus, the statement expressed by 'all immoral men are either unhappy or foolish' is of the first of these forms, and can be symbolized by 'all *P*'s are *Q*'s' and by '$(x)(Px \supset Qx)$', in which '*P*' represents the property of being an immoral man and 'Q' represents the property of being either unhappy or foolish. But it is more illuminating to symbolize it by 'all objects which are P's and Q's are either R's or S's' or by '(x)[(Px · Qx) ⊃ (Rx ∨ Sx)]', in which 'P' represents the property of being a man, 'Q' the property of being immoral, 'R' the property of being unhappy, and 'S' the property of being foolish. Similarly, the statement expressed by 'no happy man is either foolish or immoral' is of the third of these forms and can be symbolized by 'no P's are Q's' or by '(x)(Px ⊃ ∼Qx)', in which 'P' represents the property of being a happy man and 'Q' the property of being either foolish or immoral. But it is more illuminating to symbolize it by 'no object which is a P and a Q is either an R or an S', or by '(x)[(Px · Qx) ⊃ ∼(Rx ∨ Sx)]', in which 'P' represents the property of being a man, 'Q' the property of being happy, 'R' the property of being foolish, and 'S' the property of being immoral.

Consider now the statements expressed by the following sentences:

> All men are mortal.
> Men are mortal'.
> Every man is mortal.
> Any man is mortal.
> Each man is mortal.

It seems that we can symbolize them all by using '(x)(Px ⊃ Qx)', in which 'P' represents the property of being a man and 'Q' the property of being mortal. Similarly, if we consider the statements expressed by:

> No man is mortal.
> None of the men are mortal.
> No one who is a man is mortal.
> Nobody who is a man is mortal.

it seems as though we can symbolize them all by '(x)(Px ⊃ ∼Qx)', in which 'P' represents the property of being a man and 'Q' the property of being mortal.

This is not to say that there is no difference in meaning between the different sentences in the first list or between the different sentences in the second list. Looking back at the first list, we see some of the difference when we consider the apparent internal negation of the first and the last sentences in that list. Although 'each man is not mortal' means the same thing as 'no man is mortal' and is not really the internal negation of 'each man is mortal', 'all men are not mortal' only means the same thing as 'some men are immortal' and is the internal negation of 'all men are mortal'. Nevertheless, this difference does not affect the possibility of symbolizing the statements expressed by these different sentences in the same way.

The statements that are most difficult to symbolize correctly are those asserting that some relation holds between two or more objects. So let us first look at some simple examples, and then some more complicated ones. Consider the statement expressed by 'John defeated Mary' and that expressed by 'Mary defeated John'. If we let 'a' represent John, 'b' represent Mary, and 'P' represent the relation of defeating, then we can symbolize the first of those statements as 'Pab' and the second as 'Pba'. This means, of course, that in dealing with relational statements, once we decide what the various symbols represent, we must be very careful about the order in which we write them. For the statement symbolized by 'Pab' may, given our decision as to what the symbols represent, have a truth-value different from the statement symbolized by 'Pba'.

Now let us look at some slightly more complicated cases. Consider the statements expressed by 'John defeated all the girls' and by 'all the girls defeated John'. Let 'Q' represent the property of being a girl. Then the first of these statements will be symbolized as '$(x)(Qx \supset Pax)$', whereas the second will be symbolized as '$(x)(Qx \supset Pxa)$'. Once more, the order in which you write 'x' and 'a' makes a great difference.

Even more complicated are the symbolizations of the statements expressed by 'all the boys defeated all the girls' by 'all the girls defeated all the boys', by 'some of the boys defeated some of the girls', and by 'some of the girls defeated some of the boys'. Letting 'R' represent the property of being a boy, we symbolize them by '$(x)(y)[(Rx \cdot Qy) \supset (Pxy)]$', by '$(x)(y)[(Rx \cdot Qy) \supset (Pyx)]$', by '$(\exists x)(\exists y)(Rx \cdot Qy \cdot Pxy)$', and by '$(\exists x)(\exists y)(Rx \cdot Qy \cdot Pyx)$', respectively.

But the most difficult statements to symbolize are those expressed by 'all the boys defeated some girl' and 'some boy defeated each girl'. The trouble here is that these sentences are ambiguous. Let us look at them one at a time. 'All the boys defeated some girl' might mean the same thing as 'there is one girl such that every single boy defeated her', in which case it is symbolized as '$(\exists x)(Qx \cdot (y)[(Ry) \supset (Pyx)])$'. But it might also mean the same thing as 'every boy defeated at least one girl', in which case it is to be symbolized as '$(y)(Ry \supset (\exists x)(Qx \cdot Pyx)$'. Similarly, 'some boy defeated each girl' might mean the same thing as 'there is one boy who is such that he defeated every girl', in which case it would be symbolized as '$(\exists y)[Ry \cdot (x)(Qx \supset Pyx)]$'. But it might mean the same thing as 'every girl is such that some boy defeated her', in which case it would be symbolized as '$(x)[Qx \supset (\exists y)(Ry \cdot Pyx]$'. This type of ambiguity occurs wherever we need both quantifiers to symbolize a statement.

The following table summarizes the results of this section.

Statements of this form:	*Are normally symbolized:*
All *P*'s are *Q*'s.	$(x)(Px \supset Qx)$
P's are *Q*'s.	$(x)(Px \supset Qx)$
Every *P* is a *Q*.	$(x)(Px \supset Qx)$
Any *P* is a *Q*.	$(x)(Px \supset Qx)$
Each *P* is a *Q*.	$(x)(Px \supset Qx)$
All *P*'s are *Q*'s or *R*'s.	$(x)[Px \supset (Qx \vee Rx)]$
All *P*'s and *Q*'s are *R*'s or *S*'s.	$(x)[(Px \cdot Qx) \supset (Rx \vee Sx)]$
No *P*'s are *Q*'s.	$(x)(Px \supset \sim Qx)$
No one of the *P*'s is a *Q*.	$(x)(Px \supset \sim Qx)$
No one who is a *P* is a *Q*.	$(x)(Px \supset \sim Qx)$
Nobody who is a *P* is a *Q*.	$(x)(Px \supset \sim Qx)$
Some *P*'s are *Q*'s.	$(\exists x)(Px \cdot Qx)$
There are *P*'s which are *Q*'s.	$(\exists x)(Px \cdot Qx)$
Some *P*'s are not *Q*'s.	$(\exists x)(Px \cdot \sim Qx)$
a R's *b*.	Rab
b is *R*'d by *a*.	Rab
b R's *a*.	Rba
a R's all the *P*'s.	$(x)(Px \supset Rax)$
All the *P*'s *R a*.	$(x)(Px \supset Rxa)$
All the *P*'s *R* all the *Q*'s.	$(x)(y)(Px \cdot Qy \supset Rxy)$
All the *Q*'s *R* all the *P*'s.	$(x)(y)(Px \cdot Qy \supset Ryx)$
Some of the *P*'s *R* some of the *Q*'s.	$(\exists x)(\exists y)(Px \cdot Qy \cdot Rxy)$
Some of the *Q*'s *R* some of the *P*'s.	$(\exists x)(\exists y)(Px \cdot Qy \cdot Ryx)$
All the *P*'s *R* some *Q*.	$(x)[Px \supset (\exists y)(Qy \cdot Rxy)]$
	or $(\exists y)[Qy \cdot (x)(Px \supset Rxy)]$
Some *P R*'s each *Q*.	$(\exists x)[Px \cdot (y)(Qy \supset Rxy)]$
	or $(x)[Qx \supset (\exists y)(Py \cdot Rxy)]$

7.3 Two Valid Inferences

In this section we will look at a few simple inference-forms involving quantified statement-forms and show, in an intuitive way, that they are valid. Obviously, our purpose will eventually be to use these simple forms of inference as the basis for a system that can be used to prove that a whole variety of inference-forms are valid. But for the moment, our concern is simply with these forms themselves.

It is perfectly obvious that all the following inferences are valid:

All men are mortal.
_____

If Socrates is a man, then Socrates is mortal.

All men love some girl.

If Joe is a man, then Joe loves some girl.

All evil men are either foolish of unhappy.

If Frank is an evil man, then Frank is either foolish or unhappy.

Everything is somewhere.

Joe is somewhere.

Moreover, one intuitively feels that they are all valid because they are all inferences of the same form and that form is a valid form of inference. The only question is, what is this common form?

To answer that question, let us look at each of those inferences one at a time. The first is rather clearly of the form:

$$\frac{(x)(Fx \supset Gx)}{(Fa \supset Ga)}$$

The second is rather clearly of the form:

$$\frac{(x)[Fx \supset (\exists y)(Gy \cdot Hxy)]}{Fa \supset (\exists y)(Gy \cdot Hay)}$$

The third is rather clearly of the form:

$$\frac{(x)[(Fx \cdot Gx) \supset (Hx \vee Ix)]}{(Fa \cdot Ga) \supset (Ha \vee Ia)}$$

The fourth is rather clearly of the form:

$$\frac{(x)(\exists y)(Fxy)}{(\exists y)(Fay)}$$

One could justifiably say, therefore, that these inferences are not structurally alike, that they do not have the same form. But if one did say this, one would be disregarding the fact that there are certain important structural features which they all do have in common. The premise of each of these inferences asserts that something is true of all objects, whereas the conclusion asserts that it is true of some particular object. Pictorially, they all have the following form:

$$\frac{(x) - - - x - - -}{- - - a - - -}$$

Now, it is intuitively obvious that any inference of this form is valid. After all, if its premise is true, its conclusion must be true. If its conclusion were false—if that particular object did not have that property—then how could the premise, which asserts that everything has it, be true? We have here, therefore, our first new valid form of inference, the *universal quantifier elimination form* ('UE', for short).

There are many inferences that seem to be of this form, but which really are not and are even invalid. Since people are often confused about this point and suppose that these inferences are of the UE form, we had better look at a few examples of them and see why they really are not of this form.

Consider the following inference:

> If everyone goes home, then everyone will have dinner.
> _____
> If John goes home, then John will have dinner.

Someone might well suppose that this inference is valid. Isn't it of the UE form? Doesn't the premise assert that everyone has a certain property (the property of getting dinner if they go home), while the conclusion asserts that John has that property? The answer to both these questions is no. To see this, let us symbolize this inference:

$$\frac{(x)\,Fx \supset (x)\,Gx}{Fa \supset Ga}$$

In other words, the premise really says that if it is the case that everyone has a certain property, then it will also be the case that everyone has another property; it does not say, of every person, that if he has the first property, then he will also have the second. On the other hand, the conclusion does say of John that if he has the first property, then he will also have the second one. So the inference is not of the UE form.

Note, by the way, that this inference is not even valid. Its premise can be true while its conclusion is false. The cook at home may be prepared to feed everyone, but not prepared to feed them individually (that would be too much bother). So if everyone goes home, then they will all have dinner, but if John goes home (while everyone else does not), then John will not have dinner.

Another example of an invalid inference that may seem valid because it seems to be of the UE form is:

> It is not the case that everyone is rich.
> _____
> It is not the case that Joe is rich.

This inference is clearly invalid, since the premise can be true while the conclusion is false (if, for example, Frank is poor and Joe is rich). Still, why isn't it of the UE form? The answer becomes clear when we symbolize this inference. It is of the form:

$$\frac{\sim(x)Px}{\sim Pa}$$

Even if we suppose that the conclusion says that Joe has a certain property (the property of not being rich), the premise certainly does not say that everyone has this property; it says only that it is not the case that everyone has the contrary property (the property of being rich).

How can we check to be certain we don't make this error? Look at the symbols used to express the premise and the conclusion. The symbol used to express the premise must (a) begin with a universal quantifier, and (b) the quantifier must apply to the whole formula, the symbol used to express the conclusion must be like the symbol used to express the premise, except that (c) the initial universal quantifier must be missing, and (d) all occurrences of the variable in the initial quantifier (and only those occurrences) must be replaced by the same individual constant. Conditions (c) and (d) are met in both our examples (which is why they seem to be of the UE form) but either (a) or (b) is not met. In the second case condition (a) is not met, since the symbol used to express the premise begins with a negation sign. In the first case condition (b) is not met, since the initial quantifier appies only to the first half of the formula.

Let us now look at a second valid form of inference, the *existential quantifier introduction* form of inference ('EI', for short). All the following inferences are of this form:

Joe is rich.
_____

There is someone who is rich.

Joe loves everyone.
_____

There is someone who loves everyone.

If Joe loves someone, then he loves everyone.
_____

There is someone who is such that if he loves someone, then he loves everyone.

When we symbolize these inferences, we get, for the first inference:

$$\frac{Pa}{(\exists x)Px}$$

For the second inference, we get:

$$\frac{(x)Pax}{(\exists y)(x)Pyx}$$

For the third inference, we get:

$$\frac{(\exists x)Pax \supset (x)Pax}{(\exists y)[(\exists x)Pyx \supset (x)Pyx]}$$

One could justifiably say that these inferences are not structurally alike, that they are not of the same form. But to say this would be to miss the fact that they do have certain important structural features in common. The premise of each inference asserts that a particular object has a certain property, while the conclusion says that there is an object having that property. Pictorially, they all have the following form:

$$\frac{----a----}{(\exists x)---x---}$$

It is intuitively obvious that any inference of this form is valid. For the conclusion to be false, there can be no object that has the property in question. But if the premise is true, then the object of the premise has that property. So if the premise is true, the conclusion cannot be false. We have, therefore, a second valid inference-form involving quantifiers.

As in the case of the UE form, there are, in the case of the EI form, many invalid inferences that seem to be valid because they seem to be of the EI form. To be sure that we are not fooled by these inferences, we can look at the symbol used to express the premise and the symbol used to express the conclusion. The symbol used to express the conclusion must (a) begin with an existential quantifier, and (b) the quantifier must apply to the whole formula, and the symbol used to express the premise must be like the symbol used to express the conclusion, except that (c), the initial existential quantifier must be missing and (d) all occurrences of the variable in the initial quantifier (and only those occurrences) must be replaced by the same individual constant.

Let us apply these rules to a few invalid inferences that seem to be valid because they seem to be of the EI form, thereby showing that they really are not of that form. Consider the following inference:

If Joe is rich, then Joe will help.

If there is someone who is rich, then there is someone who will help.

This inference is invalid; its premises can be true while its conclusion is false (when, for example, only Frank is rich and he won't help). But why isn't it valid? Isn't it of the EI form? The answer to both these questions is no. It isn't of the EI form, since it violates rule (b); the initial quantifier applies only to part of the formula, as can be seen graphically when we consider the symbolization of this inference:

$$\frac{Pa \supset Qa}{(\exists x)Px \supset (\exists x)Qx}$$

Intuitively, the inference is not valid, for although the premise says of some object that if it has one property (being rich), then it has another (being someone who will help), the conclusion does not say that there exists an object such that if it has the first property, it also has the second property. The conclusion says that if there is an object having the first property, then there is an object having the second.

As another example, consider the following inference:

It is not the case that Joe is rich.

It is not the case that someone is rich.

This is also an invalid inference; if Joe is poor and Frank rich, then the premise is true and the conclusion is false. Despite appearances, it is not of the EI form, as becomes clear when we symbolize it:

$$\frac{\sim Pa}{\sim(\exists x)Px}$$

This inference violates rule (a). The symbol used to express the conclusion does not begin with an existential quantifier. Therefore, the inference is not of the EI form.

7.4 Two More Valid Inference-Forms

In section 7.3, we discovered two valid forms of inference: the EI form and the UE form. In this section we must find two more inference-forms that are valid, one whose conclusion is expressed by symbols containing a universal quantifier while its premises are not (so that this will be a universal-quantifier introduction form of inference), and one whose premises are expressed by symbols containing existential quantifiers while its conclusion is not (so that this will be an existential-quantifier elimination form of inference).

Consider all the following inferences:

If John is a man, then John is mortal.
_____
All men are mortal.

If John is a man, then there is (or was) someone who is his father.
_____
All men have fathers.

If John went home, then John will have dinner.
_____
All who go home have dinner.

If John is lucky, then there will be someone whom John loves.
_____
All lucky men love someone.

Are any of them valid? It would certainly seem as though they were not. They all have a premise which asserts of some object that it has a property, and they all have a conclusion which says that everything has that property; that is, pictorially they are all of the form:

$$\frac{----a----}{(x)---x---}$$

and it would seem that no inference of that form could be valid. All that is needed to make them invalid is that it is possible that their premises are true while their conclusion is false. In this case that is certainly possible, since one object can have a property while other objects do not.

This is a great shame. It is, after all, just this type of inference-form that we are seeking as a third basic valid inference-form for our system of quantification theory. What are we to do? If this inference is not valid in general, perhaps it is valid under certain conditions. If it is, then we can adopt it as our UI form, claiming, of course, that it is a valid form only under such conditions.

Under what conditions are inferences of this form valid? It would seem that they are valid only when all objects must have the same property had by the object discussed in the premise. But when is this the case? Let us imagine we have a proof that the premise is true, though it makes no assumptions about the object discussed in the premise. Then we could equally well have used that proof to prove about any other object that it has the property in question. In that case we can certainly say that if the object discussed in the premise has the property in question, then all objects must have it. In that case, therefore, we can certainly say that inferences of our form are valid.

Thus, we shall say that any inference is of the *universal-quantifier introduction* form only when it has a premise which asserts that some object has a property, a conclusion which asserts that everything has that property, and a proof of the premise which does not rest upon any assumption about the object that the premise is discussing. When checking to see whether an inference is of this form, we look at the symbol used to express the premise and the symbol used to express the conclusion. The following requirements of those symbols must be met: They must be exactly alike except for the facts that (a) the conclusion begins with a universal quantifier containing a variable that is not in the premise, (b) that quantifier applies to the whole formula, (c) there is a constant occurring in the premise such that all its occurrences (and only those) are replaced in the conclusion by the variable mentioned in (a), and (d) the initial quantifier in the conclusion is missing in the premise. However, in addition to this, we must look at the symbols used to express the proof of the premise, and be certain that, in that proof, the symbols expressing the assumptions upon which our premise rests contain no occurrences of the individual constant mentioned in (c).

Let us go back now and look at the inferences with which we began this section. Consider the inference:

If John is a man, then John is mortal.
_____

All men are mortal.

This inference is of the form:

$$\frac{Pa \supset Qa}{(x)(Px \supset Qx)}$$

so it meets all conditions (a) through (d). But that does not make it valid without a proof of the premise that rests upon no assumptions about John. There seems to be such a proof. Assume that all men are animals and all animals are mortal. Then, if John is a man, John is an animal, and if John is an animal, then John is mortal. So if John is a man, then John is mortal. This proof rests upon no assumptions about John; its only two assumptions are that all men are animals and that all animals are mortal. So from our premise that if John is a man, then he is mortal, which rests upon these two assumptions, we can conclude, by an inference of the universal-quantifier introduction form (or, simply, of the UI form), that all men are mortal. This conclusion also rests, of course, upon the assumptions that all men are animals and that all animals are mortal.

Certainly, there are other possible proofs that if John is a man, then John is mortal. For example, one can prove from the assumptions that John is dead and that all dead things are mortal. These assumptions, however, are assumptions about John. So we cannot say that, given this proof, we can infer from the fact that if John is a man, then John is mortal that all men are mortal. Consequently, we cannot conclude that if these two assumptions are true, then all men are mortal.

The same point can be made about each of the other inferences we examined in the beginning of this section. As they stand, none are valid. But when supplemented by some proofs of their premise that do not involve any assumptions about the object discussed in the premise, we can validly infer that the conclusion is true—providing, of course, that the assumptions upon which the premise is proved are also true. On the other hand, when supplemented by other proofs of their premises that do involve some assumptions about the object discussed in the premise, we cannot validly infer that the conclusion is true—even though the assumptions upon which the premise is proved are also true.

So we now have a UI form of inference that is valid; we now need only an EE form of inference that is valid. But this is even more difficult to find. To see why, consider the following inferences, which are of a form that obviously involves the elimination of an existential quantifier:

There is someone who is blind.

Joe is blind.

There is someone who loves everyone.

Joe loves everyone.

Both these inferences have premises which say there is an object having a property and conclusions which say of an object that it has that property; that is, pictorially they are of the form:

$$\frac{(\exists x)(----x----)}{----a----}$$

It would seem that no inference of this form can be valid. The premise can easily be true while the conclusion is false when the object discussed in the conclusion does not have the property in question but some other object does.

The obvious suggestion is that we should do for this form of inference exactly what we did for the UI inference-form; we have only to find a set of conditions under which the inference is valid. These are the conditions under which the object having the property must be the object discussed in the conclusion. One such case is when the object discussed in the conclusion is the only object which exists. Indeed, under such circumstances the inference would be valid. However, there are so few cases in which this condition is met that we would have an inference-form which we could rarely use (which is almost as bad as having none at all.) Another such case is when, if one object has the property in question, all objects have it. However, we then don't need a new inference-form to infer that *a* has the property. Given that additional fact, and the premise that one object has the property, we can conclude that everything has the property and that *a* therefore has it. This last inference is of the UE form. We are looking, however, for a new inference-form whose validity ensures the validity of some additional inferences whose validity is not already ensured by that of our present inference-forms.

So a new approach is required. Upon reflection, the suggestion that most naturally occurs is to see what we can infer from premises which assert that there is an object with a given property when that premise is supplemented by additional premises. Adopting this approach, logicians have discovered the following valid form of inference, which we will call the *existential-quantifier elimination* form of inference (or, simply, the EE form of inference):

$$\frac{\begin{array}{l}(\exists x)(----x----)\\(----a----) \supset p\end{array}}{p}$$

Two conditions must be met for this inference to be valid. It must be possible to prove that the second premise is true without making any assumptions about *a*. And the statement represented by '*p*' also must not be about *a*.

To determine whether an inference is of this form, we must look at the symbols used to express the premises of this inference and the symbol used to express its conclusion. The following requirements must be met. (a) The symbol used to express the first premise must begin with an existential quantifier containing a variable which does not occur in the antecedent of the second premise, and that quantifier must apply to the whole formula. (b) The symbol used to express the second premise must be a conditional sentence whose antecedent is like the symbol used to express the first premise, except that the initial quantifier is missing and that it contains a constant such that all (and only those) its occurrences are replaced in the first premise by the variable mentioned in (a), and whose consequent does not contain that constant. In addition, however, we must examine the symbols used to express the proof of the second premise and be sure that, in the proof, the symbols expressing the assumptions upon which the premise rests contain no occurrences of the individual constant mentioned in (b).

Intuitively, it is fairly clear that such inferences will be valid. After all, since the proof of the second premise makes no assumptions about the object *a* and since its consequent is not about *a*, we could equally well have proved about any object that if the object has the property in question, then the statement represented by '*p*' will be true. In particular, we could prove about the object which does have that property (and the first premise guarantees that there is such an object) that if it has the property, then the statement represented by '*p*' will be true. So the statement represented by '*p*' must be true.

Let us now look at an inference that is of this form and is, therefore, valid. On the assumption that all men are mortal, one can obviously prove that if Joe is a man, then there is something that is mortal. Therefore, the following inference is valid:

> There is something that is a man.
> If Joe is a man, then there is something that is mortal.
> _____
> There is something that is mortal.

The conclusion rests, of course, upon the assumption that all men are mortal (the assumption that we needed to prove the second premise) and any assumptions of the first premise.

Let us check to see that this inference is of the EE form. It can be symbolized as:

$$(\exists x)(Px)$$
$$\frac{Pa \supset (\exists x)Qx}{(\exists x)(Qx)}$$

The symbol used to express the first premise does begin with an existential quantifier (containing a variable, '*x*', which does not occur in the antecedent of the second premise), and it does apply to the whole symbol. The symbol used to express the second premise is a conditional symbol. Its antecedent symbol is like '$(\exists x)(Px)$', except that the initial quantifier is missing and it contains a constant, '*a*', which is such that all and only its occurrences are replaced in the first premise by '*x*', and its consequent symbol contains no occurrences of '*a*'. Moreover, the proof we gave previously of the second premise contains no assumption about *a*, since its only assumption is that all men are mortal.

7.5 Proofs in Quantification Theory

Now that we have a few valid forms of inferences, we will use them as the basis for a system to prove that other forms of inference are valid. The method we will employ is like the method used in Chapter 6. We will show that an inference is valid by showing that if the premises of an inference of this form are true, then its conclusion is also true. We do this by producing an ordered sequence of statements, all of which either are assumptions or are validly inferable, by use of one of our fifteen inference-forms) eleven from Chapter 6 and the four new ones from this chapter), from earlier members of the sequence. The last member of the sequence must, of course, be the conclusion of the inference in question, and it must rest only upon assumptions that are premises of the inference in question. Such a proof proves that if the premises of the inference are true, then its conclusion is also true, and it proves that any inference of the form in question is a valid inference.

We shall also use this method, as we did in Chapter 6, to prove that certain statements must be true and that every statement of certain forms must be true. One of our proofs is a proof that a certain statement must be true if (a) that statement is the last member of the sequence, (b) it rests upon no assumptions, and (c) every member of the sequence either is an assumption or is derivable from the earlier members of the sequence by use of an inference that is of one of our 15 valid forms. Such a proof proves that any statement of that form must be true.

Let us look at a few simple proofs in our expanded system. Our first proof is of the validity of one of those inferences which we used, in the beginning of this chapter, to show that propositional logic is inadequate for proving, for every valid inference, that it is valid. The inference was:

All men are mortal.
Socrates is a man.
_____
Socrates is mortal.

and it is of the form:

$$(x)(Px \supset Qx)$$
$$Pa$$
$$\overline{}$$
$$Qa$$

The following proof proves that any inference of this form must be valid:

(1)	(1) $(x)(Px \supset Qx)$	Assump.
(2)	(2) Pa	Assump.
(1)	(3) $Pa \supset Qa$	UE (1)
(1)(2)	(4) Qa	CE (2)(3)

The first two steps are the assumptions that the premises of our inference are true. The third can be validly inferred from the first by an inference of the UE form. After all, the symbol expressing the premise begins with a universal quantifier and it does cover the whole symbol. Moreover, the symbol expressing the conclusion, '$Pa \supset Qa$', is like the symbol expressing the premise, '$(x)(Px \supset Qx)$', except that the universal quantifier is missing and that a constant ('a') is substituted for all (and only those) occurrences of the variable ('x') in the initial quantifier. Finally, step (4) can be validly inferred from steps (2) and (3) by an inference of the CE form.

Let us now prove that any inference of the following form is valid.

$$\frac{(x)Px}{(\exists x)Px}$$

The proof is very simple:

(1)	(1) $(x)Px$	Assump.
(1)	(2) Pa	UE (1)
(1)	(3) $(\exists x)Px$	EI (2)

Here we employ inferences of both our simple forms of inference, UE and EI. The symbol expressing the second step, 'Pa', is, so to speak, the dequantified version of the symbols expressing both the first and the third steps; that is, it is like them except that it does not contain their initial quantifiers and that it has, instead of all (and only those) occurrences of the variable in their quantifier, the same constant. Therefore, we can infer the statement it expresses from step (1) by a UE inference, and we can infer from it, by an EI inference, step (3).

So far, we have looked only at proofs that employ inferences of the simplest of our new forms. Let us now look at some proofs that employ inferences of some of our more difficult forms. For example, here is a proof that the following is a valid inference-form:

$$\frac{\begin{array}{c}(x)(Fx \supset Gx)\\ (x)Fx\end{array}}{(x)Gx}$$

The proof is as follows:

(1)	(1) $(x)(Fx \supset Gx)$	Assump.
(2)	(2) $(x)Fx$	Assump.
(1)	(3) $Fa \supset Ga$	UE (1)
(2)	(4) Fa	UE (2)
(1)(2)	(5) Ga	CE (3)(4)
(1)(2)	(6) $(x)Gx$	UI (5)

The first two steps are simply the assumption that the premises of the inference in question are true. Since '$Fa \supset Ga$' is the dequantified version of '$(x)(Fx \supset Gx)$' and 'Fa' is the dequantified version of '$(x)Fx$', steps (3) and (4) can be inferred from (1) and (2) by two inferences of the UE form. Step (5) follows from steps (3) and (4) by an inference of the CE form. Now, notice that we have a proof of the statement represented by 'Ga' that depends upon no assumptions about a. The only assumptions it depends upon are (1) and (2), and the symbols expressing these do not contain any occurrences of 'a'. Therefore, by an inference of the UI form, we can infer that $(x)Gx$.

This proof illustrates a very important point. To infer some statement *p* from some statement *q* by an inference of the UI form, we must look at a proof of *q* to see that it does not involve any assumptions of a certain type (these must not be assumptions about a certain object). The proof that we will always look at is to be found in the larger proof which we are working on. Thus, in our case the proof of (5) that we will look at, to see whether we can infer (6) from (5) by a UI inference, is the proof given for it in steps (1) through (5). This makes our task very easy. All we must do is look to the left of the symbol representing the statement *q* to see what assumptions the proof of *q* depended upon [in our case it is just (1) and (2)]; then we can easily check to see whether they are of the prohibited type.

The same thing is true of proofs employing inferences of the EE form. Let us look at one example. It is a proof that any inference of the form

$$(x)(Fx \supset Gx)$$
$$(\exists x)Fx$$
$$\overline{(\exists x)Gx}$$

is valid, and it runs as follows:

(1)	(1) $(x)(Fx \supset Gx)$	Assump.
(2)	(2) $(\exists x)Fx$	Assump.
(3)	(3) Fa	Assump.
(1)	(4) $Fa \supset Ga$	UE (1)
(1)(3)	(5) Ga	CE (3)(4)
(1)(3)	(6) $(\exists x)Gx$	EI (5)
(1)	(7) $Fa \supset (\exists x)Gx$	CI (6)
(1)(2)	(8) $(\exists x)Gx$	EE (2)(7)

Steps (1) and (2) are, of course, the assumption that the premises of the inference in question are true. Steps (3) through (7) are a proof of step (7), a proof that does not rest upon any assumptions about the object *a* [(7) only rests upon the assumption that (1) is true, and the symbol that expresses (1), '$(x)(Fx \supset Gx)$', contains no occurrences of '*a*']. So from (2) and (7) we can infer (8). For the symbol used to express (2) begins with an existential quantifier that applies to the whole formula; the symbol used to express (7) is a conditional symbol whose antecedent symbol is the dequantified version of the symbol used to express (2) and whose consequent symbol does not contain '*a*'; and, as we have just seen, the proof of (7) rests upon no assumptions containing *a*.

As a final example, let us look at a proof of the validity of the second inference with which we began this chapter, and which we used to illustrate the inadequacy of propositional logic. It was:

All horses are animals.
_____

Every head of a horse is a head of an animal.

This inference is of the form:

$$\frac{(x)(Px \supset Qx)}{(y)[(\exists z)(Pz \cdot Ryz) \supset (\exists w)(Qw \cdot Ryw)]}$$

and we will show that it is valid by proving that every inference of this form is valid. The proof is as follows:

(1)	(1) $(x)(Px \supset Qx)$	Assump.
(2)	(2) $(\exists z)(Pz \cdot Rbz)$	Assump.
(3)	(3) $Pa \cdot Rba$	Assump.
(3)	(4) Pa	AE (3)
(3)	(5) Rba	AE (3)
(1)	(6) $Pa \supset Qa$	UE (1)
(1)(3)	(7) Qa	CE (4)(6)
(1)(3)	(8) $Qa \cdot Rba$	AI (5)(7)
(1)(3)	(9) $(\exists w)(Qw \cdot Rbw)$	EI (8)
(1)	(10) $(Pa \cdot Rba) \supset [(\exists w)(Qw \cdot Rbw)]$	CI (9)
(1)(2)	(11) $(\exists w)(Qw \cdot Rbw)$	EE (2)(10)
(1)	(12) $(\exists z)(Pz \cdot Rbz) \supset (\exists w)(Qw \cdot Rbw)$	CI (11)
(1)	(13) $(y)[(\exists z)(Pz \cdot Ryz) \supset (\exists w)(Qw \cdot Ryw)]$	UI (12)

The idea was to prove (12) by a proof that involved no assumptions about b, so that we could infer (13) from (12) by an inference of the UI form. To prove (12), we assumed its antecedent [in (2)] and proved its consequent [in (11)], so that (12) follows by CI. That proof was a standard proof of the EE form. We assumed, in (3), the statement expressed by the dequantified version of the symbol that expresses (2), and proved, by (10), that if it is true, then so is (11). Since that proof involved no assumptions about a, and since (11) is not about a, (11) followed from (10) and (2) by an EE inference.

Of course, this proof is more complicated than any of the other proofs we have considered so far. But it involves no new methods of proof. Our method, based as it is on our 15 valid forms of inference, is just as adequate for handling inferences involving relational statements as it is for handling inferences involving nonrelational statements; and the inferences it employs in proofs involving one are no different from those it employs in proofs involving the other.

7.6 Some Proofs

In this section we will look at a variety of additional proofs, some of which prove that certain inference-forms are valid ones, others of which prove that statements of certain forms must be true. Our purpose in looking at these proofs is twofold. First, it will give us additional exercise in recognizing when proofs are satisfactory. Second, these inference-forms and statement-forms are well-known ones that are worth learning; hence, a proof that they are valid inference-forms, or that any statement of that form must be true, is independently worthwhile.

We will begin with some statements and inferences involving only statements of the four Aristotelian forms. As you will remember, they were as follows:

$(x)(Px \supset Qx)$	Statements of this form are called *A statements*.
$(x)(Px \supset \sim Qx)$	Statements of this form are called *E statements*.
$(\exists x)(Px \cdot Qx)$	Statements of this form are called *I statements*.
$(\exists x)(Px \cdot \sim Qx)$	Statements of this form are called *O statements*.

The first set of proofs that we will examine prove that all of the statements of the following forms must be true:

(a') $(x)(Px \supset Qx) \equiv \sim(\exists x)(Px \cdot \sim Qx)$	Law of the contradictoriness of A and O statements.
(b') $(x)(Px \supset \sim Qx) \equiv (x)(Qx \supset \sim Px)$	Law of conversion for E statements.
(c') $(\exists x)(Px \cdot Qx) \equiv (\exists x)(Qx \cdot Px)$	Law of conversion for I statements.
(d') $(x)(Px \supset Qx) \equiv (x)(\sim Qx \supset \sim Px)$	Law of contraposition for A statements.

By the way, note that Aristotelian logicians had additional statement-forms like these that they claimed were such that any statement of those forms must be true. But their claim was based upon their supposition that A statements (when expressed in a natural language) had existential import. Since we are not supposing that they have such import, we do not recognize their additional statement-forms.

Let us first look at a proof of the law of conversion for *E* statements:

(1)	(1) $(x)(Px \supset \sim Qx)$	Assump.
(1)	(2) $Pa \supset \sim Qa$	UE (1)
(3)	(3) Qa	Assump.
(3)	(4) $\sim \sim Qa$	DN (3)
(1)(3)	(5) $\sim Pa$	NE (2)(4)
(1)	(6) $Qa \supset \sim Pa$	CI (5)
(1)	(7) $(x)(Qx \supset \sim Px)$	UI (6)
	(8) $(x)(Px \supset \sim Qx) \supset (x)(Qx \supset \sim Px)$	CI (7)
(9)	(9) $(x)(Qx \supset \sim Px)$	Assump.
(9)	(10) $Qa \supset \sim Pa$	UE (9)
(11)	(11) Pa	Assump.
(11)	(12) $\sim \sim Pa$	DN (11)
(9)(11)	(13) $\sim Qa$	NE (10)(12)
(9)	(14) $Pa \supset \sim Qa$	CI (13)
(9)	(15) $(x)(Px \supset \sim Qx)$	UI (14)
	(16) $(x)(Qx \supset \sim Px) \supset (x)(Px \supset \sim Qx)$	CI (15)
	(17) $(x)(Px \supset \sim Qx) \equiv (x)(Qx \supset \sim Px)$	BI (8)(16)

Since this is a proof of a biconditional statement, we might expect that it will be inferred [as it is in step (17)] from two conditional statements, and that the main part of the proof will consist of proofs of those two conditional statements [as it does; steps (1) through (8) prove one of them, and (9) through (16) prove the other]. Since these proofs turn out to be exactly alike, we will look only at the first one. Since the statement to be proved is a conditional statement, we assume its antecedent [in step (1)] and prove, on that assumption, its consequent [in step (7)]. Since the consequent is a universal statement, we know that we can get it by an inference of the universal-introduction form from its dequantified version [step (6)]. So all we must do is prove that the dequantified version is true, [which we can do in steps (3) through (6)] without having to assume anything about the specific object it is about.

The proof of the law of contradictoriness of *A* and *O* statements is essentially of the same type, though slightly more complicated (see p. 165). Since this is a proof of a biconditional statement, we might expect that it will be inferred [as it is in step (29)] from two conditional statements [steps (16) and (28)], and that the main part of the proof will consist of proofs of these two conditional statements [as it does; steps (1) through (16) prove one, and steps (17) through (28) prove the other]. Since these proofs are quite different, let us look at them one at a time. In steps (1) through (16) we try to prove the truth of a conditional statement; so we assume the truth of its antecedent [in step (1)] and show [in step (15)] that, given this assumption, its consequent must be true. Since its consequent is a negative statement, we

(1)	(1) $(x)(Px \supset Qx)$	Assump.
(2)	(2) $(\exists x)(Px \cdot \sim Qx)$	Assump.
(3)	(3) $Pa \cdot \sim Qa$	Assump.
(3)	(4) Pa	AE (3)
(3)	(5) $\sim Qa$	AE (3)
(1)	(6) $Pa \supset Qa$	UE (1)
(1)(3)	(7) Qa	CE (4)(6)
(1)(3)	(8) $Qa \cdot \sim Qa$	AI (5)(7)
(3)	(9) $(x)(Px \supset Qx) \supset Qa \cdot \sim Qa$	CI (8)
(3)	(10) $\sim(x)(Px \supset Qx)$	NI (9)
(1)(3)	(11) $(x)(Px \supset Qx) \cdot \sim(x)(Px \supset Qx)$	AI (1)(10)
(1)	(12) $Pa \cdot \sim Qa \supset [(x)(Px \supset Qx)$ $\cdot \sim(x)(Px \supset Qx)]$	CI (11)
(1)(2)	(13) $(x)(Px \supset Qx) \cdot \sim(x)(Px \supset Qx)$	EE (2)(12)
(1)	(14) $(\exists x)(Px \cdot \sim Qx) \supset [(x)(Px \supset Qx)$ $\cdot \sim(x)(Px \supset Qx)]$	CI (13)
(1)	(15) $\sim(\exists x)(Px \cdot \sim Qx)$	NI (14)
	(16) $(x)(Px \supset Qx) \supset \sim(\exists x)(Px \cdot \sim Qx)$	CI (15)
(17)	(17) $\sim(\exists x)(Px \cdot \sim Qx)$	Assump.
(18)	(18) Pa	Assump.
(19)	(19) $\sim Qa$	Assump.
(18)(19)	(20) $Pa \cdot \sim Qa$	AI (18)(19)
(18)(19)	(21) $(\exists x)(Px \cdot \sim Qx)$	EI (20)
(17)(18)(19)	(22) $(\exists x)(Px \cdot \sim Qx) \cdot \sim(\exists x)(Px \cdot \sim Qx)$	AI (17)(21)
(17)(18)	(23) $\sim Qa \supset [(\exists x)(Px \cdot \sim Qx)$ $\cdot \sim(\exists x)(Px \cdot \sim Qx)]$	CI (22)
(17)(18)	(24) $\sim \sim Qa$	NI (23)
(17)(18)	(25) Qa	DN (24)
(17)	(26) $Pa \supset Qa$	CI (25)
(17)	(27) $(x)(Px \supset Qx)$	UI (26)
	(28) $\sim(\exists x)(Px \cdot \sim Qx) \supset (x)(Px \supset Qx)$	CI (27)
	(29) $(x)(Px \supset Qx) \equiv \sim(\exists x)(Px \cdot \sim Qx)$	BI (16)(28)

will be proving its truth by an inference of the NI form; so we assume [in step (2)] the truth of the statement of which it is a denial and prove [in step (14)] that if this statement were true, then some contradiction would also be true. Since (2) is an existential statement, we must first get the contradiction upon the dequantified version of (2) [we do that by (11)]; then we can get it [as we do by (13)] upon the original quantified statement. In steps (17) through (28) we are also trying to prove the truth of a conditional statement; so we assume [in (17)] the truth of its antecedent and show [by (27)] that its consequent must then be true. Since that consequent is a universally quantified statement, we want a proof [which we get by (26)] of a dequantified version of it so that we can infer the consequent by an inference of the UI form. And since (26) is itself a conditional statement, we assume its antecedent in (18) and get its consequent in (25).

The Aristotelian logicians spent most of their time studying the validity of *syllogisms* (inferences with two premises whose premises and conclusions were statements of one of the four Aristotelian forms). They discovered that the following fifteen syllogism forms were valid:

(1) Barbara Syllogism

$$(x)(Qx \supset Rx)$$
$$(x)(Px \supset Qx)$$
$$\overline{(x)(Px \supset Rx)}$$

(2) Baroco Syllogism

$$(x)(Rx \supset Qx)$$
$$(\exists x)(Px \cdot \sim Qx)$$
$$\overline{(\exists x)(Px \cdot \sim \check{R}x)}$$

(3) Bocardo Syllogism

$$(\exists x)(Qx \cdot \sim Rx)$$
$$(x)(Qx \supset Px)$$
$$\overline{(\exists x)(Px \cdot \sim Rx)}$$

(4) Camenes Syllogism

$$(x)(Rx \supset Qx)$$
$$(x)(Qx \supset \sim Px)$$
$$\overline{(x)(Px \supset \sim Rx)}$$

(5) Camestres Syllogism

$$(x)(Rx \supset Qx)$$
$$(x)(Px \supset \sim Qx)$$
$$\overline{(x)(Px \supset \sim Rx)}$$

(6) Celarent Syllogism

$$(x)(Qx \supset \sim Rx)$$
$$(x)(Px \supset Qx)$$
$$\overline{(x)(Px \supset \sim Rx)}$$

(7) Cesare Syllogism

$$(x)(Rx \supset \sim Qx)$$
$$(x)(Px \supset Qx)$$
$$\overline{(x)(Px \supset \sim Rx)}$$

(8) Darii Syllogism

$$(x)(Qx \supset Rx)$$
$$(\exists x)(Px \cdot Qx)$$
$$\overline{(\exists x)(Px \cdot Rx)}$$

(9) Datisi Syllogism

$$(x)(Qx \supset Rx)$$
$$(\exists x)(Qx \cdot Px)$$
$$\overline{(\exists x)(Px \cdot Rx)}$$

(10) Dimaris Syllogism

$$(\exists x)(Rx \cdot Qx)$$
$$(x)(Qx \supset Px)$$
$$\overline{(\exists x)(Px \cdot Rx)}$$

(11) Disamis Syllogism

$$(\exists x)(Qx \cdot Rx)$$
$$(x)(Qx \supset Px)$$
$$\overline{(\exists x)(Px \cdot Rx)}$$

(12) Ferio Syllogism

$$(x)(Qx \supset \sim Rx)$$
$$(\exists x)(Px \cdot Qx)$$
$$\overline{(\exists x)(Px \cdot \sim Rx)}$$

(13) Ferison Syllogism

$$(x)(Qx \supset \sim Rx)$$
$$(\exists x)(Qx \cdot Px)$$
$$\overline{(\exists x)(Px \cdot \sim Rx)}$$

(14) Festino Syllogism

$$(x)(Rx \supset \sim Qx)$$
$$(\exists x)(Px \cdot Qx)$$
$$\overline{(\exists x)(Px \cdot \sim Rx)}$$

(15) Fresison Syllogism

$$(x)(Rx \supset \sim Qx)$$
$$(\exists x)(Qx \cdot Px)$$
$$\overline{(\exists x)(Px \cdot \sim Rx)}$$

Actually, they claimed that there were nineteen valid syllogisms, but their claim about these four additional forms was based upon their supposition that *A* and *E* statements (when expressed in a natural language) had existential import. Since we are not supposing that they have such import, we do not recognize these additional inference-forms.

Let us look at the proof of the validity of several of these inference-forms. The following is a simple proof of the validity of syllogisms of the Barbara form:

(1)	(1) $(x)(Qx \supset Rx)$	Assump.
(2)	(2) $(x)(Px \supset Qx)$	Assump.
(3)	(3) Pa	Assump.
(2)	(4) $Pa \supset Qa$	UE (2)
(2)(3)	(5) Qa	CE (3)(4)
(1)	(6) $Qa \supset Ra$	UE (1)
(1)(2)(3)	(7) Ra	CE (5)(6)
(1)(2)	(8) $Pa \supset Ra$	CI (7)
(1)(2)	(9) $(x)(Px \supset Rx)$	UI (8)

In steps (1) and (2) we assume that our premises are true. In step (3) we assume the truth of the statement expressed by '*Pa*', and in step (7) we show that upon this assumption the statement represented by '*Ra*' is true. We then use inferences of the forms CI and UI to get our desired conclusion.

The proof of the validity of syllogisms of the Darii form is equally simple:

(1)	(1) $(x)(Qx \supset Rx)$	Assump.
(2)	(2) $(\exists x)(Px \cdot Qx)$	Assump.
(3)	(3) $Pa \cdot Qa$	Assump.
(3)	(4) Pa	AE (3)
(3)	(5) Qa	AE (3)
(1)	(6) $Qa \supset Ra$	UE (1)
(1)(3)	(7) Ra	CE (5)(6)
(1)(3)	(8) $Pa \cdot Ra$	AI (4)(7)
(1)(3)	(9) $(\exists x)(Px \cdot Rx)$	EI (8)
(1)	(10) $Pa \cdot Qa \supset (\exists x)(Px \cdot Rx)$	CI (9)
(1)(2)	(11) $(\exists x)(Px \cdot Rx)$	EE (2)(10)

Once more, we assume in steps (1) and (2) that our premises are true. In step (3) we assume the truth of the statement expressed by '*Pa · Qa*'. We show, by step (10), that if this statement is true, then our conclusion is true. But then, by one use of an inference of the EE form, we get our conclusion.

Finally, let us examine the following equally simple proof of the validity of syllogisms of the Ferio form:

(1)	(1) $(x)(Qx \supset \sim Rx)$	Assump.
(2)	(2) $(\exists x)(Px \cdot Qx)$	Assump.
(3)	(3) $Pa \cdot Qa$	Assump.
(3)	(4) Pa	AE (3)
(3)	(5) Qa	AE (3)
(1)	(6) $Qa \supset \sim Ra$	UE (1)
(1)(3)	(7) $\sim Ra$	CE (5)(6)
(1)(3)	(8) $Pa \cdot \sim Ra$	AI (4)(7)
(1)(3)	(9) $(\exists x)(Px \cdot \sim Rx)$	EI (8)
(1)	(10) $Pa \cdot Qa \supset (\exists x)(Px \cdot \sim Rx)$	CI (9)
(1)(2)	(11) $(\exists x)(Px \cdot \sim Rx)$	EE (2)(10)

This proof is exactly like the proof of the validity of syllogisms of the Darii form; so we need say nothing more about it.

So much for statements and inferences involving only statements of the four Aristotelian forms. Let us now look at statements and inferences involving statements that are not of the four Aristotelian forms. The first four deal with the distribution of quantifiers over conjunctions and disjunctions in the symbols expressing various statements:

(e′) $(x)(Fx \cdot Gx) \equiv (x)Fx \cdot (x)Gx$
(f′) $(\exists x)(Fx \vee Gx) \equiv (\exists x)Fx \vee (\exists x)Gx$
(g′) $(\exists x)(Fx \cdot Gx) \supset (\exists x)Fx \cdot (\exists x)Gx$
(h′) $(x)Fx \vee (x)Gx \supset (x)(Fx \vee Gx)$

Any statement that is of one of these four forms must be true. Notice, by the way, that the last two forms are forms of conditional statements and not of biconditional statements. The corresponding other conditional statements can be false.

Let us first prove that the third of the preceding statement-forms [(g′)] is a theorem. The proof is relatively simple:

(1)	(1) $(\exists x)(Fx \cdot Gx)$	Assump.
(2)	(2) $Fa \cdot Ga$	Assump.
(2)	(3) Fa	AE (3)
(2)	(4) $(\exists x)Fx$	EI (3)
(2)	(5) Ga	AE (2)
(2)	(6) $(\exists x)Gx$	EI (5)
(2)	(7) $(\exists x)Fx \cdot (\exists x)Gx$	AI (4)(6)
	(8) $Fa \cdot Ga \supset (\exists x)Fx \cdot (\exists x)Gx$	CI (7)
(1)	(9) $(\exists x)Fx \cdot (\exists x)Gx$	EE (1)(8)
	(10) $(\exists x)(Fx \cdot Gx) \supset [(\exists x)Fx \cdot (\exists x)Gx]$	CI (9)

As usual, we assumed the truth of the antecedent in step (1). We then assumed the truth of the statement expressed by the dequantified version of the symbol used to express step (1). Having done this in (2), we inferred, by (8), that if this statement is true, then so is the conclusion. The conclusion then followed quickly by one inference each of the EE and CI forms.

It might look as though we could also run the proof the other way to show that if the preceding consequent is true, then the preceding antecedent is true. The following "proof" seems to show that.

(1)	(1) $(\exists x)Fx \cdot (\exists x)Gx$	Assump.
(1)	(2) $(\exists x)Fx$	AE (1)
(1)	(3) $(\exists x)Gx$	AE (1)
(4)	(4) Fa	Assump.
(5)	(5) Ga	Assump.
(4)(5)	(6) $Fa \cdot Ga$	AI (4)(5)
(4)(5)	(7) $(\exists x)(Fx \cdot Gx)$	EI (6)

Of course it does not, for we have proved our conclusion on the assumption of (4) and (5), but we need a proof on the assumption of (1) so that we can use a CI inference to get what we want. There is no way to continue this "proof" so as to eliminate those assumptions and end with a proof of our consequent simply on the assumption of the truth of the antecedent.

The same thing happens in the case of the fourth of the preceding statement-forms [(h')]. The proof that it is a theorem is relatively simple:

(1)	(1) $(x)Fx \lor (x)Gx$	Assump.
(2)	(2) $(x)Fx$	Assump.
(2)	(3) Fa	UE (2)
(2)	(4) $Fa \lor Ga$	OI (3)
(2)	(5) $(x)(Fx \lor Gx)$	UI (4)
	(6) $(x)Fx \supset (x)(Fx \lor Gx)$	CI (5)
(7)	(7) $(x)Gx$	Assump.
(7)	(8) Ga	UE (7)
(7)	(9) $Fa \lor Ga$	OI (8)
(7)	(10) $(x)(Fx \lor Gx)$	UI (9)
	(11) $(x)Gx \supset (x)(Fx \lor Gx)$	CI (10)
(1)	(12) $(x)(Fx \lor Gx)$	OE (1)(6)(11)
	(13) $(x)Fx \lor (x)Gx \supset (x)(Fx \lor Gx)$	CI (12)

Once more, we assume the truth of the antecedent in step (1). Since it is a disjunctive statement, we assume the truth of its first disjunct in step (2) and prove in step (6) that if that disjunct is true then our consequent is true. In step (7) we assume that the second disjunct is true. We then prove in step (11) that if the second disjunct is true, then our consequent is true. So by use of one inference each of the OE and CI forms, we get our desired conclusion.

Once more, it might look as though we could also run the proof the other way to show that if the preceding consequent is true, then the preceding antecedent is true. The following "proof" seems to show that.

(1)	(1) $(x)(Fx \lor Gx)$	Assump.
(1)	(2) $Fa \lor Ga$	UE (1)
(3)	(3) Fa	Assump.
(3)	(4) $(x)Fx$	UI (3)
(3)	(5) $(x)Fx \lor (x)Gx$	OI (4)
	(6) $Fa \supset [(x)Fx \lor (x)Gx]$	CI (5)
(7)	(7) Ga	Assump.
(7)	(8) $(x)Gx$	UI (7)
(7)	(9) $(x)Fx \lor (x)Gx$	OI (8)
	(10) $Ga \supset [(x)Fx \lor (x)Gx]$	CI (9)
(1)	(11) $(x)Fx \lor (x)Gx$	OE (2)(6)(10)
	(12) $(x)(Fx \lor Gx) \supset [(x)Fx \lor (x)Gx)]$	CI (11)

Unfortunately, this proof is not satisfactory. There is something wrong with both step (4) and step (8). The proof of (3) and the proof of (7) depend upon assumptions about a; so we cannot infer (4) and (8) from (3) and (7) by inferences of the UI form.

An examination of the next four statement-forms that we want to consider teaches us about the relations between the universal and the existential quantifier. All the following statement-forms are theorems:

(i') $(x)Px \equiv \sim(\exists x) \sim Px$
(j') $(\exists x)Px \equiv \sim(x) \sim Px$
(k') $\sim(x)Px \equiv (\exists x) \sim Px$
(l') $\sim(\exists x)Px \equiv (x) \sim Px$

This means that we can always say whatever we wish by use of only one of the quantifiers. If we want to use only the existential quantifier, we replace every occurrence of '(x)' with '$\sim(\exists x)\sim$', and every occurrence of '$\sim(x)$' with '$(\exists x)\sim$', and if we want to use only the universal quantifier, we replace every occurrence of '$(\exists x)$' with '$\sim(x)\sim$' and every occurrence of '$\sim(\exists x)$' with '$(x)\sim$'.

Let us now prove that some of the preceding statement-forms are theorems. We shall begin with a proof of the first one [(i')], (see p. 171). Since this was a proof of a biconditional statement, it divides itself into two parts [(1) through (13) and (14) through (22)], each of which is the proof of a conditional statement. In (1) we assumed the truth of the antecedent of the first conditional. Since the consequent is a negative statement, we knew that

(1)	(1) $(x)Px$	Assump.
(2)	(2) $(\exists x) \sim Px$	Assump.
(3)	(3) $\sim Pa$	Assump.
(1)	(4) Pa	UE (1)
(1)(3)	(5) $Pa \cdot \sim Pa$	AI (3)(4)
(3)	(6) $(x)Px \supset (Pa \cdot \sim Pa)$	CI (5)
(3)	(7) $\sim(x)Px$	NI (6)
(1)(3)	(8) $(x)Px \cdot \sim(x)Px$	AI (1)(7)
(1)	(9) $\sim Pa \supset [(x)Px \cdot \sim(x)Px]$	CI (8)
(1)(2)	(10) $(x)Px \cdot \sim(x)Px$	EE (2)(9)
(1)	(11) $(\exists x) \sim Px \supset [(x)Px \cdot \sim(x)Px]$	CI (10)
(1)	(12) $\sim(\exists x) \sim Px$	NI (11)
	(13) $(x)Px \supset \sim(\exists x) \sim Px$	CI (12)
(14)	(14) $\sim(\exists x) \sim Px$	Assump.
(15)	(15) $\sim Pa$	Assump.
(15)	(16) $(\exists x) \sim Px$	EI (15)
(14)(15)	(17) $(\exists x) \sim Px \cdot \sim(\exists x) \sim Px$	AI (14)(16)
(14)	(18) $\sim Pa \supset [(\exists x) \sim Px \cdot \sim(\exists x) \sim Px]$	CI (17)
(14)	(19) $\sim \sim Pa$	NI (18)
(14)	(20) Pa	DN (19)
(14)	(21) $(x)Px$	UI (20)
	(22) $\sim(\exists x) \sim Px \supset [(x)Px]$	CI (21)
	(23) $(x)Px \equiv \sim(\exists x) \sim Px$	BI (13)(22)

we would infer its truth by an NI inference; so we assumed [in (2)] the statement of which it is a negation, and showed [in (11)] that if that statement were true, then some contradiction must also be true. It was a bit complicated to do that, because (2) is an existential statement; so we first had to get the contradiction on (3) [as we did in (9)] and then use an EE and a CI inference to get what we really wanted. The second half of the proof was easier. We assumed the antecedent in (14), hoping to get the consequent [which we got in (21)], since we could then get our conditional statement [as we did in (22)] by a CI inference. Since our consequent was a universally quantified statement, we first tried to get (20), from which we could infer our consequent by a UI inference. We assumed the negation of (20) in (15), showed [in (18)] that if it were true, then some contradiction would have to be true, and then got (20) by an NI and a DN inference.

Let us now look at a proof that the third of the preceding statement-forms [(k')] is a theorem (see proof, top of p. 172). Once more we are proving a biconditional statement; so the proof breaks down into two parts [(1) through (14) and (15) through (24)], each of which is a proof of a conditional statement.

(1)	(1) $\sim(x)Px$	Assump.
(2)	(2) $\sim(\exists x) \sim Px$	Assump.
(3)	(3) $\sim Pa$	Assump.
(3)	(4) $(\exists x) \sim Px$	EI (3)
(2)(3)	(5) $(\exists x) \sim Px \cdot \sim(\exists x) \sim Px$	AI (2)(4)
(2)	(6) $\sim Pa \supset [(\exists x) \sim Px \cdot \sim(\exists x) \sim Px]$	CI (5)
(2)	(7) $\sim \sim Pa$	NI (6)
(2)	(8) Pa	DN (7)
(2)	(9) $(x)Px$	UI (8)
(1)(2)	(10) $(x)Px \cdot \sim(x)Px$	AI (1)(9)
(1)	(11) $\sim(\exists x) \sim Px \supset [(x)Px \cdot \sim(x)Px]$	CI (10)
(1)	(12) $\sim \sim(\exists x) \sim Px$	NI (11)
(1)	(13) $(\exists x) \sim Px$	DN (12)
	(14) $\sim(x)Px \supset (\exists x) \sim Px$	CI (13)
(15)	(15) $(\exists x) \sim Px$	Assump.
(16)	(16) $\sim Pa$	Assump.
(17)	(17) $(x)Px$	Assump.
(17)	(18) Pa	UE (17)
(16)(17)	(19) $Pa \cdot \sim Pa$	AI (16)(18)
(16)	(20) $(x)Px \supset Pa \cdot \sim Pa$	CI (19)
(16)	(21) $\sim(x)Px$	NI (20)
	(22) $\sim Pa \supset \sim(x)Px$	CI (21)
(15)	(23) $\sim(x)Px$	EE (15)(22)
	(24) $(\exists x) \sim Px \supset \sim(x)Px$	CI (23)
	(25) $\sim(x)Px \equiv (\exists x) \sim Px$	BI (14)(24)

This proof could have been made simpler and smaller. For we could replace (1) through (14) with:

(1)	(1) $\sim(x)Px$	Assump.
(2)	(2) $\sim(\exists x) \sim Px$	Assump.
	(3) $\sim(\exists x) \sim Px \equiv (x)Px$	TI (i')
	(4) $\sim(\exists x) \sim Px \supset (x)Px$	BE (3)
(2)	(5) $(x)Px$	CE (2)(4)
(1)(2)	(6) $(x)Px \cdot \sim(x)Px$	AI (1)(5)
(1)	(7) $\sim(\exists x) \sim Px \supset [(x)Px \cdot \sim(x)Px]$	CI (6)
(1)	(8) $\sim \sim(\exists x) \sim Px$	NI (7)
(1)	(9) $(\exists x) \sim Px$	DN (8)
	(10) $\sim(x)Px \supset (\exists x) \sim Px$	CI (9)

This simplification is made possible by our method of theorem-introduction. By this method we can introduce, at any point in a proof, any instance of a theorem, which is exactly what we did here in step (3). Steps (3) through (5) in the second proof take the place of (3) through (9) in the first. Note, by the way, that (3) through (9) appear in the proof of (i'). This illustrates the fact that we can use theorem-introduction simply because introducing the theorem is merely a shorthand for proving it again.

In general, then, now that we have 12 new theorems (as well as all the theorems from Chapter 6), we should watch for the possibility that we can save ourselves several steps in a proof by introducing an instance of a theorem.

Finally, let us look at three theorems dealing with the relation between statements expressed by symbols that are exactly alike except for an interchange of quantifiers:

(m') $(x)(y)Fxy \equiv (y)(x)Fxy$
(n') $(\exists x)(\exists y)Fxy \equiv (\exists y)(\exists x)Fxy$
(o') $(\exists x)(y)Fxy \supset (y)(\exists x)Fxy$

Notice that the symbol expressing the third theorem contains a '$\supset$' rather than a '$\equiv$'. The reason is that the other conditional statement-form, '$(y)(\exists x)Fxy \supset (\exists x)(y)Fxy$', is not a theorem; statements of that form, such as the statement that if everyone is such that someone loves him, then there is someone who loves everyone, can be (as in this case) false.

The proof showing that these statements are theorems is very simple. For example, the following proof shows that (m') is a theorem:

(1)	(1) $(x)(y)Fxy$	Assump.
(1)	(2) $(y)Fay$	UE (1)
(1)	(3) Fab	UE (2)
(1)	(4) $(x)Fxb$	UI (3)
(1)	(5) $(y)(x)Fxy$	UI (4)
	(6) $(x)(y)Fxy \supset (y)(x)Fxy$	CI (5)
(7)	(7) $(y)(x)Fxy$	Assump.
(7)	(8) $(x)Fxa$	UE (7)
(7)	(9) Fba	UE (8)
(7)	(10) $(y)Fby$	UI (9)
(7)	(11) $(x)(y)Fxy$	UI (10)
	(12) $(y)(x)Fxy \supset (x)(y)Fxy$	CI (11)
	(13) $(x)(y)Fxy \equiv (y)(x)Fxy$	BI (6)(12)

The only important thing to note here is that the proof takes as long as it does only because, in using inferences of any of our four new inference-forms, the symbol expressing the conclusion can contain only one more or one less quantifier than the symbol expressing the premise(s). So we need to make (2) and (3), (4) and (5), (8) and (9), and (10) and (11) separate steps.

The proof showing that (o') is a theorem is equally simple:

(1)	(1) $(\exists x)(y)Fxy$	Assump.
(2)	(2) $(y)Fay$	Assump.
(2)	(3) Fab	UE (2)
(2)	(4) $(\exists x)Fxb$	EI (3)
(2)	(5) $(y)(\exists x)Fxy$	UI (4)
	(6) $(y)Fay \supset (y)(\exists x)Fxy$	CI (5)
(1)	(7) $(y)(\exists x)Fxy$	EE (1)(6)
	(8) $(\exists x)(y)Fxy \supset (y)(\exists x)Fxy$	CI (7)

This proof is a bit tricky since we must be sure that we do not misuse our inferences of the UI and EE forms. Here we do not, for we can infer (5) from (4) since the proof of (4) depends upon no assumptions about b. And we can infer (7) from (1) and (6) since the proof of (6) depends upon no assumptions about a and the consequent of (6) is not about a.

It might seem as though the following proof is also satisfactory:

(1)	(1) $(y)(\exists x)Fxy$	Assump.
(1)	(2) $(\exists x)Fxa$	UE (1)
(3)	(3) Fba	Assump.
(3)	(4) $(x)Fxa$	UI (3)
(3)	(5) $(\exists y)(x)Fxy$	EI (4)
	(6) $Fba \supset (\exists y)(x)Fxy$	CI (5)
(1)	(7) $(\exists y)(x)Fxy$	EE (2)(6)
	(8) $(y)(\exists x)Fxy \supset (\exists x)(y)Fxy$	CI (7)

This would be most surprising since we would then have a proof that any statement of the same form as (8) would be true, and we just saw before that such is not the case. However, it turns out that this proof is not satisfactory. In particular, we cannot infer (4) from (3) by an inference of the UI form, since (3) rests upon an assumption about b.

7.7 Strategy for Inventing Proofs

In most of the proofs we have looked at so far, it has not been too difficult to see both that it is a successful proof and that it has a clearcut organization and structure. But none of this helps us to see how these proofs were constructed or helps us to construct new proofs. In this section we will look for a series of hints for constructing proofs, for some strategies for inventing proofs.

In Chapter 6, we adopted the following strategies for inventing proofs in propositional logic:

(1) We assume, immediately, the truth of all the premises of the inference in question and guess that we will be using, if possible, inferences of the corresponding elimination-forms. We also guess that the last step will be inferred by the corresponding introduction inference, and that, earlier in the proof, the necessary premises for such an inference will occur. We then try to fill in the steps between what we guess both the beginning and the end of the proof will be like.

(2) We assume the denial of what we want to prove, get a contradiction on that assumption, and then, by use of CI, NI, and DN inferences, get our original conclusion.

We will adopt exactly these strategies in this chapter as well. The only difference is that, since we now have new types of premises and conclusions, the introduction and elimination inferences which we guess we will use may be of our new forms, and not merely of the old forms used in Chapter 6.

Let us begin by using our strategies to help us construct some proofs showing certain forms of inference to be valid. We will begin with a simple example. Let us use them to find a proof that every syllogism of the Celarent form is valid. All these inferences are of the form:

$$(x)(Qx \supset \sim Rx)$$
$$(x)(Px \supset Qx)$$
$$\overline{(x)(Px \supset \sim Rx)}$$

We know that the conclusion is a universal statement; so it will probably be inferred, by a UI inference, from the statement that $Pa \supset \sim Ra$. Since that statement is conditional, we can guess that it will be inferred by a CI inference from a proof, on the assumption that Pa, of the statement that $\sim Ra$. We also know that we will begin our proof with the assumption of our two premises and the inference of what we can infer from them by UE inferences. So far, then, we know that our proof will look like this:

(1)	(1) $(x)(Qx \supset \sim Rx)$	Assump.
(2)	(2) $(x)(Px \supset Qx)$	Assump.
(1)	(3) $Qa \supset \sim Ra$	UE (1)
(2)	(4) $Pa \supset Qa$	UE (2)
(5)	(5) Pa	Assump.
(1)(2)(5)	$\sim Ra$	
(1)(2)	$Pa \supset \sim Ra$	CI
(1)(2)	$(x)(Px \supset \sim Rx)$	UI

It is easy to see how, in this case, we can fill in the missing steps so that we get the following complete proof:

(1)	(1) $(x)(Qx \supset \sim Rx)$	Assump.
(2)	(2) $(x)(Px \supset Qx)$	Assump.
(1)	(3) $Qa \supset \sim Ra$	UE (1)
(2)	(4) $Pa \supset Qa$	UE (2)
(5)	(5) Pa	Assump.
(2)(5)	(6) Qa	CE (4)(5)
(1)(2)(5)	(7) $\sim Ra$	CE (3)(6)
(1)(2)	(8) $Pa \supset \sim Ra$	CI (7)
(1)(2)	(9) $(x)(Px \supset \sim Rx)$	UI (8)

Let us now use our strategy considerations to help us invent a proof that the following, more complicated, form of inference is valid:

$$(x)(Fx \supset Gx \cdot Hx)$$
$$\sim(\exists x)Hx$$
$$\overline{\sim(\exists x)Fx}$$

Since our conclusion is a negative statement, we guess that we will infer it by an NI inference and that, therefore, earlier in the proof there will be a proof that if the statement of which it is a negation is true, then some contradiction will also be true. Since that statement is conditional, we also guess that we will have a proof that its consequent is true, upon the assumpion of its antecedent. We also know that we will assume our premises and infer what we can from the first premise by a UE inference. So far, then, we guess that our proof will look like this:

(1)	(1) $(x)(Fx \supset Gx \cdot Hx)$	Assump.
(2)	(2) $\sim(\exists x)Hx$	Assump.
(1)	(3) $Fa \supset Ga \cdot Ha$	UE (1)
(4)	(4) $(\exists x)Fx$	Assump.
(4)	contradiction	
	$(\exists x)Fx \supset$ contradiction	CI
	$\sim(\exists x)Fx$	NI

All we must do is fill in the missing steps, after which we get the following proof:

(1)	(1) $(x)(Fx \supset Gx \cdot Hx)$	Assump.
(2)	(2) $\sim(\exists x)Hx$	Assump.
(1)	(3) $Fa \supset Ga \cdot Ha$	UE (1)
(4)	(4) $(\exists x)Fx$	Assump.
(5)	(5) Fa	Assump.
(1)(5)	(6) $Ga \cdot Ha$	CE (3)(5)
(1)(5)	(7) Ha	AE (6)
(1)(5)	(8) $(\exists x)Hx$	EI (7)
(1)(2)(5)	(9) $(\exists x)Hx \cdot \sim(\exists x)Hx$	AI (2)(8)
(1)(2)	(10) $Fa \supset [(\exists x)Hx \cdot \sim(\exists x)Hx]$	CI (9)
(1)(2)(4)	(11) $(\exists x)Hx \cdot \sim(\exists x)Hx$	EE (4)(10)
(1)(2)	(12) $(\exists x)Fx \supset [(\exists x)Hx \cdot \sim(\exists x)Hx]$	CI (11)
(1)(2)	(13) $\sim(\exists x)Fx$	NI (12)

As a third, more complicated, example let us use our strategy rules to invent a proof that the following is a valid form of inference:

$$(x)(Fx \vee Gx)$$
$$\overline{\sim(\exists x)(\sim Fx \cdot \sim Gx)}$$

Once more, our conclusion is a negative statement; so we guess again that we will infer it by an NI inference and that, therefore, earlier in the proof there will be a proof that if the statement of which it is a negation is true, then some contradiction will also be true. Since that statement is conditional, we guess that we will also have a proof that its consequent is true upon the assumption of its antecedent, so that we can infer the conditional statement by a CI inference. We also know that we will assume our premise and probably infer what we can from it by a UE inference. So far, then, we guess that our proof will look like this:

(1)	(1) $(x)(Fx \lor Gx)$	Assump.
(1)	(2) $Fa \lor Ga$	UE (1)
(3)	(3) $(\exists x)(\sim Fx \cdot \sim Gx)$	Assump.
(1)(3)	contradiction	
(1)	$(\exists x)(\sim Fx \cdot \sim Gx) \supset$ contradiction	CI
(1)	$\sim(\exists x)(\sim Fx \cdot \sim Gx)$	NI

All that remains is to fill in the missing steps. This is easily done, and we get the following proof:

(1)	(1) $(x)(Fx \lor Gx)$	Assump.
(1)	(2) $Fa \lor Ga$	UE (1)
(3)	(3) $(\exists x)(\sim Fx \cdot \sim Gx)$	Assump.
(4)	(4) $\sim Fa \cdot \sim Ga$	Assump.
	(5) $\sim(Fa \lor Ga) \equiv \sim Fa \cdot \sim Ga$	TI (g)
	(6) $\sim Fa \cdot \sim Ga \supset \sim(Fa \lor Ga)$	BE (5)
(4)	(7) $\sim(Fa \lor Ga)$	CE (4)(6)
(1)(4)	(8) $Fa \lor Ga \cdot \sim(Fa \lor Ga)$	AI (2)(7)
(4)	(9) $(x)(Fx \lor Gx) \supset [(Fa \lor Ga) \cdot \sim(Fa \lor Ga)]$	CI (8)
(4)	(10) $\sim(x)(Fx \lor Gx)$	NI (9)
(1)(4)	(11) $(x)(Fx \lor Gx) \cdot \sim(x)(Fx \lor Gx)$	AI (1)(10)
(1)	(12) $\sim Fa \cdot \sim Ga \supset [(x)(Fx \lor Gx) \cdot \sim(x)(Fx \lor Gx)]$	CI (11)
(1)(3)	(13) $(x)(Fx \lor Gx) \cdot \sim(x)(Fx \lor Gx)$	EE (3)(12)
(1)	(14) $(\exists x)(\sim Fx \cdot \sim Gx) \supset [(x)(Fx \lor Gx) \cdot \sim(x)(Fx \lor Gx)]$	CI (13)
(1)	(15) $\sim(\exists x)(\sim Fx \cdot \sim Gx)$	NI (14)

Of course, the proof would have been considerably longer and more difficult to work out if we had not thought of using De Morgan's law for disjunction. One must always remember one's theorems.

One feature of this proof deserves additional comment, particularly because it has appeared in several earlier proofs. In (8) we have derived a contradiction. Thus, we are immediately tempted to continue the proof as follows:

(1)	(9) $\sim Fa \cdot \sim Ga \supset [Fa \lor Ga \cdot \sim(Fa \lor Ga)]$	CI (8)
(1)(3)	(10) $Fa \lor Ga \cdot \sim(Fa \lor Ga)$	EE (3)(9)
(1)	(11) $(\exists x)(\sim Fx \cdot \sim Gx) \supset [Fa \lor Ga \sim (Fa \lor Ga)]$	CE (10)
(1)	(12) $\sim(\exists x)(\sim Fx \cdot \sim Gx)$	NI (11)

However, this proof would not be satisfactory. The EE inference used to derive step (10) is not legitimate, since the consequent of (9) is about *a*. So we must do what we did before, namely, use that contradiction to get still another contradiction that does not involve *a*.

We turn now to some inferences involving relational statements. Let us first use our strategy rules to construct a proof that every inference of the following form is valid:

$$(\exists x)(Fx \cdot Gx)$$
$$\underline{(x)(Fx \supset \sim Hxa)}$$
$$(\exists x)(Gx \cdot \sim Hxa)$$

Our conclusion is an existential statement; so we can guess that it will be inferred by an EI inference from the statement expressed by '*Gb* · ~*Hba*'. Since that is a conjunctive statement, we can guess that the statements expressed by '*Gb*' and '~*Hba*' will appear earlier in the proof; so we can infer it by an AI inference. We also know that our premises will occur at the beginning of the proof and will be followed by what we can infer from them by quantifier-elimination inferences. So we guess, so far, that our proof will look like this:

(1)	(1) $(x)(Fx \supset \sim Hxa)$	Assump.
(2)	(2) $(\exists x)(Fx \cdot Gx)$	Assump.
(1)	(3) $Fb \supset \sim Hba$	UE (1)
	Gb	
	$\sim Hba$	
	$Gb \cdot \sim Hba$	AI
	$(\exists x)(Gx \cdot \sim Hxa)$	EI

All that remains is to fill in the missing steps, which looks easy since it appears we will wind up with:

(1)	(1) $(x)(Fx \supset \sim Hxa)$	Assump.
(2)	(2) $(\exists x)(Fx \cdot Gx)$	Assump.
(1)	(3) $Fb \supset \sim Hba$	UE (1)
(4)	(4) $Fb \cdot Gb$	Assump.
(4)	(5) Gb	AE (4)
(4)	(6) Fb	AE (4)
(1)(4)	(7) $\sim Hba$	CE (3)(6)
(1)(4)	(8) $Gb \cdot \sim Hba$	AI (5)(7)
(1)(4)	(9) $(\exists x)(Gx \cdot \sim Hxa)$	EI (8)

Actually, however, that proof doesn't prove what we want, since we have proved our conclusion on (1) and (4) and we wanted a proof on (1) and (2).

But this poses no great problem; all we must do is add the following last two steps:

(1)	(10) $Fb \cdot Gb \supset [(\exists x)(Gx \cdot \sim Hxa)]$	CI (9)
(1)(2)	(11) $(\exists x)(Gx \cdot \sim Hxa)$	EE (2)(10)

In general, when one of our premises is an existential statement, we will have to add two steps like this.

Let us look at one final example. We are looking for a proof that all inferences of the following form are valid:

$$(x)(Fx \supset Gx \lor Hx)$$
$$(x)[Gx \supset (\exists y)(Ixy)]$$
$$\underline{(x)[Hx \supset (\exists y)(Ixy)]}$$
$$(x)[Fx \supset (\exists y)(Ixy)]$$

Our conclusion is a universal statement; so we can guess that we are likely to infer it by a UI inference from the statement expressed by '$(Fa \supset (\exists y) Iay)$'. And since that statement is conditional, we can guess that it will be inferred, by a CI inference, from a proof of its consequent on the assumption that its antecedent is true. We also know that our proof will begin with our three premises, followed by their consequences according to the appropriate UE inferences. So far, therefore, we guess that our proof will look like this:

(1)	(1) $(x)(Fx \supset Gx \lor Hx)$	Assump.
(2)	(2) $(x)[Gx \supset (\exists y)(Ixy)]$	Assump.
(3)	(3) $(x)[Hx \supset (\exists y)(Ixy)]$	Assump.
(1)	(4) $Fa \supset Ga \lor Ha$	UE (1)
(2)	(5) $Ga \supset (\exists y)Iay$	UE (2)
(3)	(6) $Ha \supset (\exists y)Iay$	UE (3)
(7)	(7) Fa	Assump.
(1)(2)(3)(7)	$(\exists y)Iay$	
(1)(2)(3)	$Fa \supset (\exists y)Iay$	CI
(1)(2)(3)	$(x)[Fx \supset (\exists y)(Ixy)]$	UI

All that remains is to fill in the missing steps, after which we get the final proof shown at the top of p. 180.

In all our examples we have been able to figure out a proof by use of our first strategy, and we have not yet had to use the strategy of indirect proof.

(1)	(1) $(x)(Fx \supset Gx \lor Hx)$	Assump.
(2)	(2) $(x)[Gx \supset (\exists y)(Ixy)]$	Assump.
(3)	(3) $(x)[Hx \supset (\exists y)(Ixy)]$	Assump.
(1)	(4) $Fa \supset Ga \lor Ha$	UE (1)
(2)	(5) $Ga \supset (\exists y)Iay$	UE (2)
(3)	(6) $Ha \supset (\exists y)Iay$	UE (3)
(7)	(7) Fa	Assump.
(1)(7)	(8) $Ga \lor Ha$	CE (4)(7)
(9)	(9) Ga	Assump.
(2)(9)	(10) $(\exists y)Iay$	CE (5)(9)
(2)	(11) $Ga \supset (\exists y)Iay$	CI (10)
(12)	(12) Ha	Assump.
(3)(12)	(13) $(\exists y)Iay$	CE (6)(12)
(3)	(14) $Ha \supset (\exists y)Iay$	CI (13)
(1)(2)(3)(7)	(15) $(\exists y)Iay$	OE (8)(11)(14)
(1)(2)(3)	(16) $Fa \supset (\exists y)Iay$	CI (15)
(1)(2)(3)	(17) $(x)[Fx \supset (\exists y)(Ixy)]$	UI (16)

However, in some cases we must. A good example occurs when we set out
to prove that all inferences of the following form are valid:

$$\frac{\sim(x) \sim Fx}{(\exists x)Fx}$$

Using our normal strategy considerations, we would guess that since our
conclusion is an existential statement, it should be inferred, from the statement expressed by '*Fa*', by an EI inference. We also know that we will begin
the proof with our premise and anything derivable from it by the elimination
inferences. So far, then, we would guess that the proof would look like this:

(1)	(1) $\sim(x) \sim Fx$	Assump.
(1)	Fa	
(1)	$(\exists x)Fx$	EI

But nothing suggests itself as to how we can fill in the proof. So we must try
our second strategy. We guess, then, that the proof will look like this:

(1)	(1) $\sim(x) \sim Fx$	Assump.
(2)	(2) $\sim(\exists x)Fx$	Assump.
(1)(2)	contradiction	
(1)	$\sim(\exists x)Fx \supset$ contradiction	CI
(1)	$\sim \sim(\exists x)Fx$	NI
	$(\exists x)Fx$	DN

The only question now is how we are to get the contradiction. If we could get the statement of which (1) is a denial, we would have a contradiction. So perhaps our proof will look like this:

(1)	(1) $\sim(x) \sim Fx$	Assump.
(2)	(2) $\sim(\exists x)Fx$	Assump.
(2)	$(x) \sim Fx$	
(1)(2)	$(x) \sim Fx \cdot \sim(x) \sim Fx$	AI
(1)	$\sim(\exists x)Fx \supset [(x) \sim Fx \cdot \sim(x) \sim Fx)]$	CI
(1)	$\sim \sim(\exists x)Fx$	NI
(1)	$(\exists x)Fx$	DN

Filling in the steps is now relatively easy, and we get the following proof:

(1)	(1) $\sim(x) \sim Fx$	Assump.
(2)	(2) $\sim(\exists x)Fx$	Assump.
(3)	(3) Fa	Assump.
(3)	(4) $(\exists x)Fx$	EI (3)
(2)(3)	(5) $(\exists x)Fx \cdot \sim(\exists x)Fx$	AI (2)(4)
(2)	(6) $Fa \supset [(\exists x)Fx \cdot \sim(\exists x)Fx]$	CI (5)
(2)	(7) $\sim Fa$	NI (6)
(2)	(8) $(x) \sim Fx$	UI (7)
(1)(2)	(9) $(x) \sim Fx \cdot \sim(x) \sim Fx$	AI (1)(8)
(1)	(10) $\sim(\exists x)Fx \supset [(x) \sim Fx \cdot \sim(x) \sim Fx]$	CI (9)
(1)	(11) $\sim \sim(\exists x)Fx$	NI (10)
(1)	(12) $(\exists x)Fx$	DN (11)

7.8 Semantical Tableaux for Quantification Theory

In the last three sections we have extended the method of proof that we developed for propositional logic to quantification theory. In this final section we will extend our method of semantic tableaux from propositional logic to quantification theory. Once more, the method of semantic tableaux provides us with a mechanical method for proving validity and theorem-hood. But it will not provide us, in the case of quantification theory, with a method that always enables us to conclude (when it is true) that either an inference-form is not a valid form or a statement-form is not a theorem. The reasons for this will emerge as we proceed.

The basic idea for constructing semantic tableaux remains the same. We continue to construct a table with two sides, one for true statements and the other for false statements. We will put the symbols representing the premises on the true side, and the symbols representing the conclusion on the false side. We will then see what else, given our initial assumptions, must be true (and put the symbols for those statements on the true side) and what else must be false (and put the symbols for those statements on the false side). If it turns out that some statement must be true or false (i.e., if same symbol appears on both sides of the table), then our initial assumption has led to a contradiction, and we can conclude that the conclusion cannot be false when the premises are true—that is, that the inference (and inference-form) in question is valid. But if, at the end, it turns out that there is no contradiction, then we will conclude that the inference (and inference-form) in question is not valid.

Similarly, if we are trying to see whether some statement-form is a theorem, we begin by assuming that a statement of that form is false (and put the symbol representing it on the false side.) If we can get a contradiction from that assumption (i.e., if the same symbol appears on both sides of the table), then that statement (and statements of that form) must be true, and that statement-form is a theorem. But if, at the end, we wind up with no contradiction, then the statement in question can be false and the statement-form in question is not a theorem.

There is only one important difference between the semantical tableaux for propositional logic and those for quantification theory. In the case of propositional logic, our construction always came to an end. At some point in the construction, either a contradiction appeared (in which case we knew that the inference-form was valid or the statement-form was a theorem) or there was nothing else that we could do (in which case we know that the inference-form was not valid or the statement-form was not a theorem). In the case of quantification theory, however, the construction may not come to an end. There are cases in which no contradiction appears at any given point but in which, no matter how far we go in the construction of the table, there is still more to do. In such cases we will not know whether the inference-form is valid or whether the statement-form is a theorem. In other words, in these cases there will be some invalid inferences whose invalidity cannot be shown by use of our tableaux and some nontheorems whose nontheoremhood cannot be shown by use of our tableaux.

All that remains to do is provide the additional rules for operating with tableaux when formulas beginning with quantifiers appear in them. To state these rules, we need the following two symbols:

$A[x]$	A formula A that contains the variable x in an initial quantifier
$A[x/\!\!-\!\!]$	A formula like $A[x]$, except that the initial quantifier is dropped and it contains the constant, which occurs in—wherever $A[x]$ contains x.

The following are the additional rules:

If the line in the table that you want to operate on is of the form:	*Then you add to the table the corresponding symbol(s) of the form:*

True	False
$(\exists x)A$	

True	False
$A[x/—]$ for some constant which has not yet occurred in the table. If such a formula has already occurred, do nothing.	

True	False
	$(\exists x)A$

True	False
	$(x) \sim A$

True	False
$(x)A$	

True	False
$A[x/—]$ for every constant that has already occurred in the table. If none has, use any constant you want. In any case, if later on we add a new constant to the table, we also add $A[x/—]$ for that constant.	

True	False
	$(x)A$

True	False
	$(\exists x) \sim A$

Let us now look at a variety of examples of the use of tableaux in connection with quantification theory. As a very simple example, let us look at the following table, which shows that every inference of the form

$$\frac{(x)Px}{(\exists x)Px}$$

is valid:

True	False
(1) $(x)Px$	
(2)	$(\exists x)Px$
(3) Pa	
(4) $(x) \sim Px$	
(5) $\sim Pa$	
(6)	Pa

In step (1) we put the symbol representing the premise in the true column, and in step (2) we put the symbol representing the conclusion in the false column. Since we have a symbol of the form '$(x)A$' in the true column, we put a symbol ('Pa') in the true column that is like the symbol of the form 'A', except for the fact that it lacks the initial quantifier and contains, instead of 'x', some individual constant (in this case, 'a'). Note that since no individual constant occurs in the table before step (3), we write in step (3) only one new symbol in the true column. We have, in step (2), an existentially quantified statement, the symbol for which appears in the false column. Therefore, in step (4) we write in the true column the appropriate symbol of the form '$(x)\sim A$'; in this case, that symbol is '$(x) \sim Px$'. We then must deal, in step (5), with that universally quantified symbol, and we write '$\sim Pa$'; it is the only symbol of the appropriate form. Finally, since that symbol is of the form '$\sim A$', we write the corresponding symbol of the form 'A' in the false column. We now have a contradiction since 'Pa' appears in both columns. Therefore, inferences of this form must be valid.

Let us now look at a slightly more complicated inference. We want to show that every inference of the form

$$(x)(Fx \supset Gx)$$
$$\underline{(\exists x)(Fx \cdot Hx)}$$
$$(\exists x)(Gx \cdot Hx)$$

is valid, which is shown by the following table:

	True		False	
(1) $(\exists x)(Fx \cdot Hx)$				
(2) $(x)(Fx \supset Gx)$				
(3)			$(\exists x)(Gx \cdot Hx)$	
(4) $(x) \sim (Gx \cdot Hx)$				
(5) $Fa \cdot Ha$				
(6) Fa				
Ha				
(7)	$Fa \supset Ga$			
(8) $\sim Fa$	Ga			
(9)			Fa	
(10) $\sim(Ga \cdot Ha)$	$\sim(Ga \cdot Ha)$			
(11)			$Ga \cdot Ha$	$Ga \cdot Ha$
(12)			Ga | Ha	Ga | Ha

In steps (1) through (3) we put the symbols expressing the premises in the true column and the symbols expressing the conclusion in the false column. Since we have a symbol of the form '$(\exists x)A$' in the false column, we put, in step (4), the corresponding symbol of the form '$(x) \sim A$' in the true column. In step (5) we dequantify the symbol introduced in step (1). Since the result is a symbol of the form '$A \cdot B$', we write both symbols expressing the con-juncts in step (6) in the true column. In step (7) we dequantify the symbol introduced in step (2). Since the result is a symbol of the form '$A \supset B$', we make two subcolumns in the true column (and two corresponding ones in the false column) and, in step (8), begin one of those columns with the symbol of the form '$\sim A$' and the other with the symbol of the form 'B'. In step (9) we write, in the left subcolumn of the false column, the appropriate symbol of the form 'A'. Now, in step (10) we dequantify the symbol introduced in (4). The result is a symbol of the form '$\sim A$', so in step (11) we write the appropriate symbol of the form 'A' in the false column. Finally, since that symbol is of the form '$A \cdot B$', we make two new subcolumns for each sub-column in the false column and begin one with the symbol of the form 'A' and the other with the symbol of the form 'B'. We now have a contradiction. The first two subcolumns on the false side contain 'Fa', which appears in every subcolumn on the true side. The fourth subcolumn on the false side contains 'Ha', which appears in every subcolumn on the true side. And the third contains 'Ga', which appears in every subcolumn on the corresponding right-hand side of the true column.

Now let us look at an example of an inference-form that is invalid and whose invalidity can be shown by use of our tableaux. The following table shows that there can be inferences of the form

$$\frac{(\exists x)(Px \cdot Qx)}{(x)(Px \cdot Qx)}$$

which are invalid:

	True	False	
(1)	$(\exists x)(Px \cdot Qx)$		
(2)		$(x)(Px \cdot Qx)$	
(3)	$(\exists x) \sim (Px \cdot Qx)$		
(4)	$Pa \cdot Qa$		
(5)	$\sim(Pb \cdot Qb)$		
(6)		$Pb \cdot Qb$	
(7)	Pa		
	Qa		
(8)		Qb	Pb

In steps (1) and (2) we put the symbol expressing the premise in the true column and the symbol expressing the conclusion in the false column. Since we have a symbol of the form '$(x)A$' in the false column, we put the corre-sponding symbol of the form '$(\exists x) \sim A$' in the true column in step (3). In steps (4) and (5) we dequantify the symbols introduced in steps (1) and (3).

Notice that we must use a different constant ('*b*') the second time. In dequantifying a symbol beginning with an existential quantifier, we must always use a constant that has not yet appeared in the table. Since we have a symbol of the form '~*A*' in the true column we put the appropriate '*A*' in the false column in step (6). We now have two symbols of the form '*A* · *B*', one in the true column and one in the false column. In steps (7) and (8) we take care of them. We now have nothing more to do, and since no contradiction has turned up, we must conclude that such inferences can be invalid.

In all the examples we have considered so far, we have not dealt with any statements which are relational in structure, nor have we been concerned with theoremhood. Let us now rectify these omissions by looking at a familiar example and showing by the following table that every statement of the form

$$(\exists x)(y)Fxy \supset (y)(\exists x)Fxy$$

must be true:

True	False
(1)	$(\exists x)(y)Fxy \supset (y)(\exists x)Fxy$
(2) $(\exists x)(y)Fxy$	$(y)(\exists x)Fxy$
(3) $(\exists y) \sim (\exists x)Fxy$	
(4) $(y)Fay$	
(5) $\sim(\exists x)Fxb$	
(6)	$(\exists x)Fxb$
(7) $(x) \sim Fxb$	
(8) Faa	
Fab	
(9) $\sim Fab$	
$\sim Fbb$	
(10)	Fab
	Fbb

In step (1) we put the symbol that represents the statement in question in the false column. Since it is of the form '*A* ⊃ *B*', we put the antecedent symbol in the true column and the consequent symbol in the false column. Since we have a symbol of the form '(*y*)*A*' in the false column, we put, in step (3), the appropriate symbol of the form '(∃*y*) ~ *A*' in the true column. In steps (4) and (5) we requantify the symbols occurring in the true column. We now have a symbol of the form '~*A*' in the true column; so we put the corresponding symbol of the form '*A*' in the false column. This gives us a symbol of the form '(∃*x*)*A*' in the false column; so we put, in step (7), the corresponding symbol of the form '(*x*) ~ *A*' in the true column. We now have, from steps (4) and (7), two symbols beginning with universal quantifiers in the true column, and two individual constants ('*a* and '*b*') have appeared in the table. So in steps (8) and (9) we write the two dequantified symbols for each of our original quantified ones. Since this leaves us with two symbols of the form '$\sim A$', we put, in step (10), the appropriate symbols of the form '*A*' in the false column. We now have a contradiction since '*Fab*' occurs in both columns; so we can conclude that such statements must be true and that the statement-form in question is a theorem.

Let us look at one final example of a table constructed to enable us to see whether the statement-form

$$(x)(\exists y)Fxy \supset (\exists x)(y)Fxy$$

is a theorem. The table is as follows:

True	False
(1)	$(x)(\exists y)Fxy \supset (\exists y)(x)Fxy$
(2) $(x)(\exists y)Fxy$	$(\exists y)(x)Fxy$
(3) $(y) \sim (x)Fxy$	
(4) $(\exists y)Fay$	
(5) $\sim(x)Fxa$	
(6)	$(x)Fxa$
(7) $(\exists x) \sim Fxa$	
(8) Fab	
(9) $\sim Fca$	
(10) $(\exists y)Fby$	
$(\exists y)Fcy$	
(11) Fbd	
Fce	
(12) $(\exists y)Fdy$	
$(\exists y)Fey$	
.	
.	
.	

The beginning of its construction is not far different from the beginning of the last table. In step (1) we put the symbol that represents the statement in question in the false column. Since it is of the form '$A \supset B$', we put, in step (2), the antecedent symbol in the true column and the consequent symbol in the false column. Since we have a symbol of the form '$(\exists y)A$' in the false column, we put, in step (3), the corresponding symbol of the form '$(y) \sim A$' in the true column. In steps (4) and (5) we dequantify the symbols occurring in the true column. We have a symbol of the form '$\sim A$' in the true column; so we put the corresponding symbol of the form '*A*' in the false column. This gives us a symbol of the form '$(x)A$' in the false column; so in step (7) we put the corresponding symbol of the form '$(\exists x) \sim A$' into the true column. We now have, from steps (4) and (7), two symbols beginning with existential quantifiers in the true column. Thus, in steps (8) and (9) we write in the true column dequantified versions of these, taking care to use in each case (as we must) new individual constants. But now we must return to the symbol in step (2) that began with a universal quantifier and introduce two new dequantified versions of it, each containing one of our new constants. We do that in step (10). We now have two new symbols beginning with existential quantifiers in the true column. Therefore, in step (11) we introduce dequantified versions of them, taking care (as we must) that we use new constants. But then we must return once more to the symbol in step (2) that begins with a universal quantifier and introduce two new dequantified versions of it, and so on. It looks as though our table will never end.

We have here an example of the special feature of tableaux for quantification theory: the feature that they might not end. When, as in this case, they do not end, our method is not able to tell us whether the inference in question is valid, or whether the statement in question must be true. Unfortunately, this is not a shortcoming of our method only. It can be shown, though by methods far more advanced than any we have encountered in this book, that any method will have the same drawback. This is a basic fact about quantifiers and not merely a shortcoming of a particular method of studying them.

EXERCISES FOR CHAPTER 7

Part I

A. For each of the following inferences, indicate some statemental and some quantificational form of which it is an instance. Also indicate which, if any, of these forms are valid.

(1) All men are animals.
   All animals are mortal.
   _____
   All men are mortal.

(2) If Socrates is a man, then Socrates is mortal.
   Socrates is a man.
   _____
   Socrates is mortal.

(3) Joe is the brother of Frank.
   _____
   Frank is the brother of Joe.

(4) Either all men love someone or there are some unloved men.
   Not all men love someone.
   _____
   There are some unloved men.

(5) All men are such that either they love someone or they are unhappy.
Joe is a man and he loves no one.

Joe is unhappy.

(6) All men have a brother.

Someone is everyone's brother.

B. For each of the following formulas, indicate which of its constituent symbols are individual constants, which are individual variables, which are quantifiers, and which are predicates:

(1) *Fa*
(2) *(x)Fx*
(3) *(x)Fxa*
(4) *(x)(y)(Fx ⊃ Gxy)*
(5) *(x)(∃y)(Fx · Gxya)*
(6) *(∃x)[Fxa ∨ (y)(Gyx)]*
(7) *Fa ∨ (x)Gx*
(8) *Fa ∨ Gb*

C. Symbolize each of the following statements and indicate which (if any) of the four Aristotelian statement-forms it is an instance of.
1. Every girl is romantic or unhappy.
2. Some girls are not both romantic and unhappy.
3. Every girl is not happy.
4. Some girls love someone.
5. It is not the case that every girl is romantic.
6. Some books are not interesting.
7. Either some books are interesting or all books are.
8. Each book is very interesting.
9. Any book is as interesting as the other.
10. No book is interesting.

D. Symbolize each of the following relational statements:
1. Joe is older than Harry and Harry is older than Frank.
2. All sophomores are older than Joe.
3. Joe is older than all freshmen.
4. All sophomores are older than any freshman.
5. Some sophomore is older than some freshman.
6. Some sophomore is older than every freshman.
7. Every sophomore is older than some freshman.
8. There is no sophomore who is older than every freshman.
9. Some sophomores are older than every freshman and some are older than every male freshman.
10. Either Joe is older than every freshman or Joe is older than every sophomore.

E. Which of the following inferences are of the UE form?

(1) $\underline{(x)(\exists y)(Fxy)}$
   Fab

(2) $\underline{(x)[Fx \supset (\exists y)(Gxy)]}$
   $Fa \supset (\exists y)(Gay)$

(3) $\underline{(x)(y)(Fxy)}$
   Fab

(4) $\underline{Fa \cdot (x)(Gx)}$
   $Fa \cdot Ga$

(5) $\underline{(x) \sim Fx}$
   $\sim Fa$

(6) $\underline{(x)(Fx) \cdot (x)(Gx)}$
   $Fa \cdot Ga$

F. Which of the following inferences are of the EI form?

(1) $\underline{\sim Fab}$
   $(\exists x) \sim (Fax)$

(2) $\underline{\sim Fab}$
   $\sim(\exists x)(Fax)$

(3) $\underline{\sim Fab}$
   $(\exists x)(\sim Fxx)$

(4) $\underline{Fa \cdot Ga}$
   $(\exists x)(Fx) \cdot Ga$

(5) $\underline{Fa \vee Ga}$
   $(\exists x)(Fx \vee Ga)$

(6) $\underline{Fa \cdot Ga}$
   $(\exists x)(Fx) \cdot (\exists x)(Gx)$

G. Which of the following inferences are of the UI form? You may assume that there is a proof of the premise that does not rest upon any assumptions about the object(s) the premise is talking about.

(1) $\underline{(x)(Fxx)}$
   Faa

(2) $\underline{Faa}$
   $(x)(Fxa)$

(3) $\underline{Faa}$
   $(x)(Fxx)$

(4) $\underline{Fa \vee Ga}$
   $(x)(Fx) \vee (x)(Gx)$

(5) $\underline{Fa \vee Ga}$
   $(x)(Fx \vee Ga)$

(6) $\underline{Fa \vee Ga}$
   $(x)(Fx \vee Gx)$

H. Which of the following inferences are of the EE form? You may assume that the proof of the second premise does not depend upon any assumptions about any object that the antecedent of that premise is concerned with.

(1) $(\exists x)(Fx \cdot Gx)$
$(Fa \cdot Ga) \supset Hb$
———
Hb

(2) $(\exists x)(Fx \cdot Gx)$
$(Fa \cdot Gb) \supset Hc$
———
Hc

(3) $(\exists x)(Fx \cdot Gx)$
$(Fa \cdot Ga) \supset Ha$
———
Ha

(4) $\sim(\exists x)(Fx \cdot Gx)$
$\sim(Fa \cdot Ga) \supset Hb$
———
Hb

(5) $(\exists x)(Fx) \cdot (\exists x)(Gx)$
$(Fa \cdot Ga) \supset Hb$
———
Hb

(6) $(\exists x)(Fx \cdot Gx)$
$(Fa \supset Hb) \cdot (Ga \supset Hb)$
———
Hb

I. Prove that the following inference-forms are valid. You may use theorems from Chapter 6 only.

(1) $(x)[Fx \supset (Gx \vee Hx)]$
$(x)(Gx \supset Ix)$
$(x) \sim Ix$
———
$(x)(Fx \supset Hx)$

(2) $(x) \sim (Fx \vee Gx)$
$(\exists x)(Hx \equiv Fx)$
———
$(\exists x) \sim Hx$

(3) $(x)(Fx \supset \sim Gx)$
$(\exists x)(Gx \vee Hx)$
———
$(\exists x)(\sim Fx \vee Hx)$

(4) $(x)[(Fx \vee Gx) \cdot Hx]$
$(\exists x) \sim Gx$
———
$(\exists x)(Fx \cdot Hx)$

(5) $(x)(Fx \equiv Gx)$
$(x)(Gx \equiv Hx)$
$(\exists x) \sim Hx$
———
$(\exists x) \sim Fx$

(6) $(x)(y)[(Fx \cdot Fy) \supset Gxy]$
$(x)(y)(Hxy \supset \sim Gxy)$
———
$(x)(y)[Hxy \supset (\sim Fx \vee \sim Fy)]$

J. Prove that the following statement-forms are theorems. You may use theorems from Chapter 6 only.

(1) $(\exists x)(Px \cdot Qx) \equiv (\exists x)(Qx \cdot Px)$
(2) $(x)(Px \supset Qx) \equiv (x)(\sim Qx \supset \sim Px)$
(3) $(x)(Fx \cdot Gx) \equiv (x)Fx \cdot (x)Gx$
(4) $(\exists x)(Fx \vee Gx) \equiv (\exists x)Fx \vee (\exists x)Gx$
(5) $(\exists x)Px \equiv \sim(x) \sim Px$
(6) $\sim(\exists x)Px \equiv (x) \sim Px$
(7) $(\exists x)(\exists y)Fxy \equiv (\exists y)(\exists x)Fxy$

K. Symbolize all the following inferences and prove that they are valid:

(1) There is an uneducated wise man.

Not all wise men are educated.

(2) A man is wise if and only if he is educated.

If there is someone who is uneducated, then there is an unwise person.

(3) Someone is either educated or wise.
If anyone is educated, he must have gone to college.

Someone either went to college or is wise.

(4) Everyone either is wise or (is educated and has a college degree).
There is someone who is educated but does not have a college degree.

There is someone who is wise.

(5) Everyone is such that he is not both educated and wise.
There is someone who is educated and has a college degree.

There is someone who is unwise but who has a college degree.

(6) A wise man knows everything.
There is someone who does not know something.

There is someone who is not a wise man.

(7) There is some one person who knows everything.
If one knows something, one is not surprised by it.

There is some one person who is not surprised by anything.

L. For each of the inference-forms in Exercise I and the statement-forms in Exercise J, show by the method of semantic tableaux that it is valid or that it is a theorem. You may skip I(6) and J(7).

M. Using the method of semantic tableaux, show, if possible, that the following (if inference-forms) are not valid or (if statement-forms) are not theorems:

(1) $(x)(Fx \vee Gx)$

$(x)Fx \vee (x)Gx$

(2) $(\exists x)Fx \cdot (\exists x)Gx$

$(\exists x)(Fx \cdot Gx)$

(3) $(\exists x)(y)Fxy$

$(x)(\exists y)Fxy$

(4) $\dfrac{(y)(\exists x)Fxy}{(\exists x)(y)Fxy}$

(5) $(x)(Fx \lor Gx) \supset (\exists x)Fx$

(6) $(x)(Fx \supset Gx) \supset (x)(Fx \cdot Gx)$

(7) $(\exists x)(Fx \lor Gx) \supset (\exists x)(Fx \cdot Gx)$

Part II

1. If the quantificational form of an inference contains more of the structure of that inference than its statemental form, why do we bother with the statement-forms of inferences?

2. Can you think of any valid inference-forms that are neither statement-forms of the type studied in Chapter 6 nor quantification-forms of the type we studied in this chapter?

3. It is sometimes said that quantification theory breaks down the distinction between properties and relations. Is there any basis for such a claim? If there is, is that good or bad?

4. In our system individual variables cannot occur in a symbol without the appearance in that symbol of a corresponding quantifier. What is the rationale for this stipulation?

5. In symbolizing an *A* or *E* statement, we use '$\supset$', whereas in symbolizing an *I* or *O* proposition, we use '$\cdot$'. Why does this difference exist?

6. What is the difference in meaning between 'all', 'any', 'every', and 'each'?

7. In light of our examination of Aristotelian logic in this chapter, contrast its strength with that of quantification theory, and explain why the latter is stronger.

8. Assume, as did most Aristotelian logicians, that *A* and *E* statements have existential import. In light of that assumption, prove that an *A* statement and its corresponding *E* statement cannot both be true (they are *contraries*) although they can both be false (and they are not therefore *contradictories*). Also explain why these proofs cannot be given if we do not make that assumption.

9. Assume, as did most Aristotelian logicians, that *A* and *E* statements have existential import. In light of that assumption, prove that an *A* statement entails the corresponding *I* statement and an *E* statement entails the corresponding *O* statement. Also explain why these proofs cannot be given if we do not make that assumption.

10. Given that *A* statements in quantification theory have no existential import, how can we infer from '$(x)(Fx \supset Gx)$' that '$(\exists x)(Fx \supset Gx)$' is true? What does this do to our definition of validity?

11. Show how the validity of the EI form of inference suggests a connection between the existential quantifier and disjunction. Similarly, show how the validity of the UE form of inference suggests a connection between the universal quantifier and conjunction.

12. In light of your answer to (11), explain why two of our forms are restricted and two are not.

13. Find four additional syllogistic forms of inference that are valid when A and I statements are understood to have existential import.

14. By comparing the examples in the text with the examples in Exercise M of Part I, explain what type of statements are such that their tableaux do not end.

15. Critically evaluate the following argument: Even if a table does not end, we still know that the inference in question is not valid or that the statement in question may be true, for we recognize that the table is just repeating itself endlessly. Thus, contrary to what is said in this chapter, the method of semantic tableaux still will always enable us to determine mechanically that some inference is invalid or that some statement may be false.

APPENDIX TO PART TWO

And-Elimination

$$\frac{p \cdot q}{p} \qquad \frac{p \cdot q}{q}$$

And-Introduction

$$\frac{\begin{array}{c} p \\ q \end{array}}{p \cdot q}$$

Or-Elimination

$$\frac{\begin{array}{c} p \vee q \\ p \supset r \\ q \supset r \end{array}}{r}$$

Or-Introduction

$$\frac{p}{p \vee q} \qquad \frac{q}{p \vee q}$$

Negation-Elimination
(*modus tollens*)

$$\frac{\begin{array}{c} p \supset q \\ \sim q \end{array}}{\sim p.}$$

Negation-Introduction
(*reductio ad absurdum*)

$$\frac{p \supset (q \cdot \sim q)}{\sim p}$$

Conditional-Elimination
(*modus ponens*)

$$\frac{\begin{array}{c} p \supset q \\ p \end{array}}{q}$$

Conditional-Introduction

$$\frac{\text{Given assumptions } A_1, \ldots, A_n,}{\text{Given assumptions } A_1, \ldots, A_n, p \supset q.}$$

q can be inferred from p.

Biconditional-Introduction

$$\frac{\begin{array}{c} p \supset q \\ q \supset p \end{array}}{p \equiv q}$$

Biconditional-Elimination

$$\frac{p \equiv q}{p \supset q} \qquad\qquad \frac{p \equiv q}{q \supset p}$$

Double Negation

$$\frac{\sim\sim p}{p} \qquad\qquad \frac{p}{\sim\sim p}$$

PRINCIPAL THEOREMS OF PROPOSITIONAL LOGIC:

(a) $p \vee (q \vee r) \equiv (p \vee q) \vee r$ Associative law for disjunction
(b) $p \cdot (q \cdot r) \equiv (p \cdot q) \cdot r$ Associative law for conjunction
(c) $p \vee q \equiv q \vee p$ Commutative law for disjunction
(d) $p \cdot q \equiv q \cdot p$ Commutative law for conjunction
(e) $p \cdot (q \vee r) \equiv (p \cdot q) \vee (p \cdot r)$ Distributive law for conjunction over disjunction
(f) $p \vee (q \cdot r) \equiv (p \vee q) \cdot (p \vee r)$ Distributive law for disjunction over conjunction
(g) $\sim(p \vee q) \equiv \sim p \cdot \sim q$ De Morgan's law for disjunction
(h) $\sim(p \cdot q) \equiv \sim p \vee \sim q$ De Morgan's law for conjunction
(i) $p \supset q \equiv \sim q \supset \sim p$ Law of contraposition
(j) $p \equiv p$ Law of identity
(k) $p \vee \sim p$ Law of excluded middle
(l) $\sim(p \cdot \sim p)$ Law of contradiction
(m) $[\sim p \cdot (p \vee q)] \supset q$ Law of disjunctive syllogisms

ADDITIONAL INTERESTING PROPOSITIONAL INFERENCE-FORMS:

(1) Disjunctive syllogism

$$\frac{\begin{array}{c} p \vee q \\ \sim p \end{array}}{q}$$

(2) Hypothetical syllogism

$$\frac{\begin{array}{c} p \supset q \\ q \supset r \end{array}}{p \supset r}$$

(3) Constructive dilemma

$$\frac{\begin{array}{c} p \supset q \\ r \supset s \\ p \vee r \end{array}}{q \vee s}$$

(4) Destructive dilemma

$$p \supset q$$
$$r \supset s$$
$$\underline{\sim q \lor \sim s}$$
$$\sim p \lor \sim r$$

ADDITIONAL BASIC QUANTIFICATIONAL INFERENCE FORMS:

Universal-Elimination

$$\frac{(x)—x—}{—a—}$$

Where (1) the premise begins with a universal quantifier that applies to the whole formula; and (2) the conclusion is like the premise, except that the initial quantifier is missing and all (and only those) occurrences of the variable in it (in the premise) are replaced in the conclusion by the same constant.

Universal-Introduction

$$\frac{—a—}{(x)—x—}$$

Where (1) the conclusion begins with a universal quantifier that contains a variable which is not in the premise and the quantifier applies to the whole formula; (2) the conclusion is like the premise, except for its initial quantifier and its containing the variable in that quantifier in all (and only those) places in which some one constant occurred in the premise; (3) the premise rests upon no assumption involving that constant.

Existential-Elimination

$$(\exists x)(—x—)$$
$$\underline{(—a—) \supset p}$$
$$p$$

Where (1) the first premise begins with an existential quantifier whose variable not occur in the antecedent of the second premise and applies to the whole formula; (2) the second premise is a conditional whose (a) antecedent is like the first premise, except that the initial quantifier is missing and that it contains a constant such that all (and only its) occurrences are replaced in the first premise by the variable in the initial quantifier, (b) consequent does not contain that constant; (3) the second premise rests upon no assumptions involving that constant.

Existential-Introduction

$$\frac{\text{---}a\text{---}}{(\exists x)\text{---}x\text{---}}$$

> Where (1) the conclusion begins with an existential quantifier that applies to the whole formula; (2) the premise is like the conclusion, except that the initial quantifier is missing and all (and only those) occurrences of the variable in it in the conclusion are replaced in the premise by the same constant.

PRINCIPAL THEOREMS OF QUANTIFICATION THEORY:

(a′) $(x)(Px \supset Qx) \equiv \sim(\exists x)(Px \cdot \sim Qx)$ Law of contradictoriness of A and O statements

(b′) $(x)(Px \supset \sim Qx) \equiv (x)(Qx \supset \sim Px)$ Law of conversion for E statements

(c′) $(\exists x)(Px \cdot Qx) \equiv (\exists x)(Qx \cdot Px)$ Law of conversion for I statements

(d′) $(x)(Px \supset Qx) \equiv (x)(\sim Qx \supset \sim Px)$ Law of contraposition for A statements

(e′) $(x)(Fx \cdot Gx) \equiv (x)Fx \cdot (x)Gx$

(f′) $(\exists x)(Fx \lor Gx) \equiv (\exists x)Fx \lor (\exists x)Gx$

(g′) $(\exists x)(Fx \cdot Gx) \supset (\exists x)Fx \cdot (\exists x)Gx$

(h′) $(x)Fx \lor (x)Gx \supset (x)(Fx \lor Gx)$

(i′) $(x)Px \equiv \sim(\exists x) \sim Px$

(j′) $(\exists x)Px \equiv \sim(x) \sim Px$

(k′) $\sim(x)Px \equiv (\exists x) \sim Px$

(l′) $\sim(\exists x)Px \equiv (x) \sim Px$

(m′) $(x)(y)Fxy \equiv (y)(x)Fxy$

(n′) $(\exists x)(\exists y)Fxy \equiv (\exists y)(\exists x)Fxy$

(o′) $(\exists x)(y)Fxy \equiv (y)(\exists x)Fxy$

SOME ADDITIONAL IMPORTANT QUANTIFICATIONAL INFERENCE-FORMS:

(1) Barbara Syllogism

$$\frac{\begin{array}{l}(x)(Qx \supset Rx)\\(x)(Px \supset Qx)\end{array}}{(x)(Px \supset Rx)}$$

(2) Baroco Syllogism

$$\frac{\begin{array}{l}(x)(Rx \supset Qx)\\(\exists x)(Px \cdot \sim Qx)\end{array}}{(\exists x)(Px \cdot \sim Rx)}$$

(3) Bocardo Syllogism

$$\frac{\begin{array}{l}(\exists x)(Qx \cdot \sim Rx)\\(x)(Qx \supset Px)\end{array}}{(\exists x)(Px \cdot \sim Rx)}$$

(4) Camenes Syllogism

$$\frac{\begin{array}{l}(x)(Rx \supset Qx)\\(x)(Qx \supset \sim Px)\end{array}}{(x)(Px \supset \sim Rx)}$$

(5) Camestres Syllogism

$$\frac{\begin{array}{l}(x)(Rx \supset Qx)\\(x)(Px \supset \sim Qx)\end{array}}{(x)(Px \supset \sim Rx)}$$

(6) Celarent Syllogism

$$\frac{\begin{array}{l}(x)(Qx \supset \sim Rx)\\(x)(Px \supset Qx)\end{array}}{(x)(Px \supset \sim Rx)}$$

(7) Cesare Syllogism

$$(x)(Rx \supset \sim Qx)$$
$$(x)(Px \supset Qx)$$
$$\overline{(x)(Px \supset \sim Rx)}$$

(8) Darii Syllogism

$$(x)(Qx \supset Rx)$$
$$(\exists x)(Px \cdot Qx)$$
$$\overline{(\exists x)(Px \cdot Rx)}$$

(9) Datisi Syllogism

$$(x)(Qx \supset Rx)$$
$$(\exists x)(Qx \cdot Px)$$
$$\overline{(\exists x)(Px \cdot Rx)}$$

(10) Dimaris Syllogism

$$(\exists x)(Rx \cdot Qx)$$
$$(x)(Qx \supset Px)$$
$$\overline{(\exists x)(Px \cdot Rx)}$$

(11) Disamis Syllogism

$$(\exists x)(Qx \cdot Rx)$$
$$(x)(Qx \supset Px)$$
$$\overline{(\exists x)(Px \cdot Rx)}$$

(12) Ferio Syllogism

$$(x)(Qx \supset \sim Rx)$$
$$(\exists x)(Px \cdot Qx)$$
$$\overline{(\exists x)(Px \cdot \sim Rx)}$$

(13) Ferison Syllogism

$$(x)(Qx \supset \sim Rx)$$
$$(\exists x)(Qx \cdot Px)$$
$$\overline{(\exists x)(Px \cdot \sim Rx)}$$

(14) Festino Syllogism

$$(x)(Rx \supset \sim Qx)$$
$$(\exists x)(Px \cdot Qx)$$
$$\overline{(\exists x)(Px \cdot \sim Rx)}$$

(15) Fresison Syllogism

$$(x)(Rx \supset \sim Qx)$$
$$(\exists x)(Qx \cdot Px)$$
$$\overline{(\exists x)(Px \cdot \sim Rx)}$$

PART THREE

THE THEORY
of
INDUCTION

CHAPTER 8

The Process of Generalization

8.1 *Samplings and Generalizations*

Suppose you were the President of the United States and that you wanted to know what percentage of the electorate supported an action you had recently taken. The usual way to find out would be by running a poll. How does a polling service conduct such a poll? Obviously they do not question every registered voter in the country. What they do is to query a relatively small number of voters, determine what percentage supports the presidential action, and infer that the same percentage of voters supports the action.

The same process would be used to determine, for example, what percentage of marijuana smokers winds up taking heroin. Investigators would not interview every person who has ever smoked marijuana; they would poll a relatively small number of such people, determine what percentage of them had gone on to heroin after having smoked marijuana, and then infer that the same percentage of marijuana smokers in general winds up taking heroin.

The use of this process is not confined to such formal cases. Consider the case of the girl who buys a few dresses manufactured by the *XYZ* company, discovers that they tend to wear out very quickly, and decides that she won't buy any more dresses from that company. Although she may not be consciously aware of all the steps, she has, in effect, carried out this process of investigation. She has examined a small number of the dresses manufactured by the *XYZ* company, determined that a relatively large percentage of them wear out very quickly, inferred that this is true for a similarly high percentage of all the dresses manufactured by the *XYZ* company, and therefore concluded that she ought not to buy their dresses.

The procedure we have been describing is called the *sampling process*. It is used to determine what percentage of a certain class of objects (in our examples: voters, marijuana smokers, or *XYZ*-made dresses) has a given property (in our examples: approving of a presidential action, taking heroin, of wearing out quickly). In this process you examine a relatively small number of objects that belong to the class in question (these examined objects are usually called the *sample*), determine what percentage of them have the property in question, and then infer (by a mode of inference known as *generalization*) that the same percentage of all members of that class (usually called the *population*) has the property in question.

Generalization, the inference mode that is part of the sampling process, can be represented schematically as follows:

$n\%$ of the examined objects from the class of objects having property A also have property B.

$n\%$ of the objects in the class of objects having property A also have property B.

Or, more simply,

$n\%$ of the examined A's are also B's.

$n\%$ of all A's are B's.

The first, and, in a way, the most important thing to note about generalizations is that they are never deductively valid inferences. It is easy to see how the premise of a generalization could be true and the conclusion false; all that is required is that there be some nonexamined A's and that the percentage of these A's that are B's not be equal to n. Thus, in the following case the premise of the generalization is true but the conclusion is false. There are 10 A's. We examine 8 and discover that 6 are also B's. But the other 2 A's are not B's. So if we were to make the following inference (which we very well might do if we didn't know about the other 2 A's),

75 % of the examined A's are B's.

---

75 % of all A's are B's.

we would have an inference with a true premise and a false conclusion. This is possible because there are unexamined A's (two of them), and the percentage of those A's that are also B's (0 %) is different from the percentage of examined A's that are also B's (75 %).

What premises could we add to the premise of a generalization to turn the resulting inference into a valid deductive inference? We saw previously that two conditions must be present before a generalization can have a true premise but a false conclusion. So all we need is a premise denying that one of these conditions applies. In other words, we can turn a generalization into a valid deductive inference by making it conform to one of the following two forms:

$n\%$ of the examined A's are also B's.
There are no unexamined A's.

$n\%$ of all A's are B's.

$n\%$ of the examined A's are also B's.
The percentage of unexamined A's that are also B's is the same as the percentage of examined A's that are B's.

$n\%$ of all A's are B's.

We shall consider inferences of the second form in the last section of this chapter. We shall now concentrate upon inferences of the first form (the so-called *generalization by complete enumeration*), and see why it is so seldomly used to establish the truth of conclusions of the type that we are considering.

To use such an inference to establish the truth of its conclusion, the premises of the inference must be true and we must know that the premises are true. Both these requirements usually pose insurmountable practical problems. First, it is often practically impossible to examine all the A's (and, therefore, for it to be true that there are no unexamined A's). Consider, once more, our President trying to discover what percentage of citizens approves of a given action he has taken. It would be far too difficult, expensive, and time consuming actually to ask every citizen for his opinion. But even if he could do this, it would not be enough, for to know that he had done it, he would have to run additional checks to make sure that he hadn't missed anyone, which would be an even more difficult task. So establishing general propositions by use of generalization by complete enumeration is usually not a viable alternative.

Let us consider a case in which we might actually use a generalization by complete enumeration to establish the truth of a general conclusion. Imagine that there are a certain number of people in a room and that we want to establish how many of them speak English. In this case we could readily examine all the members of the population because they are relatively few and accessible. Moreover, and equally important, since the population is confined to the objects in one room, we are able to determine that we have examined every member of the population. But this case is clearly an exception, for generalization by complete enumeration is usually not viable.

At the other extreme there are cases in which it is theoretically, not merely practically, impossible to establish any conclusion through generalization by complete enumeration. These are the cases in which the population is infinitely large (in which case it is impossible that there be no unexamined A's) or in which it is possible that it is infinitely large (in which case it is impossible for one to know that there are no unexamined A's). An example of such a case would be Newton's law of gravity, which discusses all objects that exist, have existed, or will exist. We don't know whether there are an infinite number of objects that exist sometime in the history of the universe, but if there are, then it is theoretically impossible to examine all the objects in the population which Newton's law discusses. Even if there aren't an infinite number, as long as we aren't certain whether there are only a finite number of objects in the history of the universe, it would be theoretically impossible to know that we have examined all the objects in our population.

Let us return now to the ordinary invalid generalizations. The second extremely important point to note about them is that although they are all invalid, some, but not all, are such that their premises give us good reasons for believing the conclusion. To see that this is so, contrast the following two cases: Joe, the local barber, has polled his first ten customers in a given week, and discovered that 60% approve of a given presidential action. He concludes that 60% of the American public approves of that action. The *QED* polling company polls 2,000 persons spread throughout the country— young and old, rich and poor, white and black, and so on. They find that 50% of their sample approves of the President's action, and conclude that 50% of the American public approves of the action. Joe's evidence gives us little reason for believing his conclusion, but the evidence amassed by the *QED* company gives us good reason for believing its conclusion.

We shall say that an inference is *sound* if knowledge of the truth of its premises gives one good reason to believe in the truth of its conclusion; all other inferences will be said to be *unsound*. We can then rephrase our second point about ordinary generalizations as follows: Although all ordinary generalizations are invalid, some of them, but not all, are sound. This chapter is concerned with the theory of the soundness of generalizations.

Before turning to that theory, however, we ought to note two more points about soundness. First, since there are invalid but sound inferences, there can be sound inferences whose premises are true but whose conclusion is false (in the preceding case even the very good generalization made by the *QED* company might be wrong). This means that believing in the conclusions of sound inferences with true premises is riskier than believing in only the conclusions of valid inferences with true premises: You can be wrong in the first case, but not in the second. Second, soundness, unlike validity, is a matter of degree. Some sound inferences give good reasons for believing in their conclusions, some give even better, and deductively valid sound inferences give the best reasons for believing in their conclusions. Any complete theory of the soundness of generalizations should, therefore, include a theory of degrees of soundness.

8.2 Good and Bad Samples

Why was Joe's generalization about the percentage of the American public that supports the President's action an unsound inference, whereas the generalization by the *QED* polling company was sound? The logical form of the two generalizations was, after all, the same. The difference was obviously in the sample. Joe's sample was much too small, and he didn't have a proper variety of individuals. The *QED* sample on the other hand, was both larger and more diversified. Thus as a preliminary account, we can say that the soundness of a generalization depends upon the type of sample that is used, and that a sample must be both large enough and varied enough if the generalization is to be sound. We still have to determine what is meant by 'large enough' and 'varied enough'.

First, as to the size of the sample, what size is large enough? To answer that question, we must remind ourselves of a few elementary facts from the theory of probability. In particular, we want to remember why large samples are better than small samples.

Let us imagine that we have a population of 100 A's and we want to know how many of them are B's. We examine a sample of 20 and find 4 B's. We are now in a position to exclude the suggestion (*hypothesis*) that 80% of the A's are B's by arguing as follows. Assume the truth of the hypothesis. Then, unless there was something unusual about the sample, the most likely occurrence would be 16 B's and 4 non-B's. Still quite possible, although progressively less likely, is the observation of 17 (15) B's and 3 (5) non-B's, 18 (14) B's and 2 (6) non-B's, and 19 (13) B's and 1 (7) non-B's. However, given our hypothesis, the odds are so great against our seeing only 4 B's in a normal sample that if we do observe only 4 B's, we can rule out the possibility that our hypothesis is true. Remember, of course, that this argument is not conclusive; what is very unlikely can occur. But this is just another way of saying that arguments from samples are never valid, and it is still true that our argument is sound, that is, that our argument gives us good reasons for supposing that the hypothesis in question is false.

Although we can use the preceding argument to rule out the hypothesis that 80% of the A's are B's, we could hardly use it to rule out the hypothesis that 30% of the A's are B's. It is true that if 30% of the A's are B's, the most likely observation would have been 6 B's and 14 non-B's. But on that hypothesis the likelihood of observing only 4 B's is still great enough that we wouldn't rule out the hypothesis on the basis of that observation. The situation is quite different when our sample rises to 80. Let us imagine that we then observe 16 *B*'s and 64 non-*B*'s. Then we are in a position to rule out the hypothesis that 30% of the *A*'s are *B*'s. If that hypothesis were true, the most likely observation would have been 24 *B*'s, with one or two more or less still reasonably likely. But on that hypothesis the chances of observing only 16 *B*'s are so small (unless there is something odd about the sample) that we can rule it out.

Generalizing from this example, we can say the following: If we have a sample in which *n*% of the *A*'s are *B*'s, then, as the size of the sample increases, (1) we are able to exclude more and more hypotheses stating that the percentage of *A*'s in the total population which are also *B*'s is other than *n*, and (2) the remaining hypotheses all say that the percentage of *A*'s in the total population which are also *B*'s is $n \pm a$ (where *a* gets smaller and smaller as the size of the sample increases). In other words, as the size of the sample increases, the reasonably possible differences between the percentage of *A*'s in the sample that are also *B*'s and the percentage of *A*'s in the total population that are also *B*'s become increasingly smaller.

In the preceding example we rejected hypotheses when, given the truth of the hypothesis, the odds against observing the sample that we did observe were too high. How high is 'too high'? The normal answer in statistics is that the odds are 19 to 1; that is, that the odds are great enough so that we will be wrong in only one out of twenty cases. But the statistician is quick to admit that if we are dealing with a more important case, in which the cost of a mistake is high, then we may want to be more cautious and not reject a hypothesis on the basis of a sample until the odds against observing such a sample, given the truth of the hypothesis, are much greater. And if we are dealing with a more trivial case, in which the cost of an error is minimal, we may be less cautious and start rejecting hypotheses on the basis of a sample when the odds against observing such a sample, given the truth of the hypothesis, are less than 19 to 1. In other words, the point at which we start rejecting hypotheses will vary from case to case. We shall call those odds for a given sampling process the *rejection point* employed in that sampling process.

Returning now to the question of how large the sample must be before the generalization based upon it is sound, an obvious suggestion is that it is sound when all other hypotheses would be rejected, given the rejection point for our process, on the basis of the sample. In other words, it is sound to infer that the percentage of *A*'s in the population that are *B*'s is the same as the percentage of *A*'s in the sample that are *B*'s only when, on the basis of the sample, all other possibilities can be rejected.

The trouble with this rule is that we are almost never in a position to reject all other hypotheses. Consider, once more, the *QED* polling company, which has sampled 2,000 Americans and discovered that 1,000 (or 50%) approve of an action that the President took. We would want to say, providing the sample is properly varied, that the company could soundly infer by generalization that 50% of the American public approves of the action. But on the basis of this sample, given any reasonable rejection point, we would not be in a position to reject the alternative hypothesis that 50.000001% of all Americans approve of the action. So, given our rule, we would be forced to reject as unsound a generalization that is obviously sound.

The obvious reply to this objection is that the difference between the two hypothesis is normally insignificant, and the fact that we could not reject this variation of the 50% hypotheses doesn't bother us. More generally, when in advancing a hypothesis about the percentage of A's that are B's, we say that $n\%$ are B's, we really mean $n\%$, give or take a little. We can formalize this flexibility by advancing our hypotheses in the form $n \pm a\%$ of the A's are B's, meaning that the percentage of A's that are B's is somewhere between $n + a\%$ and $n - a\%$. In our example, if we assume that we don't care about anything less than 0.1%, we might advance our 50% hypothesis as $50 \pm \frac{1}{10}\%$ of all Americans approve of the President's policy. In other words, our hypothesis is really that the percentage of Americans approving of the action is somewhere between 49.9% and 50.1%. Of course, a isn't always $\frac{1}{10}$. It can be more or less, depending upon how precise we require our information.

Therefore, all generalizations will really be of the form:

$n\%$ of the examined A's are also B's.

$n \pm a\%$ of all A's are B's.

Since they are of this form, thereby eliminating the problem of being perfectly precise, we can lay down the rule that a sample is large enough so that generalizations based upon it can be sound if, given the rejection point for the sampling process in question, all hypotheses asserting that the percentage of all A's that are B's is y (where y is greater than $n + a$ or less than $n - a$) would, on the basis of the sample, be rejected.

We are now in a position to explain why some generalizations are sounder than others. Let us imagine we have a generalization G_1 based upon a sample S_1, and a generalization G_2 based upon a sample S_2. And let us imagine that if our rejection point is 19 to 1, both these generalizations are sound. Let us also imagine, however, that if our rejection point were 99 to 1, only G_1 would remain sound; G_2 would be unsound. Therefore, if we were being cautious about rejecting hypotheses, we could no longer infer the conclusion of G_2, but we could still infer the conclusion of G_1. In other words, we can infer from the sample that is the basis of G_2 the conclusion of G_2 only if we are prepared to risk mistakes we needn't make in order to infer the conclusion of G_1 from the sample that is the basis of G_1. For this reason we can say that G_1 is sounder than G_2 and that our knowledge of the truth of the premises of inference G_1 gives us better reasons for believing its conclusion than the reasons offered by our knowledge of the truth of the premises of inference G_2 for believing its conclusion.

Let's consider now the second important difference between Joe's poll and the poll conducted by the *QED* polling company. What de we mean by samples that are 'varied enough', and how do we obtain them? You will recall that the object of those polls was to find out what percentage of American voters approved of a given presidential action. To make it more concrete, let us suppose that the action in question was the sending of American soldiers to fight in Cambodia. Now, certain groups of citizens are more likely than others to approve of that action. According to actual opinion polls, Southerners are more likely to approve than Northeasterners, people without a college education are more likely to approve than college graduates; men are more likely to approve than women, and so on. If we have a sample that is drawn solely from the groups more likely to favor this presidential action, then it would be unsound to generalize from that sample to the whole population of American voters. Thus, if Joe's barber shop were located in a Southern working-class district, and his customers were men only, Joe's sample would most likely yield a percentage out of proportion to the total population. The same would be true, i.e., the sample would not be diverse enough, if Joe's barber shop were located in a student center on a Northeastern college campus.

The sample used by the *QED* company was properly varied because it contained a correct representative proportion from each group of American voters, whereas Joe's sample did not.

Note that it is not sufficient that a sample contain members from each of the important groups. It must contain the correct representative percentage of them. It is easy to see why this is so. We would not be satisfied with a sample containing only one Republican among a group of ardent Democrats. We would still feel that this would probably give us too high a percentage of disapprovers in the sample. We need a sample that contains a right percentage of Republicans and Democrats; namely, the same percentage of Republicans and Democrats as the percentage in the total population of American voters.

Note also that we are concerned only with groups that are significant in the circumstances. We are not concerned with whether the sample contains the right percentage of say brunettes, people over six feet, and so on, because we have reason to believe that height, or hair color, are unlikely to affect political opinions. Thus, for the purpose of our investigation, those groups are unimportant.

We can now generalize and formalize this account of variety as follows. We first need some definitions:

(1) *A characteristic of a population of all and only A's* is a set of properties $P_1, \ldots, P_n$ such that every member of the population has one, and only one, of these properties.

(2) *A significant characteristic of a population of all and only A's for the sake of investigation about being a B* is one which is such that, for any two properties P_1 and P_2 in the characteristic, the likelihood of an A which is a P_1 being a B is different from the likelihood of an A which is a P_2 being a B.

(3) *A grouping of members of the population of all and only A's for the sake of investigating about being a B* is a group of members which has, for each significant characteristic of a population of all and only A's, the same property in that characteristic.

Intuitively, each of the members of the grouping is alike in all respects that are relevant to the likelihood of its being a B. Let us suppose that we are trying to determine, from a sampling, the percentage of A's that are also B's. We shall say that we have a *properly varied sample* when, for every grouping of members of the population of all and only A's for the sake of investigating about being a B, the percentage of members of the sample that are members of that grouping is the same as the percentage of members of the total population that are members of the grouping. In all other cases the sample is not properly varied.

There are two approaches to choosing one's sample (two *sampling techniques*) to achieve a properly varied sample. One, which is most obvious but, for reasons to be explained, not often used, is of the method of *sampling by matching*. When using this method to pick a sample of the population of A's in order to see what percentage are B's, we (1) determine what are the significant characteristics of the population of A's for the sake of investigating about being a B and what are the resulting groupings, (2) determine the percentage of the total population that belongs to each of these groupings, and (3) pick, by any method we please, a sample which has, for each grouping, the same percentage of members. When this process is successful, we have *matched* the sample to the population; when it is not, we have *mismatched* them.

The advantage of this method of sampling is obvious. When carried out properly, we are guaranteed a properly varied sample. However, there are severe practical limitations on its use. It requires us to know all the significant characteristics and to know, for every relevant grouping, the percentage of the population belonging to this grouping. Such information is often simply not available.

The other approach to choosing the sample is *random sampling*. This is not a method of sampling but a requirement of the method of sampling employed. The requirement is that the method be *random;* that is, that there be an equal chance, at each stage, for each as-yet-unpicked member of the population to be picked as a member of the sample. When a method is random, the resulting sample is a *random sample.* If the method is not random, it is a *biased* method, and the resulting sample is a *biased sample.*

There is, of course, no guarantee that a random sample will be a properly varied sample; indeed, it usually isn't. But if it is large enough (say, as large as is required to be the basis for sound generalizations), the odds are very strong that it will be close enough to being a properly varied sample that we can use it as the basis for sound generalizations.

We say that a method for choosing a sample *works* in a given case when it is either a random method or a sampling by matching that has matched (or come close to matching—the exact details of this is something that we needn't worry about now) the sample to the population in that case. We can then summarize our discussion of varied samples by saying that our requirement (stated on page 207) for the soundness of generalizations should really read as follows: A generalization is sound when (a) it is based upon a sample chosen by a method that worked in the case in question, and (b) the sample is large enough so that, given the rejection point for the sampling process in question, all hypotheses asserting that the percentage of all A's that are B's is y (where y is greater than $n + a$ or less than $n - a$) would, on the basis of the sample, be rejected.

8.3 Indirect Evidence and Analogies

So far, we have been considering the way in which, by generalization, we can soundly infer the truth of certain general statements on the basis of relatively small samples. In our discussion we have supposed that the only relevant evidence is what we have observed in the sample. This is not, however, what is usually the case. We often approach the problem of what percentage of A's are B's with good reasons—having nothing to do with inferences by generalization—for expecting certain types of answers (and perhaps even just one answer); this does, and should, affect the way we assess the evidence from the sample.

This can happen in one of two ways. One occurs when we have reason to believe that the percentage of A's that are B's is $n \pm a\%$, and we observe that the percentage of A's that are B's in some sample is $n \pm a\%$. Then, even though we would not normally be justified in generalizing from this sample that the percentage of A's that are B's in the total population is $n + a\%$, we might in this case. What happens in such a case, (to put it crudely), is that the small amount of evidence generalized from the sample (the amount which is normally insufficient to justify such a conclusion) is joined with the evidence we already have indepenent of the generalization from the sample, and together they are sufficient to justify drawing such a conclusion about the total population. The second way occurs when we have reason to believe that the percentage of A's that are B's is $n \pm a\%$, and we observe that the percentage of A's that are B's in a relatively large sample chosen by a method that works is $y \pm a$ (where $y \pm a$ differs significantly from $n \pm a\%$). Then, even though we would normally be justified in concluding by generalization from this sample that the percentage of A's that are B's in the total population is $y \pm a$, we would not be in this case. What happens in such a case, to put it crudely, is that the strength of the evidence generalized from the sample is vitiated by the strength of the evidence we have independent of the generalization from the sample, and on the basis of both of them, we are not justified in drawing such a conclusion about the total population.

Naturally, the extent to which this independent evidence can strengthen or weaken the evidence from samples depends upon the strength of the independent evidence. Note that if the independent evidence is strong enough, it could justify certain general conclusions about populations, and in such a case we would have no reason to generalize from a sample of the population to see whether the conclusion is true.

All of this means that the theory of the soundness of generalizations developed in section 8.2 is really only a theory of their soundness when there is no evidence other than the evidence generalized from the sample. And what we have said so far in this section suggests that in order to develop a theory of the soundness of generalizations when there is evidence other than that generalized from the sample, we must (a) determine what these alternative sources of evidence are, (b) determine how their strength, in each case, could be measured, and (c) decide how to add or subtract (roughly speaking) that strength from the strength of the generalization. Since the solutions to problems (b) and (c) are still not adequately worked out, we will only consider problem (a) in this section. In particular, we will consider two main alternative sources of evidence, analogy and indirect support by way of theories.

Let us return once more to our example of the QED polling company. Imagine that, a week before the President had sent soldiers into Cambodia, the QED company had run a poll to determine the percentage of voters that support the use of American soldiers to fight Communism in South Vietnam, and that they had determined that $n \pm a\%$ of American citizens approve. A few days after the American troops are sent to Cambodia, QED company begins to poll different groupings to determine their reaction. Let us imagine that they first poll a "hawkish" grouping then a "dovish" grouping, and finally a middle-of-the-road grouping, and that they discover (a) that the groupings hold the same opinion about Cambodia that they held about South

Vietnam; i.e., that the percentage in each grouping which approves of the President's action in Cambodia is more or less the same as the percentage in each grouping which approved of the use of American soldiers in South Vietnam, and (b) that, when combining these three groupings, they find that the percentage of Americans sampled so far which approve of the presidential action is $n \pm a$. The sample so far (since it includes only three of the groupings of American citizens) does not match the population of American citizens. If we were only taking into account the evidence from this sample of three groupings, we would hardly be justified in concluding, on the basis of a generalization from the sample of the three groupings, that the percentage of American citizens which approves of sending American soldiers to Cambodia is $n \pm a$. But there is more evidence to take into account; namely the previous poll on the reasonably similar (although certainly not the same) issue of the use of American soldiers in South Vietnam, which showed that $n \pm a\%$ of American citizens approve of that. And we must also take into account that the members of the three groupings we have already sampled seem to have the same views on the two issues. Given this additional evidence, we might soundly infer from the sample that $n \pm a\%$ of Americans approve of sending American soldiers to fight in Cambodia.

The additional evidence in this case is evidence by analogy. We are arguing, in effect, that $n \pm a\%$ of the American citizens have the property of approving the President's sending American soldiers to fight in Cambodia on the grounds that $n \pm a\%$ have a similar property, namely, approving of the use of American soldiers to fight in South Vietnam. These two properties are obviously similar in many respects, and as our sample so far shows, they are also shared by the same percentage of American citizens belonging to several very different groupings.

Using this example as our model, we can formalize the structure of *arguments from analogy* as follows:

(1) Let A and A' be two similar properties (perhaps even the same).
(2) Let B and B' be two similar properties (perhaps even the same).

$n \pm a\%$ of the A's are B's.
_____
$n \pm a\%$ of the A''s are B''s.

In our example A and A' are identical (the property of being an American citizen), whereas B (the property of approving of the use of American soldiers in South Vietnam) is similar to B' (the property of approving the sending of American soldiers to fight in Cambodia).

When are two properties similar? Presumably, when they have a lot in common; that is, when there are many things true about one that are also true about the other, and when there are not so many things true about one

manner (the B's), and (b) the general statement that 100% of all mixtures of two or more gases in a given container (the C's) are such that their pressure is the sum of the pressure that would be exerted by each of the gases if it alone were in the container (the D's). Now, let us imagine that neither the kinetic theory nor any of these consequences had ever been tested before, and that we wanted to see whether (a) and (b) were true. We would presumably begin by testing a sample of the total population of the A's to see whether they were all also B's. Let us now imagine that this has been done and that we can now soundly infer (a) to be true. But if (a) is true, we have some (though certainly not conclusive) evidence for the truth of the kinetic theory; after all, the best evidence for a theory is that its consequences turn out to be true. But (b) is also a consequence of the kinetic theory; if the kinetic theory is true, (b) must be true as well. So if we have some evidence for the truth of the kinetic theory, we also have some evidence for the truth of (b). That is to say, before we even begin testing a sample of the C's to see whether they are D's, we already have some (though certainly not conclusive) reasons for believing that 100% of the C's are D's. These reasons are the indirect support by way of theories for the hypothesis that 100% of the C's are D's.

Although there are many cases in which we can clearly get indirect support for a general statement by use of a theory, the logic of this method of supporting general propositions is very obscure. The trouble lies in distinguishing the legitimate cases from the illegitimate ones. To see why this is so, let us return to our example of the kinetic theory. We had inferred by generalization that (a) is true. We then argued that this gives us some (though not conclusive) reason for supposing that the kinetic theory is true, since (a) is a consequence of this theory. This point clearly presupposes the plausible principle that if we can infer by generalization that H_1 is true and H_2 entails H_1, then we have some (though not necessarily conclusive) reason for supposing that H_2 is true. Let us call this principle the *converse consequence principle for evidence from samples*. We then argued that if we have some reason to believe that the kinetic theory is true, then we also have some reason to believe that (b) is true, since (b) is a logical consequence of the kinetic theory. This point clearly presupposes the plausible principle that if we have some reason to believe, because of a generalization, that H_2 is true and H_1 is a consequence of H_2, then we have some reason to believe that H_1 is true. Let us call this principle the *special consequence principle for evidence from samples*. It would seem, therefore, that the possibility of getting indirect support through theories for a general statement exists because of the truth of these two principles, which is why we are in trouble. For these two principles allow too many illegitimate cases. Indeed, we can easily show that if they are both true, then any sample from which we can soundly infer by generalization the truth of any general statement G_1 provides us with some reason for believing the truth of any other generalization G_2, no matter how unrelated G_1 and G_2 are. By the converse consequence condition for evidence from samples, the evidence for G_1 is also evidence for $G_1 \cdot G_2$ (which clearly entails G_1). Therefore, by the special consequence condition for evidence from samples, it is also evidence for G_2 (a consequence of $G_1 \cdot G_2$). This is a marvellous method of collecting evidence to support a treasured belief for which one is having difficulty finding evidence. All one needs is to have a sample that supports any other general statement, and that sample provides some (though, unfortunately, not conclusive) evidence for the belief.

Obviously, this will not do. At least one of the principles, no matter how plausible it seems, must be dropped, and other principles must be found so that, on the basis of the new principles, we can construct a theory enabling us to distinguish legitimate cases of indirect support by use of theories from illegitimate cases. However, no such theory is presently available.

It is clear by now that the whole theory of additional evidence for general statements is in much worse shape than the theory of the soundness of inference by generalization to general statements. Nevertheless, we often cannot get along without this additional evidence. Consider, for instance, the medical researchers who would like to test a sample of human beings who have a given disease to discover what percentage of the population of human beings having that disease will be cured by taking a new drug. Since this drug has never been used on humans before, we could never know by a generalization that it will not harm people who take it. Yet we must have good reasons for believing that this is so before we can let the researchers run the experiment. The only reasons we could have are either based upon analogies or derived indirectly through theories. Therefore, these additional types of evidence play an essential role in such a case, and in many others like it.

8.4 Skepticism about Generalizations

In this chapter we have attempted to sketch the outlines of a theory for the soundness of generalizations. In particular, we have tried to show why those generalizations normally recognized as sound are sound. In doing so we have, of course, assumed that there are such things as sound generalizations; that is, we have assumed that there are generalizations such that knowledge of the truth of their premises gives us good reasons for believing in the truth of their conclusion. But is this really so? Are there such generalizations? In this last section we will consider this fundamental issue.

Let us consider the following argument against the soundness of any generalization. All generalizations assume that the unexamined members of the population are like the sample. Indeed, we saw in section 8.1 that, with such an assumption, a generalization can be turned into a valid deductive inference. But how could we know that this is so? If we knew so much about the whole population, we would not need to bother sampling it at all. Clearly, we do not know that this is so, but if we don't, then why should we suppose that knowing about the sample gives us good reasons for our beliefs about the population; that is, why should we suppose that any generalizations are sound?

This is an important skeptical argument. By casting doubt upon the process of generalization, we cast doubt upon all those general beliefs which we all hold and which guide our actions in life. (We entrust ourselves to a bus driver without worrying that he will intentionally involve us in an accident, because we have inferred, by generalizing from past experience, that he won't. Such examples could be multiplied *ad nauseam*.) It therefore behooves us to consider it carefully.

If we formalize the argument, it seems to come down to the following:

(1) In a generalization we argue from the fact that $n\%$ of the A's in the sample are B's to the conclusion that $n \pm a\%$ of the A's in the population are B's.

(2) This argument is sound only if we have some reason to believe that the whole population is like the sample.

(3) However, we don't have that information; we couldn't have it unless we already knew what percentage of the A's in the population are also B's. If we knew that, we wouldn't have to bother with a generalization to find it out.

(4) Therefore, the generalization is not sound, and it makes no difference how large or varied the sample is.

The key steps, of course, are (2) and (3). Some have challenged step (2). They claim that if we have reason to believe that the population is like the sample, we would have a valid deductive argument to prove our conclusion; but if we don't have such reasons, it only follows that we don't have such a deductive argument. It does not follow that we don't have a sound argument for the truth of the conclusion. According to this challenge to step (2), then, the skeptical argument fails, because it insists that the only sound argument for a conclusion is a valid argument proving the truth of the conclusion.

One thing is certainly right about this objection: there is a difference between a sound argument and a valid argument, and the fact that we must know that something is true in order to have a valid deductive argument to prove a conclusion does not mean that we must know it is true in order to have a sound argument for the conclusion. Nevertheless, this is not sufficient to meet the skeptical challenge, for the skeptic can always reply: I grant I have not proved that you must know that the population is like the sample in order to have a sound argument for the conclusion that $n \pm a\%$ of the A's in the total population are also B's. That does not follow, as you righly point out, from the fact that you must know that the population is like the sample in order to have a valid argument to prove that conclusion true. Nevertheless, if you don't know that the population is like the sample, why does knowledge about the sample give you good reasons for your beliefs about the population? As long as that question remains unanswered, we still ought to be skeptical about generalizations.

This reply of the skeptics can also be put as follows: The issue before us is whether knowledge about a sample gives us good reasons to believe certain conclusions about the whole population. There is no doubt that it would if we also had good reasons to believe that the population is like the sample. It may do so, as the objector to step (2) points out, even if we don't know that the population is like the sample. But then again it may not, and until we are shown that it does provide us with good reasons for beliefs about the whole population, we ought to be skeptical about the process of generalization and about conclusions based upon generalizations.

Other critics of this skeptical argument have challenged step (3). They agree we cannot know that the population is like the sample by comparing the two to see whether the same percentage of the A's in each are also B's. After all, if we could do that, then we would already know what percentage of the A's in the total population are also B's, and we wouldn't need to make any generalization to find that out. But, they claim, there are other ways of knowing that the population is like the sample. We could know that this was so, not by a comparison of the two in each particular case, but by virtue of our knowledge of a general correspondence in the world between samples and populations. In other words, there is a principle which we know to be true—often called the *principle of the uniformity of nature*—that says that all (most, some) populations resemble all (most, some) samples drawn from them; and because we know that this principle is true, we have good reasons for believing, on the basis of the sample, certain general claims about the entire population.

What would such a principle be like? It surely is not the principle that:

(a) every population is like every sample drawn from it.

For we all know that populations are usually not like mismatched samples, biased samples, or insignificant samples. It isn't even true that:

(b) every population is like every significantly large sample drawn from it by a method that works.

For if our rejection point is 19 to 1, then we in effect concede that, even with our significantly large sample drawn by a method that works, we will be wrong in supposing that the population is like the sample once every 20 times. So perhaps the most plausible principle of the uniformity of nature would be something like:

(c) every population is like most significantly large samples drawn from it by a method that works.

We can therefore reformulate this objection to step (3) as follows. We are not certain that the population will resemble the sample, even though the sample is large enough and though it was chosen by a method that works. But our principle of the uniformity of nature tells us that, in most such cases, the population does resemble the sample. So that gives us good, though not conclusive, reasons for supposing that the population will be like the sample in the case in question. Therefore, our knowledge of the sample gives us good reasons for holding certain beliefs about the population, and our generalizations are sound.

This is a powerful objection to step (3), but it is not entirely satisfactory. For what proof have we for supposing that the principle of the uniformity of nature, even in the plausible form of (c), is true? Indeed, the skeptic can give us good reasons for doubting the possibility of ever coming to know that (c) is true. After all, (c) is of the form 'all A's are B's' (where 'A' is the property of being a population and 'B' the property of resembling most significantly large samples drawn by a method that works). And like all statements of that form, the usual way of coming to know that (c) is true is by sampling the population of A's—that is, by drawing a generalization from what one observes in a sample. But this means that we are in trouble. To know that (c) is true, we must generalize from a sample. But to be justified in doing that, we must know that (c) is true. We are in a vicious circle; we will never come to know that (c) is true, and therefore the challenge to step (3) fails.

Where do we stand? Well, unless we can find some other way of coming to know that (c) is true, we cannot challenge step (3). Furthermore, our challenge to step (2) has already failed. Since these were the only two questionable steps, it looks as though the skeptic has succeeded in his argument.

This is an untenable position. We have an argument for something (skepticism about generalizations) that seems conclusive, and yet we are not convinced. We all tend to think that, despite the powerful skeptical argument, some generalizations are sound. But does our belief indicate a logically developed suspicion of skeptical arguments or simply a basic need to be able to make and believe certain assumptions? This question is left for each of us to answer as best he can.

EXERCISES FOR CHAPTER 8

Part I

A. Which of the following inferences are generalizations? Why aren't the other ones generalizations?

1. 80% of American bachelors read *Playboy;* therefore, 80% of the bachelors in our class read it.
2. 80% of the bachelors in our class read *Playboy;* therefore, 80% of the bachelors in the other class read it.
3. 80% of American bachelors read *Playboy;* therefore, 80% of European bachelors read it.
4. 80% of American bachelors read *Playboy;* therefore, 80% of all bachelors read it.
5. 80% of all bachelors read *Playboy;* therefore, 80% of all Americans read it.

B. Which of the following conclusions could, if true, actually be established by use of a generalization by complete enumeration. Which cannot? Explain why in each case.

1. All the coins in my pocket are nickels.
2. The next coin I will take out of my pocket is a nickel.
3. All coins are nickels.
4. The next coin that everyone in this room takes out of his pocket will be a nickel.
5. The next coin that everyone takes out of his pocket will be a nickel.
6. All American presidents are male.
7. All living American Presidents are males.
8. All past American Presidents are males.
9. All planets have elliptical orbits.
10. All planets of our sun have elliptical orbits.

C. Which of the following inferences (none of which are valid) are sound? Why are they sound?

1. I see a table in front of me and there are no special circumstances that typically cause perceptual illusions; therefore, there is a table in front of me.
2. 80% of all teenagers like *XYZ* toothpaste; therefore, my teenage nephew John does.
3. The color of that book is like the color of the book I saw last week; therefore, it probably is that book.
4. Fires can be caused by people carelessly disposing of matches; therefore, this fire was caused by a match carelessly disposed of.
5. I feel a pain very much like those I felt some time ago when I had a toothache; therefore, I have a toothache.
6. I remember hearing you say that, and you say that you did; therefore, you did say it.
7. The newspaper says that it happened; it happened.

8. A lot of girls dye their hair; therefore, Sally will do it as well.

9. I see a man across the street; therefore, there is a man across the street.

10. Accidents can be caused by a drunken driver losing control of his car, and the driver of the red car was drunk; therefore, this accident was caused by his losing control of his car.

D. If you are sampling by matching, from which groups should you take at least some members of your sample if you were testing the following hypotheses? In each case, justify your answer.

1. 80% of the students in this class read a newspaper daily.
2. 60% of American students oppose the war in Vietnam.
3. 90% of the people on welfare are lazy.
4. 70% of practicing Catholics use birth control.
5. 80% of all adults think that students are trouble makers.
6. 50% of all policemen hate students.
7. 90% of college presidents are business stooges.
8. 60% of all men are trying to oppress women.
9. 20% of all husbands do not cheat on their wives.
10. 90% of logic students are brilliant thinkers.

E. None of the following generalizations are sound. In each case, explain why.

1. Everyone I met today is angry at the President; so the whole country must be.

2. In the last three years, 70% of people writing letters to the *New York Times* were against the war in Vietnam; so 70% of the country must be.

3. We ran a poll in my home town, and 90% of the town favors the President; so he must be a very popular President.

4. We've polled a large sample of people randomly chosen from the list of homeowners in America, and 70% are opposed to increased welfare payments; so 70% of America must be opposed to them.

5. 35% of the voters in this state voted for immediate withdrawal from Vietnam; so 35% of this state must be for immediate withdrawal.

6. 80% of a randomly drawn sample of Americans who responded to our questions were strongly for or against the war in Vietnam; so 80% of Americans must have strong feelings on the matter.

F. For each of the following hypotheses, there is some evidence, independent of any evidence from samples, that supports either it or its denial. In each case indicate what this independent evidence is and why it supports the hypothesis or its denial:

1. All men are immortal.
2. Australia is colder in June than in December.
3. There is a good deal of silicon on Mars.
4. The moon is made of green cheese.
5. We'll have a few bad snowfalls this winter.
6. All additional works of Beethoven that will be discussed will be of high quality.

7. A good percentage of books you will read in the next few years will be for your courses.

8. 40 % of the students in the class cannot read.

G. Assess the strength of the following arguments by analogy:

1. Most people who read *Gone With the Wind* liked it; most people would probably like other novels about the South in the Civil War.

2. Millions of children like *Sesame Street;* they would probably like other educational programs.

3. The last seven quiz shows on television were failures; the next one will also be a failure.

4. Most of Neil Simon's comedies are great successes; the next one will probably also be a success.

5. A majority of Americans are sorry we entered Vietnam; a majority would therefore be sorry if we got involved in another war.

6. A majority of Americans voted Democratic in 1970; a majority will vote Democratic in 1972.

7. A Conservative won in New York in 1970; a Conservative will win there in 1972.

8. Most Americans have in the past opposed measures that sound like Socialism; most will oppose socialized medicine if it is proposed now.

H. Does the validity of each of the following arguments, if it is valid, depend upon the truth of the converse consequence principle for evidence from samples or the truth of the special consequence principle for evidence from samples?

1. There is evidence from samples that all men are sometimes worried about their masculinity; therefore, there is also such evidence that your male relatives are worried.

2. There is evidence from samples that everyone loves someone; therefore, there is also such evidence that everyone loves everyone.

3. There is evidence from samples that everyone loves someone; therefore, there is also such evidence that everyone is loved by someone.

4. There is evidence from samples that all men are sometimes worried about their masculinity; therefore, there is also such evidence that some men are always worried.

5. There is evidence from samples that all men are sometimes worried about their masculinity; therefore, there is also such evidence that all men are always worried.

Part II

1. We have seen that sound, nonvalid inferences are not, in certain ways, as satisfactory as valid inferences. In what ways are they more satisfactory?

2. What is wrong with the following claim: There are some generalizations that are not generalizations by complete enumeration but that are still

valid. After all, if we examine thousands of ravens under all types of conditions and they are all black, it must be the case that they are all black. So the generalization from the description of our sample to our claim about the population is valid.

3. Critically evaluate the following objections to current political pollsters:
   (a) We cannot have any confidence in their results, because out of the whole population of America, they test only a few thousand people.
   (b) We cannot have any confidence in their results, because they have been wrong in the past.
   (c) We cannot have any confidence in their results, because there are many groups (with small membership—say, a few thousand in each) with special views none of whose members are polled.

4. What factors should lead us to choose a higher rejection point? What factors should lead us to choose a lower rejection point?

5. Consider the following argument: Let us imagine that we choose our sample by a random method and that the sample is large enough. In some cases, contrary to what was claimed in the text, the generalization to the population will still be unsound. This will be so in the not-too-frequent cases in which we get, by our random selection process, a sample that is clearly not properly varied.

6. Invent a variety of methods for randomly choosing samples from a given population.

7. What reasons are there for belief in the truth of the converse consequence principle and the special consequence principle? We have seen that they cannot both be true. In light of your answer to the first part of this question, which do you think is false? Are either of them true?

8. Consider the following reply to the skeptic about generalizations: People have been making generalizations for a long time and they have had great success with them. The method of making generalizations works; therefore, we should not be skeptical about it. Is this reply satisfactory?

9. Consider the following reply to the skeptic: You have shown that I have no reason to believe in the uniformity of nature. But there is also no reason to believe that nature is *not* uniform. Therefore, there is no reason to prefer skepticism over belief in generalizations. This reply rests upon a serious confusion. What is it?

CHAPTER
9

Causality
and Causal Knowledge

When some event has occurred, we often want to know what other event caused it to happen. Sometimes, but not usually, this is simply a matter of intellectual curiosity. We may want to know what event e_1 caused the event e_2 to happen so that by bringing about an event like e_1, we can make an event like e_2 happen again. Thus, if one wanted to produce a revolution, one might enquire about the cause of previous revolutions so as to bring about, by repeating such causes, a new revolution. Or one could use the same information in the opposite way. If one wanted to prevent a new revolution one would try to prevent the occurrence of events similar to those which caused earlier revolutions. More generally, one might want to know what event e_1 caused the event e_2 to happen in order to prevent the future occurrence of events like e_2 by eliminating the future occurrence of events like e_1. We have, therefore, two cases in which the search for causal knowledge—for knowledge of what caused a particular event to occur—is motivated by a desire to influence the course of future events.

This is not the only practical reason for seeking the cause of the occurrence of a particular event. We sometimes engage in this search to assess responsibility for the occurrence of the event so that we can reward or punish the appropriate individuals. Thus, we may want to know whether it was Joe's action or Frank's action that produced the automobile accident, because we want to know who should pay for the resulting damages. Of course, there is more to assessing responsibility than this. Even if Joe's action caused the event to occur, Joe may not be responsible; he may have a legitimate excuse that frees him from responsibility. Nevertheless, the first step in assessing responsibility is finding out whose action caused the event to occur.

Given all these practical needs for causal knowledge, it is not surprising that we are often called upon to make *causal judgments*, judgments of the form 'e_1 caused e_2'. This does not mean, however, that the logic of these judgments is particularly clear. In this chapter we shall see that it is very difficult to explain what such a judgment means, and that it is equally difficult to state the conditions under which we can soundly infer from some evidence that e_1 caused e_2.

9.1 Necessary and Sufficient Conditions and the Regularity Theory of Causality

Before turning directly to our problem, we should introduce some helpful philosophical terminology. We shall say that the occurrence of an event e_1 is a *sufficient condition* for the occurrence of an event e_2 when the following conditions are satisfied:

1. e_2 occurs shortly after e_1
2. e_1 is of a type E_1; e_2 is of a type E_2
3. every occurrence of an event of type E_1 is followed shortly thereafter by an occurrence of an event of type E_2. (This can be stated as: E_1's are sufficient for E_2's.)

We shall say that the occurrence of an event e_1 is a *necessary condition* for the occurrence of an event e_2 when the following conditions are satisfied:

1. e_1 occurs shortly before e_2
2. e_1 is of a type E_1; e_2 is of a type E_2
3. every occurrence of an event of type E_2 is preceded shortly before by an occurrence of an event of type E_1. (This can be stated as: E_1's are necessary for E_2's.)

To clarify these concepts, let us imagine that there have been only four occurrences of those types of events in the following order (where the events in parentheses occurred shortly before or after each other): (E_1^*, E_2), $(E_1, E_2)^*$. In this case events of type E_1 are both sufficient and necessary for the occurrence of events of type E_2, since both E_1's are followed shortly afterward by an E_2, and both E_2's are preceded shortly before by an E_1. On the other hand, events of type E_2 are neither sufficient nor necessary for the occurrence of events of type E_1, since there is an E_2^* (the second one) not followed by an E_1, and an E_1 (the first one) not preceded by an E_2.

The situation is very different in the following case: (E_2, E_1), (E_1, E_2). In this case events of neither type are either sufficient or necessary for the occurrence of events of the other type. There is an E_1 (the first one), not followed shortly afterward by an E_2, and an E_2 (the second one) not followed shortly afterward by an E_1. Similarly, there is an E_1 (the second one) not immediately preceded by an E_2, and an E_2 (the first one) not immediately preceded by an E_1.

We now take up one final point about our definition of necessary and sufficient conditions. As we have defined these notions, the occurrence of a particular event is necessary or sufficient for the occurrence of another event because of some general relation between a type of event to which one belongs and a type to which the other belongs. But particular events belong to many different types. Thus, a particular event e_1, such as the French Revolution, belongs to the type revolution (E_a), the type event that occurred in 1789 (E_b), the type famous historical event (E_c), etc. Similarly, another event e_2, such as Louis XVI's negative response to the demands for moderate reforms, belongs to many types—actions of kings (E_1), refusals of kings to meet legitimate demands (E_2), and so on. Thus, even if we only want to know whether Louis XVI's negative response to the demands for moderate reform was a necessary and/or sufficient condition for the occurrence of the French Revolution, we must find out whether E_1's are always followed shortly thereafter by E_a's, E_b's, and so on, and whether E_2's are always followed shortly thereafter by E_a's, E_b's, and so on. In other words, answering such a question is not easy.

What has all this to do with causal judgments? As the last example may have suggested, many philosophers think that judgments of the form 'e_1 causes e_2' are equivalent to judgments of the form 'e_1 is a necessary condition for e_2', or 'e_1 is a sufficient condition for e_2', or 'e_1 is both a necessary and a sufficient condition for the occurrence of e_2'. That is to say, many philosophers think that causality is the same relation as necessary conditionhood, or sufficient conditionhood, or some combination of the two. And since these relations are based upon the regular occurrence of certain patterns of events, these theories are called the *regularity theories of causality*.

It is easy to see what intuitions led to the suggestion of such a theory. When we say that e_1 caused e_2, we certainly seem at least to be suggesting that it was because of e_1 that e_2 occurred, and that e_2 would not have occurred unless e_1 had occurred. But what does that last statement mean? One simple suggestion is that e_2 is of a type of event such that it does not occur unless an event of another type (of which e_1 is a member) has occurred first; that is, e_1 is a necessary condition for the occurrence of e_2. Similarly, when we say that e_1 caused e_2, we certainly seem to be suggesting that e_1 made e_2 happen, that once e_1 occurred, e_2 had to occur. But what does that last statement mean? One obvious suggestion is that e_1 is of a type of event such that when they occur, an event of a certain other type (of which e_2 is a member) always occurs shortly afterward; that is, e_1 is a sufficient condition for the occurrence of e_2.

The preceding remarks were not meant as arguments for the truth of one of the regularity theories but merely as intuitive motivations for such theories. These motivations are reinforced by another very powerful advantage of the regularity theories: these theories give a simple account of the soundness of inferences to the conclusion that e_1 is the cause of e_2. If one of the regularity theories is true, then one of the following inferences will be valid:

NECESSITY REGULARITY THEORY

> e_1 occurred shortly before e_2.
> e_1 is an event of type E_1.
> e_2 is an event of type E_2.
> E_1's are necessary for E_2's.
> _____
> e_1 caused e_2.

SUFFICIENCY REGULARITY THEORY

> e_1 occurred shortly before e_2.
> e_1 is an event of type E_1.
> e_2 is an event of type E_2.
> E_1's are sufficient for E_2's.
> _____
> e_1 caused e_2.

NECESSITY AND SUFFICIENCY REGULARITY THEORY

> e_1 is an event of type E_1.
> e_2 is an event of type E_2.
> e_1 occurred shortly before e_2.
> E_1's are necessary and sufficient for E_2's.
> _____
> e_1 caused e_2.

Moreover, it is easy to see how we could establish the truth of all the premises. The first three can be established merely by examining e_1 and e_2. The last premise is of the form '100% of the A's are B's', and can be established by the method of sampling discussed in Chapter 8. So, given the truth of one of the regularity theories of causality, we can see how to establish the truth of our causal judgments. This is a definite advantage of such a theory.

9.2 Mill's Methods

So far we have considered the question of from what premises we can soundly infer, according to the regularity theory, the conclusion that e_1 caused e_2. But, when we first inquire about the cause of an event e_2, we are not yet in a position to collect evidence for a hypothesis such as e_1 caused e_2. We first need a hypothesis. We can, of course, think up any hypothesis we want and try to collect evidence for it. However, that task would soon become wearisome. It would be much better if we could find a method of investigation that suggests likely hypotheses about the cause of e_2. We could then check these hypotheses (and perhaps even soundly infer the truth of one of them) by the methods described in section 9.1.

Such a method of investigation, based upon the regularity theory of causality, is known as *Mill's method*, after the nineteenth-century philosopher John Stuart Mill, who first suggested a version of it. This method is governed by several rules, which we shall now examine singly.

The first rule is the *canon of agreement*, which says that if we want to find the cause of an event e_2 of type E_2, we should look at several occurrences of events of type E_2; if we discover that the only thing that they have in common is that they are preceded by an event of type E_1, we should suggest as a hypothesis that the cause of e_2 was the event e_1 of type E_1 that preceded e_2. For example, let us suppose that we want to discover the cause of a sudden increase in the rate of inflation in a given year. The canon of agreement tells us to look at a variety of other cases of sudden increases in the rate of inflation as well. If we discover that the only thing all these cases have in common is that they were all preceded by a sharp increase in the government's budgetary deficit, we should, according to our canon, suggest as a hypothesis that the cause of the present sudden increase in the rate of inflation is the increase in the government's spending deficit that preceded it.

This is obviously a perfectly reasonable way of proceeding, but what is the rationale behind it? If we suppose that causes are necessary conditions, the rationale is apparent. By discovering that the only thing that the E_2's have in common is that they are preceded by E_1's, we have shown that only E_1's could be necessary for E_2's. This makes it plausible that the event e_1 of type E_1 that preceded e_2 was a necessary condition for the occurrence of e_2; that is, according to the regularity theory, it was the cause of e_2.

Although this is a reasonable way of proceeding to find a plausible hypothesis about the cause of e_2, it would not be a sound inference if one were to infer from the observations in question that e_1 is the cause of e_2 or even that e_1 is a necessary condition for the occurrence of e_2. Such an inference would be of the form:

e_1 is of type E_1.
e_2 is of type E_2.
The only thing that precedes all the E_2's that we have observed is an event of type E_1.
e_1 occurs shortly before e_2.

---

e_1 is a necessary condition for the occurrence of e_2, i.e., according to one regularity theory, e_1 is the cause of e_2.

Unquestionably, we could have inferred soundly from the third premise that only E_1's could be necessary for E_2's, but this does not mean that we could soundly infer that they are (and that, therefore, e_1 is necessary for the occurrence of e_2). Whether we can depends, as we saw in Chapter 8, upon whether the sample of E_2's observed is large enough and was chosen by a method that works.

However, this should not bother us. In following the canon of agreement, we were simply trying to find a plausible hypothesis for the cause of e_2. Once we have that hypothesis, it is easy enough to check its truth by use of the sampling method.

We should adopt the same approach toward our second rule, the *canon of difference*, which says that if we want to find the cause of an event e_2 of type E_2, we should look at circumstances which are similar to those surrounding the occurrence of e_2 but in which an event of type E_2 did not occur. If we find one identical with the circumstances surrounding the occurrence of e_2 except that in the circumstances surrounding e_2 there was an event e_1 of type E_1 but that in the other circumstances there was no event of type E_1, we suggest as a hypothesis that the cause of e_2 was e_1. For example, imagine that we want to discover the cause of a senator's voting a certain way on a bill. The canon of difference tells us to look at very similar circumstances in which he voted the opposite way but in which the two circumstances are identical except for one factor. Let us imagine that the Senate had voted on the bill a day earlier, that the senator had voted the other way, and that the only thing different in the two cases was that before the second vote the President had promised the senator he would campaign for the senator's re-election if he changed his vote. If we discover this, then according to the canon of difference, we should suggest as a hypothesis that the President's promise caused the senator to vote the other way.

This procedure is certainly reasonable; but what is the rationale behind it? If we suppose that causes are sufficient conditions, the rationale is apparent. Of all the types of events such that one event of that type occurred before e_2, only E_1's can be sufficient for E_2's. The rest cannot, because an event of each of those types occurred in the similar circumstances in which no event of type E_2 occurred. This makes it plausible that the event e_1 of type E_1 was the cause of e_2.

Although this is a reasonable way of proceeding to find a plausible hypothesis about the cause of e_2, it would not be a sound inference if one were to infer from the observations in question that e_1 is the cause of e_2 or even that e_1 is a sufficient condition for the occurrence of e_2. Such an inference would be of the form:

> e_1 occurred shortly before e_2.
> e_1 is of type E_1.
> e_2 is of type E_2.
> There are circumstances C_a in which no event of type E_2 occurred and which are otherwise exactly like the circumstances in which e_2 occurred, except that no event of type E_1 occurred in them.
>
> ---
>
> e_1 is a sufficient condition for the occurrence of e_2, i.e., according to one regularity theory, e_1 is the cause of e_2.

Unquestionably, we could have inferred soundly from the fourth premise that, considering only those types of events an instance of which occurred shortly before e_2, only E_1's could be sufficient for E_2's. But that does not mean that we could soundly infer that they are (and that, therefore, e_1 is sufficient for the occurrence of e_2). We could soundly infer this only from the observation of a large enough sample of E_1's, chosen by a method that works, that are all followed by E_2's.

Once more, however, the fact that this inference is not sound should not bother us. In following the canon of difference, we were simply trying to find a plausible hypothesis for what caused e_2. Once we have that hypothesis, it is easy enough to check its truth by use of the sampling method.

A third canon is the *joint canon of agreement and difference*. It simply tells you to do what one and then the other of the canons tells you to, and if each of these operations suggests that the same e_1 is the cause of e_2, to advance as plausible the hypothesis that e_1 is the cause of e_2. It is easy to see the rationale for such a procedure even on the most demanding version of the regularity theory—the one requiring causes to be both necessary and sufficient conditions.

The canons, as we have stated them so far, are a bit unrealistic. When do we ever find several cases of an occurrence of type E_2 having only one thing in common? There will always be many other (what we would think of as irrelevant) traits that they share. And when do we ever find two sets of circumstances exactly alike except in one respect? There will be many other (what we would think of as irrelevant) respects in which they differ. Thus, returning to our examples, we see it is highly like that, in addition to being preceded by a sharp increase in the government's budgetary deficit, all the examined increases in the rate of inflation took place on earth. And, in our example of the senator, the circumstances surrounding the two votes differ, in addition to the fact that only one was preceded by the presidential promise, in that they took place at different times.

Obviously, we want to modify our canons so that, in the canon of agreement, 'the only thing they have in common' would be replaced by 'the only relevant thing they have in common', and, in the canon of difference, 'exactly alike' would be replaced by 'exactly alike in all relevant respects'. But what does 'relevant' mean here? Roughly, something is relevant in this context if its presence or absence could be necessary or sufficient for the occurrence of the event for whose cause we are searching. Thus, if we are to use these canons, we must approach the search for the cause with an idea of the possible candidates and of what can be disregarded. How we obtain this knowledge, and how exactly we use it, are difficult problems that we need not consider now.

There is one other, but very different, canon that Mill suggested, which can only be followed in connection with certain types of events. Some events occur to different extents, whereas others do not. Thus the landing of men on Mars in the 1970s will either occur or not occur, but the decrease in the rate of inflation in one year can either not occur or occur to many different degrees, depending upon the extent of the decrease. (We shall not attempt here to give a formal account of this distinction.) This *canon of concomitant variation*, deals only with events that occur to a greater or lesser degree. It says that if we want to find the cause of an event e_2 of type E_2, we should look at a variety of events of type E_2 that occurred in different degrees. Then, if we find that each was preceded by an event of type E_1 and that the extent to which the event of type E_1 occurred was directly proportional to the extent to which the event of type E_2 occurred, we should advance as a plausible hypothesis that the cause of e_2 was the event e_1 of type E_1 that occurred shortly before e_2. Let us return once more to our example of the sudden increase in the rate of inflation. If we examine it and other increases and discover that they were all preceded by an increase in the government's budgetary deficit, and that the greater the increase in the deficit, the greater the increase in the rate of inflation, then, according to the canon of concomitant variation, it would be plausible to advance the hypothesis that the cause of the increase in the rate of inflation with which we are concerned is the increase in the government's budgetary deficit shortly preceding the increased inflation.

This is, once more, a perfectly reasonable way of proceeding. But what is the rationale behind it? If you think that causes are necessary conditions, you would argue that all the E_2's that we have examined are preceded a short time before by E_1's; thus E_1's could be necessary for E_2's. Of course, other things may have preceded all the E_2's, and it may be they, and not E_1's, which are necessary for E_2's. But E_1's are probably necessary, and their occurrence is to a greater extent necessary for the occurrence of an E_2 to a greater extent, since this assumption provides a good explanation of the observed concomitant variation. Therefore, advance as a plausible hypothesis that e_1 caused e_2.

Once more, although this is a reasonable way of proceeding to find a plausible hypothesis about the cause of e_2, one could not soundly infer from the observations in question either that E_1's are necessary for E_2's or that the occurrence of an E_1 to a greater extent is necessary for the occurrence of an E_2 to a greater extent, and one certainly could not soundly infer that e_1 caused e_2. The trouble is familiar by now: in following the canon, we normally will not have chosen our sample by a method that works, and our sample will not normally be large enough. But, of course, that should not bother us. In following the canon of concomitant variation, we were simply trying to find a plausible hypothesis for what caused e_2. Once we have that hypothesis, it is easy enough to check its truth by use of the sampling method.

9.3 Shortcomings of the Regularity Theory

In the last two sections we have constructed a theory about the way to discover causal hypotheses and about the soundness of inferences to their truth. This theory was based upon the regularity theory of causality, and the fact that such a reasonable and elegant theory could be constructed using it as its basis certainly counts in favor of the truth of the regularity theory.

However, we cannot leave things as they are. Unfortunately, the regularity theory is open to many serious objections that force us at least to modify it. In doing so, however, we will also be forced to modify our theory of discovering, and inferring the truth of, causal hypotheses.

Two major types of objections have been raised against the regularity theories. The first argues that we cannot explain causality in terms of de facto regularities. The second argues that causes are neither necessary nor sufficient for their effects. Let us look at each of these objections.

What was the intuitive motivation for the regularity theories? In section 9.1 we saw that they were attempts to explain what it meant to say that the effect would not have occurred if the cause had not occurred and that if the cause occurred the effect had to occur. According to the regularity theories, this means that events like the effect are always, as a matter of fact, preceded, a short time before, by other events like the cause, and events like the cause are always, as a matter of fact, followed shortly thereafter by other events like the effect. In other words, the regularity theories explain the necessities involved in causality by appeal to matter-of-fact, de facto regularities. It is just this feature of regularity theories that is criticized by the first set of objections. They claim that there is something more to the necessities involved in causality than mere de facto regularities.

The proponents of such a claim usually begin their argument by presenting a few examples. Consider, as one example, the case in which whenever (and only when) the twelve-o'clock lunch bell rings in one factory, all the workers in another factory stop work and prepare for lunch. We will call the former type of event E_1 and the latter type E_2. Now, imagine that one day someone inquires as to the cause of the workers' stopping work that day at the second factory at twelve o'clock (e_2). He is told that it is the ringing of the lunch bell just before then at the other factory (e_1). We would all, presumably, laugh at such an answer; however, it seems to be correct according to all regularity theories. For e_1 is of a type (E_1) and e_2 of a type (E_2) such that E_1's are necessary and sufficient for E_2's; that is, E_1's are, as a matter of fact, always followed shortly thereafter by E_2's, and E_2's are, as a matter of fact, always preceded shortly before by E_1's. So according to the regularity theory, e_1 is the cause of e_2, which is clearly wrong. The trouble, of course, is due to the fact that the regularity theory requires merely that there be a de facto regularity between E_1's and E_2's.

In this first counterexample to the regularity theory, we had two events regularly related to each other but only by accident. Another type of counterexample can be raised from the relation between an indicator and the event it indicates. For example, consider the rain falling around my house now, as I write this sentence. What is the cause of this rainfall (e_2)? We would normally reject the answer that it was caused by the fall of my barometer some hours ago (e_1). We would say that e_1 indicates the imminent occurrence of e_2, but does not cause it to occur. But should we say this according to the regularity theory? After all, e_1 is of a type E_1 (certain types of falls in barometric readings), and e_2 is of a type E_2 (rainfalls in areas where there are working barometers), such that, as a matter of fact, E_1's are always followed shortly thereafter by E_2's and E_2's are always preceded shortly before by E_1's; that is, e_1 is necessary and sufficient for e_2. So according to all regularity theories, we must conclude that the fall of the barometer is the cause, as well as the indicator, of the rainfall. Once more, the regularity theory involves these false claims because it supposes that all that is required is a de facto regular relation between E_1's and E_2's.

On the basis of these examples, we can conclude that the regularity of the relation between E_1's and E_2's must be something more than de facto. What this something more is we will consider in the next section. We now want to look at the second set of criticisms, the claims that causes are not really either necessary or sufficient conditions.

The claim that causes are necessary conditions runs into trouble because of the existence of those types of events that can be caused by more than one type of event. Schematically, what happens is this: E_2's can be caused by E_1's (even if an E_1' has not occurred recently) or by E_1''s (even if an E_1 has not occurred recently). Now we have an event e_2 of type E_2 that was preceded shortly before both by an event e_1 of type E_1 and by an event e_1' of type E_1'. Both these earlier events could have caused e_2; how we decide which one did is a difficult issue that we need not fully enter into now. However, we have to say that causes are not necessary conditions, since neither of these events is necessary: e_1 is not, for there are cases of E_2's (some of the ones caused by E_1''s) not preceded by E_1's, and e_1' is not, for there are cases of E_2's (some of the ones caused by E_1's) not preceded by E_1''s.

The following is a good example of this sort of phenomenon. A television may stop working for any one of a large number of reasons; that is, there are many types of events that can cause a television to stop working. But none of these are necessary for a television to stop working. Imagine that your television stopped working and that events of several of these other types (say, a tube blowing and an electrical connection being disrupted) had occurred immediately before. One of these events caused your set to stop working; we leave aside for now the issue of which one. But none of these events are necessary for your television to stop working. So causes are not necessary conditions.

The claim that causes are sufficient conditions has been objected to on the basis of a very different type of consideration—that causes do not produce their effects unless certain other conditions are present. Schematically, the objection runs as follows: When an event e_1 of type E_1 causes an event e_2 of E_2, it does so only because certain additional conditions, C_1, C_2, ..., are present. When they are not present, then an E_1 can occur without being followed by (because it caused) the occurrence of an E_2. So e_1 is the cause of e_2, although E_1's are not sufficient for E_2's; therefore, causes are not sufficient conditions.

If we look once more at our instance of the sudden increase in the rate of inflation, we can see a good example of this type of problem. We wanted to say that the increase was caused by an increase in the government's budgetary deficit, but it is simply not true that every increase in the government's budgetary deficit is followed shortly thereafter by an increase in the rate of inflation. It probably will not be so if price controls are strictly enforced, or if the supply of money is decreased, and so on. Thus, the increase in the budgetary deficit is not sufficient for the increase in the rise of the rate of inflation, but it is the cause of it. Therefore, causes are not sufficient conditions.

It is often felt that these arguments show that causes are neither necessary nor sufficient for their effects, but this interpretation is a mistake; the arguments are not really valid. The argument that causes are not necessary really came down to:

(1) e_1 is of type E_1, e_1' is of type E_1', and e_2 is of type E_2.
(2) Neither E_1's nor E_1'''s are necessary for E_2's.
(3) Therefore, neither e_1 nor e_1' is necessary for e_2.
(4) But one of them is the cause of e_2.

_____

(5) There are causes that are not necessary conditions.

The argument is not valid, because (3) does not follow from (1) and (2). For (1) and (2) can be true and (3) still be false if there is some class of events E_1^* such that all E_1's and E_1''s belong to it and such that E_1^*'s are necessary for E_2's. In our example of the television set's not working, the E_1^* might be something like the class of events that are disruptions of one of the essential structural features of a television set (where that notion is independently defined). A very similar thing happens with the argument that causes are not sufficient for their effects. That argument really came down to:

(1) e_1 is of type E_1 and e_2 is of type E_2.
(2) But E_1's are not sufficient for E_2's.
(3) Therefore, e_1 is not sufficient for e_2.
(4) But e_1 is the cause of e_2.

_____

(5) There are causes that are not sufficient conditions.

Once more, (3) does not follow from (1) and (2). For (1) and (2) can be true and (3) still false if e_1 belongs to some other type E_1^* such that E_1^*'s are sufficient for E_2's. The most obvious class of events that could be the E_1^*'s is the class of E_1 events that occur under conditions $C_1, C_2, \ldots$ (where they are the conditions that must be present in order that an event of type E_1 can cause an event of type E_2). In our example of the increase in the rate of inflation, E_1^* might be something like the class of increases in the government's budgetary deficits not accompanied by strict price controls, or the decrease in the money supply.

    We conclude, therefore, that although there are good reasons, because of the problem with mere de facto regularities, to suppose that necessary and sufficient conditions are not necessarily causes, we can continue to suppose that causes are necessary and/or sufficient conditions. The first half of this conclusion, however, is enough to make us modify our definition of causality. We shall see in the next section that this already requires some change in our account of how we soundly infer hypotheses of the form 'e_1 causes e_2', and of how we discover such hypotheses.

9.4 A More Plausible Account of Causal Inference

Let us begin our attempt to solve the problems raised in section 9.3 by reconsidering the problem of merely de facto regularities. Why do we suppose that the ringing of the lunch bell at one factory does not cause the workers to stop working at the second factory? Partly, it is because we can explain the regular relation between these two kinds of events without supposing that events of one kind cause events of the other. The bell rings at one factory at twelve o'clock. This is the lunch time of the workers at the second factory, which is why they stop working. Given this explanation, we can, imagine hypothetical circumstances in which the regular relation no longer holds. For example, if the workers at the second factory were to start taking their lunch at twelve-thirty, the regular relation in question would no longer hold. The ringing of the lunch bell at one factory would no longer always be followed shortly afterward by the workers at the second factory stopping work, and the stopping of work in the second factory would no longer always be preceded, shortly before, by the ringing of the lunch bell at the first factory.

A very similar account could be given of our reluctance to suppose that the fall of the barometer causes the rain. We can explain the regular relation between these two kinds of events without supposing that events of one kind cause the events of the other. Instead, both the rainfall and the fall in the barometer reading result from the same atmospheric conditions. Given this explanation, we can imagine hypothetical circumstances in which the regular relation no longer holds. For example, if an unpleasant neighbor wanted to deceive me about the weather, he might make a machine which he could put near my barometer at night and which would create artificial atmospheric conditions around the barometer. Although it was working, the barometer would then give completely inaccurate indications; rainfall might be preceded by a rise in the barometric reading, and falls in barometric readings might be followed by good weather.

If we were to generalize from these two examples, we could offer the following analysis of our problem: If events of a type E_1 are, as a matter of fact, necessary and sufficient for the occurrence of events of type E_2, it may be so because E_1's cause E_2's, or it may be due to something else. If the latter is true, then there are hypothetical circumstances (ones in which the something else broke down) in which E_1's would have occurred without the occurrence, shortly thereafter, of E_2's, and/or E_2's would have occurred without the occurrence, shortly before, of E_1's.

On the basis of that analysis, we might introduce the following new account of the causal relation. We shall say that the occurrence of an event

e_1 is an *unconditionally sufficient condition* for the occurrence of an event e_2 when e_2 occurs shortly after e_1 and when e_1 is of a type E_1 and e_2 of a type E_2 such that, under all possible conditions, an occurrence of an event of type E_1 would be followed shortly thereafter by an occurrence of an event of type E_2 (we shall also say then that E_1's are unconditionally sufficient for E_2's). We shall also say that the occurrence of an event e_1 is an *unconditionally necessary condition* for the occurrence of an event e_2 if e_1 occurred shortly before e_2 and e_1 is of a type E_1 and e_2 of a type E_2 such that, under all possible conditions, an occurrence of an event of type E_2 would be preceded by the occurrence, shortly before, of an event of type E_1 (we shall also say then that E_1's are unconditionally necessary for E_2's). Given these definitions, we can then introduce our new theories of causality, the *unconditional regularity theories*, which state that judgments of the form 'e_1 causes e_2' are equivalent to judgments of the form 'e_1 is an unconditionally necessary condition for e_2', of the form 'e_1 is an unconditionally sufficient condition for e_2', or of the form 'e_1 is an unconditionally necessary and sufficient condition for e_2'.

These definitions are not entirely clear. They involve the notoriously difficult concept of all possible conditions and presuppose that we understand claims about what would be the case if . . . , as well as claims about what is the case. Nevertheless, they are clear enough for our present purposes.

How does this new definition of the causal relation affect our theory of causal inference? According to the regularity theory, you could infer that e_1 caused e_2 from the premises that e_1 was an E_1, e_2 an E_2, and that E_1's were necessary (sufficient, necessary and sufficient—depending upon which version of the regularity theory you maintained) for E_2's. The first two statements could be established by observation, and the last could be soundly inferred from a large enough sample chosen by a method that works. This was possible because the last statement said only that all members of a certain class of events have a certain property (being preceded or followed by an event of another class), which is just the type of statement that can be soundly inferred from a sample by generalization. The situation is very different, however, according to the unconditional regularity theory. According to that theory, you can infer that e_1 caused e_2 from the premises that e_1 was an E_1, e_2 an E_2, and that E_1's are unconditionally necessary (sufficient, necessary and sufficient—depending upon which version of the unconditional regularity theory you maintain) for E_2's. This last statement does not merely say, however, that all members of a certain class of events have a certain property (being preceded or followed by events of another class). It claims that all potential members of that class would have that property as well. This is a stronger conclusion than the one we can soundly infer by generalization. How do we know, then, that such stronger statements are true?

There is another way of looking at this problem. According to the unconditional regularity theory, to know that statements of the form 'e_1 caused

e_2' are true, we must know the truth of statements of the form 'E_1's are unconditionally necessary (sufficient, necessary and sufficient) for E_2's'. One might think that we could soundly infer the truth of the last type of statement from the observation that, in a large enough sample chosen by methods that work, E_2's are always preceded shortly before by E_1's (E_1's are always followed shortly thereafter by E_2's, or both). Actually, however, we are only entitled to infer from that observation that E_1's are necessary (sufficient, necessary and sufficient) for E_2's. What additional premises do we need to infer the unconditional necessity (sufficiency, necessity and sufficiency)?

One way to approach this question is to reflect further upon our reasons for rejecting the claim that the sounding of the lunch bell was unconditionally necessary and sufficient for the workers' at the other factory going to lunch. We did reject this claim—asserting that it was only necessary and sufficient—because we felt that we had a good explanation of the regular connection between the two types of events and that under certain hypothetical conditions (e.g., the changing of the lunch hour at the second factory), the regular connection would no longer obtain. This suggests the following: When we soundly infer by generalization that E_1's are necessary (sufficient, necessary and sufficient) for E_2's, we have two ways of accounting for it. One is to suppose that they are unconditionally necessary (sufficient, necessary and sufficient). The other is to suppose that the regularity is a mere de facto one that can be explained in terms of the presence of certain conditions, and that would not hold if certain other conditions were present. We would then set out to find such an alternative explanation of the regularity. If we found it, we would conclude that it was a mere de facto regularity. But if we did not, and if we have searched diligently and intelligently for it, we would soundly conclude that the regularity in question is unconditional.

More formally, we can say that the following, according to the unconditional regularity theories of causality, is the scheme of sound inferences to the truth of causal hypotheses:

(1) In a large enough sample chosen by a method that works, all E_1's were followed shortly thereafter by E_2's (all E_2's were preceded shortly before by E_1's, both of these were the case).

(2) Therefore, E_1's are sufficient (necessary, necessary and sufficient) for E_2's.

(3) After diligent and intelligent searching, we have found no explanation of this regularity which entails that it is a mere de facto regularity; therefore, our best explanation now is that it is an unconditional regularity.

(4) Therefore, E_1's are unconditionally sufficient (necessary, necessary and sufficient) for E_2's.

(5) e_1 is an E_1 and e_2 is an E_2.

(6) Therefore, e_1 caused e_2.

This is a mode of inference that we have not so far encountered. In it, we in effect infer the truth of that hypothesis which best explains what we already know to be the case. As we shall see in Chapter 10, this fundamental and fully legitimate mode of inference is used in many of our investigations.

We conclude, therefore, that according to the unconditional regularity theory of causality, we first follow one of the rules of Mill's method to determine a plausible hypothesis for what type of event E_1 is necessary and/or sufficient for the type of event E_2, to which belongs the event e_2, whose cause we want to know. We then test such hypotheses by sampling. If we infer that one such hypothesis is true, we then try to find an explanation for the regularity in question. If the best explanation is that the regularity is an unconditional one, we conclude that the event e_1 of type E_1 that preceded e_2 was the cause of e_2.

EXERCISES FOR CHAPTER 9

Part I

A. Consider the following pairs of types of events. In each case indicate which one (if either) is necessary or sufficient for the other:

1. Bearing a child—being a woman
2. Hitting very brittle glass with a hard bat—breaking the glass
3. The car moving—there being fuel in the engine
4. Doing something—wanting to do it
5. The pressure of the gas increasing while the temperature is constant—the volume of the gas decreasing
6. Striking a match—the match lighting
7. Speeding—deservedly getting a ticket for speeding

B. Show that the following E_1'''s are not necessary or sufficient for the occurrence of the corresponding E_2'''s.

E_1'''s	E_2'''s
1. Robbing a bank	Going to jail
2. Spending more than you earn	Going into debt
3. Not doing your work	Losing your job
4. Making more money	Paying more taxes
5. Getting a ticket	Paying a fine
6. Reading a book	Knowing what the book says
7. Studying for a test	Passing that test
8. Handing in a paper	The teacher's reading the paper

C. Which of the following arguments follow the canon of agreement? Explain why the others don't:

1. The butler turned on the light in his room before the fuse blew; that must have caused the fuse to blow.
2. Every time the butler turned on the light in his room, the fuse blew; that must have caused the fuse to blow.

Causality and Causal Knowledge

3. When the butler did not turn on the light in his room, the fuse did not blow; his turning on the light must therefore have caused the fuse to blow.
4. The only thing that happened every time before the fuse blew was that the butler turned on the light in his room; that must have caused the fuse to blow.
5. The budgetary deficit went up and inflation followed; the increase in the deficit caused the inflation.
6. The year after the budgetary deficit did not increase, there was little inflation; when there was an inflation, therefore, it was caused by the increase in the deficit.
7. Checking over all recent inflations, the only thing I found that they had in common was that they were preceded by an increased budgetary deficit; so it caused the inflations.
8. Every single increased budgetary deficit was followed by an inflation; the increase, therefore, caused the inflation.

D. Explain why none of the following arguments follow the canon of difference:

1. Most inflations were preceded by increased budgetary deficits and most cases of stable prices were not; so the increased budgetary deficits caused the inflation.
2. All cases of stable prices were not preceded by increased budgetary deficits; such increases therefore cause inflation.
3. All inflations are preceded by increased budgetary deficits; such increases therefore cause the inflations.
4. All inflations were preceded by increased budgetary deficits and all cases of stable prices were not; so the increased budgetary deficits caused the inflation.
5. A major difference between cases in which there were inflations and cases in which there were stable prices was that the former, but not the latter, were preceded by increased budgetary deficits; these deficits, therefore, caused the inflations.

E. Which of the following arguments follow the canon of concomitant variation? Explain why the others don't:

1. As the number of students in the course increases, the burden on the instructor increases; therefore, the increase in enrollment causes the instructor to work harder.
2. As the number of students in the course increases, the instructor works harder; therefore, the increase in enrollment causes the instructor to work harder.
3. As the number of students in the course increases, the burden on the instructor increases; therefore the increase in enrollment causes an increase of the burden.
4. As the temperature increases and the volume remains the same, the pressure of the gas increases; so the increase in temperature caused the increase in pressure.
5. As the temperature increases and the pressure increases, the volume of the

gas remains the same; so the two increases caused the volume to remain the same.

6. As the temperature decreases and the volume remains the same, the pressure of the gas decreases; so the decrease in temperature caused the decrease in pressure.

F. Which of the following connections are due to de facto regularities, which to symptom regularities, and which to causal regularities?

1. The connection between my body temperature going down and the reading on the thermometer which is used to test my temperature going down.
2. The connection between your studying for the test in a course and the student next to you studying for that same test.
3. The connection between an increase in the budgetary deficit and a rise in the rate of inflation.
4. The connection between the Dow Jones average going down and most stocks going down.
5. The connection between your crossing the street and the man on the other side crossing the street.
6. The connection between the majority of vacations ending and the summer ending.
7. The connection between the breakdown of the power plant and the lights in the city going off.
8. The connection between the traffic lights turning red and the cars stopping.
9. The connection between the newspaper saying that *Sesame Street* is on at 4:00 and its being on then.
10. The connection between my hitting the glass with the bat and the breaking of the glass.

Part II

1. In all our discussion of causality in this chapter, we have supposed that the cause must come before the effect. Why? What, if anything, is wrong with the idea that the cause occurs at the same time, or even after the effect?
2. Consider the following objection to all regularity theories of causality. The cause of its being night now is not its being day 12 hours ago. But according to all the regularity theories, it is, since these types of events succeed each other regularly. So the regularity theory is wrong. Is this a good objection? Is it a good objection to the unconditional regularity theories?
3. Of the three regularity theories of causality, which seems most plausible?
4. In the text we explained, given the view that causes are necessary conditions, the rationale for the canon of agreement and the canon of concomitant variation. Is there any rationale for this canon if causes are sufficient, but not necessary, conditions?

5. Similarly, we explained, given the view that causes are sufficient conditions, the rationale for the canon of difference. Is there any rationale for this canon if causes are necessary, but not sufficient, conditions?

6. Many people suppose that Mill's methods tell us that certain inferences to causal conclusions are sound. We did not adopt that view of them. Why not?

7. Consider the following defense of the regularity theories of causality. The main objection to the regularity theory is that it does not draw any distinction between mere de facto regularity and real causal connections. But that is no objection, since the main point of this theory is to deny the existence of this distinction and to reduce causal connections to de facto regularities. Is this defense satisfactory?

8. Is the following a valid objection to the view that every unconditionally necessary condition is a cause? John's breathing shortly beforehand is unconditionally necessary for his proposing to Mary, but it certainly is not the cause of his proposing to Mary. So the view in question is false.

9. In light of the theory of causality developed in this chapter, how would you answer the following tricky questions about causality:
   (a) I push Joe off the Empire State Building. On his way down, you shoot him. Whose action caused his death, mine or yours?
   (b) I poison the water in Joe's glass. You, not realizing that it is already poisoned, pour it out and pour in other poisoned water. Joe drinks the water and dies. Whose action caused his death?
   (c) I poison the water in Joe's glass. You, not realizing that it is already poisoned, add more poison. Joe drinks the water and dies. Whose action caused his death?
   Given your answers to these question, do you think that we have omitted, in our discussion in the text, some important considerations about causality?

Inferences to the

Best Explanation

At the end of Chapter 9, we introduced a new mode of inference, in which we infer from the description of a certain phenomenon, and from the claim that the best explanation of the phenomenon presupposes that p, the conclusion that p is true. We shall call all such inferences *inferences to the best explanation*. In this chapter we shall be concerned with the conditions under which such inferences are sound.

10.1 The Formal Structure of Inferences to the Best Explanation

Let us begin by looking at a few examples of such inferences, such as the example of the workers at the two factories. The phenomenon in question was a regularity between the occurrences of two types of events. We claimed that the best explanation of that regularity presupposed that events of one type caused the occurrence of events of the other type (p). From these two premises, we concluded that events of one type did cause the occurrence of events of the other type (p is true).

The very same mode of inference is involved when we infer from people's behavior their thoughts, feelings, attitudes, and so on. If Joe changes his schedule and takes courses in subjects he hates, but June is in all those courses; if he frequently sends her roses; then, observing this phenomenon, and feeling that the best explanation of it presupposes that Joe is in love with June (p), we infer that he is indeed in love with her (p is true).

Detectives always use this mode of inference. If, let us say, we want to know how an accident took place, and if we observe that the tire tracks of the car going in one direction suddenly veer sharply to the other side of the road, then we immediately infer that the car going in that direction crossed into the other side of the road and that something had happened suddenly either to that driver or to his car, making the car cross to the˙other side of the road. The inference is of the following structure: The best explanation of the observed phenomenon (the way the tire tracks suddenly veer to the left and cross the road) presupposes that something happened suddenly either to the car or to the driver of that car, making the car cross to the other side of the road (*p*). Therefore, something like that did happen suddenly (*p* is true).

Finally, scientists also use the same mode of inference to support their scientific theories. The scientist infers the truth of the atomic theory of matter from the fact that it is presupposed in the best explanations we have of a variety of chemical phenomena (the ratio with which different elements combine with each other, etc.). Similarly, the scientist infers the truth of the kinetic theory of gases from the fact that its truth is presupposed by the best explanations we have of a variety of phenomena about gases (the relations between the temperature, pressure, and volume of gases, the fact that they compress and expand easily, etc.).

As we reflect upon the variety of uses for this mode of inference, we begin to suspect that perhaps all sound but nonvalid inferences may be of this form. We shall consider whether this is so in a later section of this chapter.

The first thing to note about all these inferences is that none of them are valid. Even if the phenomenon in question really did occur, and even if *p* really is presupposed by the best explanation of that phenomenon, *p* may still be false. Of course, this would mean that the best explanation is not the correct explanation, but that can certainly occur. As one might imagine, the best explanation might not be the correct explanation because there *is* no correct explanation of the phenomenon (there is no guarantee that everything is explainable). Nevertheless, some of these inferences are clearly sound, and some are clearly sounder than others. The question that we must now consider is when and why this is so.

All such inferences seem to be of the form:

(1) *q* is the case.
(2) *p* is presupposed by the best explanation of *q*.
(3) *p* is true.

It appears, as we examine the form of such inferences, that the question of the soundness of such an inference is tied up with two features of step (2): the extent to which the explanation in question is a good explanation, and the extent to which it is better than the next best explanation.

Let us look at each of these factors separately. Consider again Joe's behavior toward June. Let us imagine that we have also observed Joe sending flowers to Nancy and mooning every time Matilda walks by. Now, Joe's being in love with June might still be the best explanation we have of his behavior toward her, but it is not a very good explanation, because it makes his behavior toward Nancy and Matilda very difficult to understand. So any inference from his behavior toward June to his being in love with her is not very sound (if sound at all). This would be so even if we had no other explanation of his behavior. To generalize from this example, we state that if the explanation in question is by far the best explanation available, but is also a weak explanation, then the inference from the fact that it is the best explanation to the truth of statements presupposed by the explanation will be either unsound or only minimally sound.

Now let us imagine that the circumstances are slightly different. Joe is ignoring Nancy and Matilda and blissfully pursuing June. But we also know that Joe has often said that he would rather marry for money than for love, and that he is also aware that June is a wealthy, gullible heiress. Then, although we have the very good explanation of Joe's behavior based upon his being in love with June, and although that is the best explanation of his behavior, the existence of the alternative explanation might cast some doubt upon the conclusion that Joe loves June. And if, because of the acquisition of additional information, that alternative explanation begins to look better and better, then the soundness of the inference to the conclusion that Joe loves June seems weaker and weaker.

Generalizing from this example, we can say that even though the best explanation of the phenomenon q presupposes the truth of p, and even though it is a very good explanation, the soundness of the inference from those facts to the truth of p is weakened by the existence of a moderately good alternative explanation of the phenomenon, and it becomes progressively less sound as the alternative explanation seems better.

In other words, to assess the soundness of an inference to the best explanation, we must at least know how good the explanation in question is and how much better it is than all the alternative explanations. All this presupposes, of course, that we have a theory of what an explanation is and of when one explanation is better than the other explanation. Therefore, we turn now to a consideration of such questions.

10.2 The Theory of Explanation

What is an explanation? Let us look at a few examples of people explaining things. Last week I took my car into the garage and my mechanic explained to me what was wrong with it, why certain things had gone wrong, and how he planned to correct them. He performed three acts of explanation. In one he answered the question, 'What is wrong with the car?' In another, he answered the question, 'How would he correct those things that were wrong?' And, finally, he answered the question 'Why had those things gone wrong?' We will only concern ourselves with the third type of explanation—answers to why-questions. In other words, we will deal with answers of the form '*p* is the case because *q*' to questions of the form 'why is it the case that *p*?' Therefore, when we ask 'what makes something a satisfactory explanation?' we are really asking 'what makes something a satisfactory answer to a why-question?', and when we ask 'what makes one explanation better than another explanation?', we are really asking 'what makes one answer to a why-question better than another answer?'

The first and most obvious requirement is that '*p* is the case because *q*' is a satisfactory answer only if *q* is true. Of course, that is not enough to make it a satisfactory answer. 'The sun is shining because all men are mortal' is not a satisfactory answer to the question 'why is the sun shining?' even though it is true that all men are mortal. The important question for the theory of explanation becomes, then, What are the additional requirements for a satisfactory answer to a why-question?

One very obvious additional requirement is that *q* must be such that, when we know that *q* is so, we understand why *p* had to be the case. The trouble with such a requirement is that it seems, because of the last phrase, to presuppose an understanding of the very thing we are trying to figure out; namely, what it is to understand why *p* had to be the case. So we must look for different additional requirements.

In recent years one theory about an additional requirement has come to be accepted widely. According to that theory, *q* must be such that, given our knowledge of its truth, we would be entitled to say '*p* was to be expected'. In other words, *q* must give us good reasons for supposing that *p* is true. The intuitive motivation behind this theory is clear: *q* can be used to explain *p* when *q* shows that *p*'s truth was to be expected.

Let us call the statement expressed by the sentence symbolized by *p* that occurs in the question 'why is it the case that *p*?' the *explanandum* (the sentence describing that which is to be explained), and let us call the statement expressed by the sentence symbolized by *q* that occurs in the answer '*p* is the case because *q*' the *explanan* (the sentence describing that which explains). Then, according to the theory that we are now considering, in order for an explanation to be a satisfactory explanation, it must at least be the case that (1) the explanan is true, and (2) knowledge of the truth of the explanan gives us good reasons for believing in the truth of the explanandum.

In light of the second requirement, there are two types of satisfactory explanations. In one, the *deductive explanations*, one can infer, by a valid deductive argument, the truth of the explanandum from the truth of the explanan. In the other type, the *inductive explanations*, the truth of the explanan does not validly entail the truth of the explanandum, but there is a sound inference from the truth of the explanan to the truth of the explanandum.

Let us look at each of these types separately. The following is a simple example of a deductive explanation. Let us imagine that we see some tire tracks that suddenly veer sharply to the left and cross to the other side of the road. We want to know why they suddenly veer to the left. The answer to that question is that the car which made the tire tracks suddenly crossed over to the other side of the road, and that whenever this happens, the tire tracks also suddenly veer left and cross to the other side of the road. Of course, we might then want to know why the car suddenly crossed over, but that is another question and its answer is a different explanation.

If we look at the formal structure of this simple example, we will see the following. The explanandum is the statement expressed by 'the tire tracks suddenly veer sharply to the left and cross the road' whereas the explanan is the statement expressed by 'the car which made the tire tracks suddenly crossed over to the other side of the road, and whenever this happens, the tire tracks of that car veer sharply to the left and cross the road'. The explanan, of course, validly entails the explanandum. Most importantly, the explanan is a conjunction at least one of whose conjuncts is a general law and the rest of whose conjuncts are additional descriptions of the circumstances surrounding the event described in the explanandum.

Pictorially, we can represent the structure of our explanation as follows:

$L_1, L_2, \ldots, L_n$ (laws that are conjuncts of the explanan)
$C_1, C_2, \ldots, C_m$ (conjuncts of the explanan that describe further circumstances surrounding the occurrence described in the explanandum)
_____
explanandum

This model of a satisfactory deductive explanation of a particular event is known as the *covering-law model of deductive explanations of particular events*, and the hypothesis that all satisfactory deductive explanations of particular events fit this model is known as the *covering-law theory*. According to this theory, all satisfactory deductive explanations of particular events have as their explanan a conjunction some of whose conjuncts are general laws of nature and the rest of whose conjuncts are descriptions of the circumstances surrounding the event described in the explanandum.

Our first example was a satisfactory deductive explanation of a particular event. Let us now look at an example of a satisfactory deductive explanation of a more general truth. Imagine we have observed that as the temperature of a gas increases (decreases) so does its pressure, and vice versa. That is, imagine that we have observed that the temperature and pressure of a gas are directly proportional. Let us further imagine that we would like an explanation of this regularity. We can offer the following explanation in terms of the kinetic theory of gases. As the temperature of a gas increases (decreases) the average velocity of the molecules increases (decreases); therefore, there are more (fewer) impacts of the molecules on the walls of the gas's container, and the pressure increases (decreases). The same account, worked backward, explains why the relation holds the other way as well.

If we look at the formal structure of this example, we will see the following. The explanandum is the statement expressed by 'the pressure and temperature of a gas are directly proportional', whereas the explanan is the joint assertion of the basic postulates of the kinetic theory. The argument presented in the previous paragraph is an informal version of the valid deductive argument from the explanan to the explanandum. Most importantly, the conjuncts of the explanan are themselves general laws. None of them are descriptions of the circumstances surrounding the occurrence of a particular event, for we are not explaining the occurrence of a particular event.

Pictorially, we can represent the structure of our explanation as follows:

$$L_1, L_2, \ldots, L_n \quad \text{(laws that are conjuncts of the explanan)}$$

explanandum

This model of a satisfactory deductive explanation of a general law is known as the *covering-law model of deductive explanations of general laws*, and the hypothesis that all satisfactory deductive explanations of general laws fit this model is known as the *covering-law theory of deductive explanations of general laws*. In other words, according to this theory, all satisfactory deductive explanations of general laws have as their explanan a conjunction of several other general laws.

Let us now look at some inductive explanations. Imagine, once more, that we have observed Joe changing his schedule so that he takes the same courses as June, sending flowers to June, and so on. Let us further imagine that we want to know why he is doing all these things. A perfectly good answer is that he loves her, and men who love women often give them flowers, arrange their working schedules so that they can see them during the day, and so on.

If we look at the formal structure of this simple example, we will see the following. The explanandum is the statement expressed by 'Joe sends flowers to June, changes his schedule so that he is taking the same courses she is, and so on', whereas the explanan is the statement expressed by 'Joe loves June, and men who love women often give them flowers, arrange their working schedule so that they can see them during the day, and so on'.

One cannot validly infer the explanandum from the explanan; after all, the explanan says only that men in love often do these things, not that they always do them. Nevertheless, one should (provided one is not overly cautious) be able to infer soundly the explanandum from the explanan. Most importantly, the explanan is a conjunction at least one of whose conjuncts is a general law and the rest of whose conjuncts are descriptions of the circumstances surrounding the event described in the explanandum.

Pictorially, we can represent the structure of our explanation as follows:

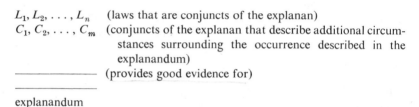

$L_1, L_2, \ldots, L_n$ (laws that are conjuncts of the explanan)
$C_1, C_2, \ldots, C_m$ (conjuncts of the explanan that describe additional circumstances surrounding the occurrence described in the explanandum)
——————————   (provides good evidence for)
————————

explanandum

This model of a satisfactory inductive explanation of a particular event is known as the *covering-law model of inductive explanations of particular events*, and the hypothesis that all satisfactory inductive explanations of particular events fit this model is known as the *covering-law theory of inductive explanations of particular events*. In other words, according to this theory, all satisfactory inductive explanations of particular events have as their explanan a conjunction some of whose conjuncts are general laws of nature and the rest of whose conjuncts are descriptions of the circumstances surrounding the event described in the explanandum.

Finally, there is a *covering-law model of inductive explanations of general laws*. Pictorially, it represents the structure of such explanations as follows:

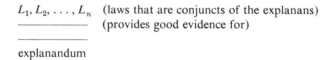

$L_1, L_2, \ldots, L_n$ (laws that are conjuncts of the explanans)
——————————   (provides good evidence for)
————————

explanandum

In explanations fitting this model, one cannot validly infer the explanandum from the explanan, but one should (provided that one is not being overly cautious) be able to infer soundly the explanandum from the explanan. Most importantly, the conjuncts of the explanan are themselves general laws. None of them are descriptions of the circumstances surrounding the occurrence of a particular event, for we are not explaining the occurrence of a particular event.

There is also the *covering-law theory of inductive explanations of general laws*, which is the hypothesis that all satisfactory inductive explanations of general laws fit this model.

Let us see where we now stand. At the end of section 10.1, we saw that we needed a theory of how good a given explanation is and of the extent to which one explanation is better than another. In this section we set out on the first step of constructing such a theory by looking at the question 'what is an explanation and what makes it satisfactory?' We saw that all satisfactory explanations must meet two requirements: the explanan must be true, and our knowledge of its truth must give us good reasons for believing the explanandum. We then introduced the covering-law theories, which state that all satisfactory explanations are of one of four types. Since these theories are plausible and widely accepted, we will work with them when necessary. In the next section we will try to construct, on the basis of this section's results, the outlines of a theory of how good an explanation is and of the extent to which one explanation is better than another.

10.3 Measuring the Quality of an Explanation

The first principle that we can certainly establish is that, if there exist two explanations of one explanandum, and one of them is satisfactory while the other is not, then the satisfactory explanation is a better explanation than the unsatisfactory one. But this is the easiest part of our job; the difficult question is that of deciding which of two different satisfactory explanations is the better one.

If we remember that we have only two requirements for satisfactory explanations, and that one of them—that the explanan be true—is equally satisfied by all satisfactory explanations, then we are inevitably led to the suggestion that the difference in quality between two satisfactory explanations is related to the way in which they satisfy the second requirement. This fits in very well with the second requirement, which states that one can soundly infer the explanandum from the explanan. As we saw when we first began talking about soundness, some sound inferences are sounder than others. Perhaps, then, we can lay down as a second principle that (all other things being equal), if there are two satisfactory explanations of one explanandum, then one is a better explanation than the other when the inference from the explanan of the former to the explanandum is sounder than the inference from the explanan of the latter to the explanandum.

By adopting this second principle, we immediately relegate inductive explanations to a lower rank than deductive explanations. For according to this second principle (all other things being equal), every satisfactory deductive explanation will be a better explanation than any satisfactory inductive explanation. For in the former, but not in the latter, type of explanation, the inference from explanan to explanandum is valid, and the soundest inference is a valid inference.

We now introduce a third principle, which states that satisfactoriness and degree of soundness are the only two factors relevant to the determination of the quality of an explanation. This principle will be defended shortly. Given this principle, we can draw two more conclusions about the ranking of explanations. (1) All satisfactory deductive explanations are equally good as explanations. After all, the inference from the explanan to the explanandum in every satisfactory deductive inference is equally sound, since they are all valid and validity does not admit of degrees. (2) We can rank satisfactory inductive explanations according to the soundness of the inference from their explanan to their explanandum without taking anything else into account. Therefore, the ranking of all explanations will look like this:

Rank 1   All satisfactory deductive explanations

              All satisfactory inductive explanations ranked according to the degree of soundness of the inference from explanan to explanandum

Rank 0   All unsatisfactory explanations

An examination of an example or two will help clarify all these points. Let us imagine that we are trying to explain why Joe, a student with average intelligence who did only a fair amount of work, managed to pass his exams. Let us further imagine that Joe took his exams honestly. We are considering two explanations. One is that Joe did a fair amount of work and that was enough. After all, most students with his intelligence who did a fair amount of work passed all their exams. The other is that Joe had copies of the exam in advance, and everyone who did that passed all his exams. Formally, the two explanations can be set out as follows:

(1) Joe is a student of average intelligence who did a fair amount of work.
(2) Most students of average intelligence who did a fair amount of work passed all their exams.

Joe passed all his exams.

(1) Joe had copies of all his exams in advance.
(2) Everyone who had copies of all his exams in advance passed all of them.

Joe passed all his exams.

Notice that the second of these explanations is a deductive explanation, whereas the first is merely an inductive explanation. Nevertheless, the first is a far better explanation than the second, since the second is not even satisfactory [its step (1) is false, since Joe took his exams honestly], whereas the first is more than merely satisfactory. Because its premises give us very good evidence for its conclusion, the inference from the explanan to the explanandum is very sound, and the explanation is very good.

Notice that the situation would be quite different if Joe had the exams in advance. Then, even though he did do a fair amount of work and would probably have passed the exams without cheating, the fact that he had the exams in advance would still be the basis of the better explanation: Joe probably would have passed even if he had not cheated, but he did pass because he cheated.

So far we have sketched the outline of a theory for comparing two explanations to determine which is better. But this outline also gives us an intuitive outline of a theory of the evaluation of an explanation. A weak but satisfactory explanation is a satisfactory explanation such that most other satisfactory explanations are better. But as the percentage of satisfactory explanations better than a given explanation becomes smaller, we can speak of that explanation as being better and better. Similarly, one explanation E_1 is only slightly better than another explanation E_2 if only a small percentage of explanations are better than E_2 but worse than E_1. As that percentage grows larger and larger, however, we can speak of E_1 as being better than E_2 to a greater and greater extent. Of course, all these notions are only sketched intuitively, but that is enough for our present purposes.

Of course, this whole theory depends upon our three principles. The first two are rather clearly satisfactory, but the third could be questioned. If the third were false—that is, if we had to take into account some other factor when we evaluated explanations—then much of what we said could be false. For it would then be possible, for example, for a satisfactory inductive explanation to be better than a satisfactory deductive explanation, because the inductive explanation might be so much better in this other respect that it would outweigh the fact that the inference from explanan to explanandum is sounder in the case of the deductive explanation. So we really must consider the question of whether there is some other factor relevant to the determination of the quality of an explanation.

What could this other quality be? Two possibilities suggest themselves. One is the likelihood that the explanan is true, and the other is the explanatory power of the explanan. Let us look at each of these suggestions separately.

Consider the following case. I toss a die two times, and the three-face does not come up either time. Why did this happen? Let us imagine that we are considering two explanations. One says that the die is made a certain way, that such dies are almost always fair dies, and that, therefore, in two-thirds of the cases in which you toss them only twice, the three-face does not come up. The other says that the die is made a certain way, that such dies are heavily biased against the three-face coming up, and that, therefore, in practically all cases in which you toss them only twice, the three-face does not come up. Let us further imagine that there is independent evidence about the way in which the die was constructed, evidence that made it more likely that the die was a fair die. Surely we would then prefer the former explanation to the latter, even though the inference from the explanan to the explanandum in the latter explanation is sounder. So we see from this example that we must consider something else beside satisfactoriness and soundness—namely, the likelihood that the explanan is true.

Although this case calls our attention to a legitimate point, it does not show that any third factor is taken into account when we decide which of the two explanations is the better one. The former explanation is preferred to the latter because, in light of the information about the likelihood of the explanan being true, we decide that the former is a satisfactory explanation (since its explanan is true) and that the latter is not a satisfactory explanation (since its explanan is false). The only legitimate point made by this example is that we often come to the question of evaluating two or more explanations without being certain whether their explanans are true, and, therefore, without being certain whether they are satisfactory explanations. In such cases we must deal with such issues first, and, in doing so, we must consider how likely it is that the various explanans are true.

Now let us consider the suggestion that the additional factor to be considered is the explanatory power of the explanan. Since the phenomenon we will examine is found more often in the developed sciences, we will use a scientific example. Let us imagine that we are studying the properties of chlorine, and we discover that chlorine combines with sodium in a ratio of one to one. Two explanations are offered for this phenomenon. One is that chlorine belongs to the halogen family of elements, sodium belongs to the alkaline metals family, and all halogens combine with alkaline metals in a ratio of one to one. The other is that bromine combines with sodium in a one-to-one ratio, and that chlorine combines in a one-to-one ratio with everything that bromine combines with in that ratio. Now, both these explanations are satisfactory deductive explanations. Therefore, according to our three principles, they are equally good explanations. Nevertheless, there certainly seems to be a difference between them. The explanan of the first is much more informative than the explanan of the second: It could be used to explain more, (and is thus said to have greater *explanatory power*). So shouldn't we add the factor of the explanatory power of the explanan to the list of factors that we should consider when evaluating explanations?

Although this is a powerful argument, the answer to this question must be no. The argument for including the explanatory power of the explanan as a factor confuses two concerns: that of the value of the explanation (which we are concerned with) and that of the value of the explanan for scientific understanding (with which we are not now concerned). Undoubtedly, the discovery of the truth of the explanan in the first explanation was a far greater scientific advance than the discovery of the truth of the explanan in the second explanation. This was true precisely because the first explanan has greater explanatory power than the second. But it does not then follow that explanations using the first explanan are better than explanations using the second.

This point can also be put as follows: To say that one explanan has greater explanatory power than a second is to say that we can use one explanan to explain more than the second explanan can explain. It seems foolish, however, to conclude on this basis that one explains better than the other. Why should that which explains more explain better?

We conclude, therefore, that neither of these two additional factors— the likelihood that the explanan is true and the explanatory power of the explanan—should be taken into account when we evaluate the quality of an explanation. Perhaps other factors should be considered. Indeed, the last example remains puzzling, and one is left with the feeling that it does point toward some additional factor. Yet until we have a plausible additional factor, we should stick to the hypothesis that all three of our principles are true.

10.4 Evaluating Inferences to the Best Explanation

In section 10.1 we saw that in order to decide about the soundness of an inference to the best explanation, we at least have to know how good the best explanation was, and how much better it was than the next best explanation. The better the best explanation is, and the greater the extent to which it is better than the next best explanation, the sounder is the inference in question. Having outlined, in sections 10.2 and 10.3, a theory for evaluating the quality of the best explanation and for telling how much better it is than that next best explanation, we may now start evaluating inferences to the best explanation.

But the situation is not so simple. To see why, let us go back to one of our initial examples, the detective looking at the tire tracks and trying to determine how the accident took place by determining why the tire tracks suddenly veer to the left and cross the road. He realizes that he can explain the direction of the tire tracks on the assumption that the car that made the tracks suddenly swerved to the left and crossed the road. For whenever cars do that, we get the type of tire tracks that he observes. In other words, he has this explanation:

(1) The car that was driving on this side of the road suddenly swerved to the left and crossed the road, leaving tracks.
(2) Whenever cars do that, the resulting tire tracks veer to the left and cross the road.

---

(3) The tire tracks veer to the left and cross the road.

The detective infers from the explanandum, and from the fact that it is presupposed by his best explanation [since it is step (1) of that explanation], the conclusion that the car suddenly did swerve to the left and cross the road. Is this a sound inference to the best explanation?

In light of the information we are given, it seems sound, but why? To begin with, the explanation seems to be a rather good one. But that, of course, isn't enough. How much better is it than the alternatives? Let us look at an alternative explanation. The car in question never swerved to the left and crossed the road. It was the other car that crossed the road. But after the accident, and before the detective arrived, the man in the second car returned to the scene of the accident, wiped out the true tire tracks that made him look responsible, and made these new tracks by any one of a variety of dependable methods. This alternative explanation comes down to:

(1') The man in the second car made these tracks by a dependable method to make it look as though the first car had.
(2') Whenever someone makes tire tracks by a dependable method to make it look as though some car swerved to the left and crossed the road, the tire tracks veer to the left and cross the road.

(3') The tire tracks veer to the left and cross the road.

Both these explanations are deductive; the explanan of each validly entails the explanandum. So we cannot say that the first explanation is better than the second because of the soundness of the inference from explanan to explanandum. Why, then, should we suppose that the first is a better explanation than the second? Only if it is (and to a considerable degree), could the detective soundly infer that (1) is true.

One is tempted to say that we should suppose the first explanation is better than the second explanation because (1) is true, and, therefore, the first explanation is satisfactory, whereas (1') is false, and, therefore, the second explanation is unsatisfactory. Although this may be true, we cannot simply give that answer. For, we do not know whether (1) is true—that is, what we are trying to find out by our inference to the best explanation. So why should we suppose that the first explanation is better than the second explanation?

The best we can say is the following. In light of our general experience about the world, it is much more likely that (1) and not (1') occurred. Indeed, (1') is so much less likely to be true, even given the occurrence of the tire tracks, that we conclude it is probably false. Consequently, the second explanation is unsatisfactory; the first may not be, so we prefer the first to the second.

The problem we ran into in this case is one that we always face when we are evaluating inferences to the best explanation. We cannot merely evaluate all the competing explanations, because to do so, we must know whether their explanans are true, which is what we are trying to infer by our inference. What we do instead is the following. We first look at all the possible explanations and rule out those (such as the second one above) whose explanan is much less likely to be true, in light of all the evidence, than the explanans of other potential explanations. We then take all the remaining explanations, assume (one at a time) that the explanan is true, decide (given that assumption) which would be the best explanation, and infer the truth of its explanan.

Another way of looking at this will help clarify this vital point. We saw in section 10.3 that the likelihood that the explanan is true does not affect the value of the explanation. But we also saw that, to evaluate two or more explanations without being certain whether their explanans are true, we must deal with such issues first by taking into account the likelihood (given all the evidence) that the different explanans are true. Now, we are always in that type of situation when we are considering different inferences to the best possible explanation. The purpose of the inferences is to determine which of the explanans is true; we don't know that in advance. So we first rule out all the explanations except those whose explanans are most likely to be true. We then infer the truth of the explanan of that remaining explanation which would be the best explanation if its explanan were true. The soundness of this inference depends upon how good an explanation it would be, on how much better it would be than its competitors, and on the likelihood that the explanan is true.

Let us look at one more example so that we can see how this more complicated process of evaluating inferences to the best explanation works. We will consider, once more, the question of whether we can soundly infer from Joe's behavior that he loves June. Let us, for the sake of simplicity, suppose that there are only three explanations of Joe's behavior: love (Joe loves June), golddigging (Joe wants to marry June for her money and is trying to convince her that he loves her), and the mad-joke explanation (Joe has a poor sense of humor and considers it is very amusing to make girls suppose that he loves them). First, let us take the simple case in which we see Joe changing his schedule, sending roses, and not doing anything that counts against the view that he loves June. Certainly, in such a case, given all our knowledge of human beings and of all his behavior, the only explanan likely to be true is that of the love explanation: we therefore rule out all the other possible explanations. The love explanation would be the best of the remaining explanations if its explanan were true; so we infer that its explanan is true. How sound is this inference? The love explanation is a rather good explanation, and it certainly has no close competitors (it has no serious ones at all); so it is a rather sound inference.

Now let us take the more complicated case in which we begin to find independent evidence that Joe wants to marry for money and has no scruples about misleading people. When that evidence is sufficient so that, in light of all the evidence, it is also reasonably likely that the explanan of the golddigger explanation is true (almost as likely that the explanan of the love explanation is true), the situation changes drastically. We now have two explanations whose explanans are likely enough to be true so that they can be taken seriously. The only explanation that can be ruled out is the mad-joker explanation. We then ask ourselves the following question. Assuming first that the explanan of the love explanation is true, how good an explanation would that be? Next, assume that the explanan of the golddigger explanation is true: how good an explanation would the golddigger explanation then be? Then, we infer the truth of the explanan of that explanation that would be the better one. How sound would the second inference be? Not as sound as the first one. To be sure, the better explanation (whichever one it is) looks like a rather good explanation, and it is reasonably likely that its explanan is true, but it doesn't look much better than the next best one.

Finally, let us look at the even more interesting case in which we also observe Joe paying attention to Matilda and sending flowers to Nancy (let us suppose he is doing it in such a way that many people know about his behavior toward all three girls). The love explanation remains a possibility although its explanation is not as likely as before, and the same is true for the golddigger explanation. But for the first time, the mad-joker explanation enters into the picture as a real possibility. All this new evidence has made it somewhat likely that its explanan is true (likely enough to be considered, especially since the explanans of the other two are now less likely.) So we must ask, about all three of the explanations, how good each would be as an explanation if it were the case that its explanan were true? We infer the truth of the explanan of that explanation that would be the best. But this inference will not be very sound, for two reasons. First, as in the last case, the best explanation is not significantly better than the next best explanation, and the likelihood of each explanan is not great. In addition to that, none of them are very good explanations. The love explanation has difficulty explaining Joe's fickleness, and the other two have difficulty explaining the fact that he doesn't hide his attentions to the other girls. How can he convince June that he loves her if she finds out that he is sending flowers to Nancy and showing affection for Matilda?

In light of what we have seen in this section, perhaps it may be best to represent the form of inferences to the best explanation as follows:

(1) q is the case.
(2) In light of the evidence available, the explanations with explanans most likely to be true are $E_1, E_2, \ldots, E_n$.
(3) E_i would be a better explanation, if its explanan is true, than would any of these other explanations, if their explanans were true.
(4) p is presupposed by E_i.

(5) p is true.

And in evaluating the soundness of such inferences, unlike evaluating the soundness of the explanation, we must take into account three factors: (1) the likelihood that the explanan of E_i is true, (2) how good an explanation E_i is, and (3) to what extent E_i is better than the next best explanation.

10.5 Are All Inferences Inferences to the Best Explanation?

Having analyzed the logic of inferences to the best explanation, and having seen the factors that help determine when it is a sound inference, we are left with considering the issue of whether all sound inferences are inferences to the best explanation. In section 10.1 we saw that there was a wide variety of sound inferences which, upon examination, turned out to be inferences to the best explanation, suggesting to us that perhaps all sound inferences are really of this form.

Note that both generalization-inferences and inferences to causal hypotheses can plausibly be construed as being of that form. Let us look first at generalizations. Remember that they are of the form:

$n\%$ of the observed A's are B's.

$n \pm a\%$ of all A's are B's.

and they are sound when the sample is large enough and it is chosen by a method that worked. Now, the question that we must consider is whether the conclusion of such an inference, when sound, is the best explanation of the premise of such an inference. If it is, then we can construe such an inference as being an inference to the best explanation.

The explanation in question would be of the following form:

(1) $n \pm a\%$ of all A's are B's.
(2) The sample we are considering is large enough and was drawn by a method that worked.

---

(3) $n\%$ of the observed A's are B's.

Of course, it is not a deductive inference but an inductive one. Is it now the best explanation? Unquestionably, the inference from explanan to explanandum is very sound. So, assuming for a moment the truth of the explanan, we would have a very good explanation. The only question is whether some other explanation could be better, and it could be so only if its explanan were true. Consider, for example, the explanation that we deliberately picked out a sample that had $n\%$ of B's. But it, and all other such explanations, are wholly unsatisfactory, for we know that the sample was chosen by a method that works, and therefore part of their explanan is false. So it looks as though this would be the best explanation.

We can also put this point as follows: Any explanation of (3) must be compatible with the fact that the sample is large enough and drawn by a method that works. Given that, it looks as though the best explanation will be the one we are considering. After all, given this fact, if some percentage other than $n \pm a$ of the A's are B's, we would have great difficulty explaining, rather than a good explanation of, the fact that $n\%$ of the observed A's are B's.

Formally, we would infer that $n \pm a\%$ of the A's are B's, as follows:

(1) It is the case that we have observed in a large enough sample chosen by a method that worked that $n\%$ of the A's are B's.
(2) In light of the evidence available, the explanations with explanans most likely to be true are those with an explanan compatible with the fact that the sample is large enough and chosen by a method that worked.
(3) The explanation we are considering would be a better explanation, if its explanan were true, than would any of these other explanations, if their explanans were true.
(4) But the hypotheses that $n \pm a\%$ of all A's are B's is presupposed by the explanation we are considering [since it is step (1) of it].

---

(5) $n \pm a\%$ of all A's are B's.

This shows us, then, that all sound generalizations can be construed as sound inferences to the best explanation.

It is now extremely easy to see that all sound inferences to the truth of causal hypotheses can be construed as sound inferences to the best explanation. For, as we saw in Chapter 9, they had two parts: a sound generalization and a sound inference to the best explanation. Inasmuch as all sound generalizations can be construed as sound inferences to the best explanation, it follows that sound inferences to the truth of causal hypotheses are simply two sound inferences to the best explanation.

This means that all the sound inferences we have studied in this part of the book are inferences to the best explanation, which reinforces the idea that all sound inferences are of that form. Nevertheless, it is wrong to conclude that all sound inferences are of this form. To begin with, many valid inferences cannot be so construed. Consider the simple inference from the statement that Joe went home and had dinner ($p \cdot q$) to the statement that Joe went home (p). This is certainly not an inference to the best explanation, since his going home hardly explains why he went home and had dinner ('because he went home' does not answer the question 'why did he go home and have dinner?'). Such examples of valid (and therefore sound) inferences that are not inferences to the best explanation could be multiplied *ad nauseum*.

But perhaps we can save our thesis by confining it to sound but not valid inferences? We could then claim that all sound, nonvalid inferences are inferences to the best explanation. Even that will not do. For one can soundly infer from the fact that A's are usually followed by B's, and the fact that an A has occurred, the conclusion that a B will soon occur. Thus, if one knows that increases in the government's budgetary deficit are usually followed by increases in the rate of inflation and that there has just been an increase in the budgetary deficit, one can soundly infer that there will be an increase in the rate of inflation. But these are not inferences to the best explanation. The increase in the rate of inflation does not explain the observed increase in the budgetary deficit. If anything, these are inferences *from* the best explanation.

Therefore, we conclude that inferences to the best explanation are only one type of sound nonvalid inferences. There exist other types; however, the study of their logic will be left to another occasion.

EXERCISES FOR CHAPTER 10

Part I

A. Show how each of the following inferences is an inference to the best explanation:

1. He must be at home since, when I called his house, I heard a man's voice in the background.
2. Louis XIV must have loved her or he wouldn't have made their illegitimate son a duke.
3. The mayor obviously said that; it says so on page one of the newspaper.
4. Something must have spoiled in the bin; there's an awful smell there.

5. Look at all those ravens flying south; ravens must migrate southward in the fall.
6. He must be upset; he hasn't smoked that many cigars in months.
7. I see the chair; so it must be there in front of me.
8. Caesar must have crossed the Rubicon; all Roman historians say that he did.

B. Why are each of the following inferences to the best explanation unsound inferences?

1. She must love me because she is always nice to me.
2. Although she won't marry me and can't give a good reason for it, she must love me because she always says she does and she's known to be very truthful.
3. Although he constantly hits her, he soon makes up; so he must love her.
4. The pressure of the gas has gone up; so the temperature must have increased.
5. The pressure of the gas has gone up; so the temperature must have decreased.

C. Which of the following explanations are answers to what-questions; which are answers to how-questions; and which are answers to why-questions?

1. You fix the machine by pressing the button.
2. The cause of the accident was his carelessness.
3. He did it to save her.
4. Sodium combines with chlorine in a one-to-one ratio because of their atomic structure.
5. You can get to his house by going down the block.

D. In the following explanations, what is the explanandum and what are the explanans?

1. Socrates drank the hemlock and that's why he died. All men who drink hemlock die.
2. He did it to save his life; wouldn't you?
3. People can't stand him because he is a bore.
4. When there are too many people in the park, you must expect to have the trouble that we had.
5. Mary doesn't feel well; she has measles.
6. John went home and found Mary with another man; so he killed her.
7. I want peace in the world because I want to live without fear. That's why I work for the cause.
8. The glass broke because he threw the bottle at it and it is brittle.

E. Which of the following are deductive explanations and which are inductive explanations?

1. John got paresis because he had syphillis years ago.
2. The pipes crashed because the water in them froze during the cold weather.

3. People continue to believe things long after it's clear that they're wrong because they don't like to admit that they made a mistake.
4. The coming of day is caused by the rotation of the earth.
5. 90 % of all people love her; that's why most women do.
6. You didn't get five 6's in a row when you threw the dice five times because that is very unlikely.

F. What are the covering laws explicitly or implicitly used in each of the following explanations?

1. The intensification of student dislike of the college president was due to their feelings that he wasn't attending to what they said.
2. The temperature of the room went up because he turned the steam on.
3. The cat has a heart because it needs an organ to pump blood through its body.
4. He killed the soldier because the soldier was trying to kill him.
5. The glass broke when he threw the rock at it because it's brittle.

G. Compare the explanatory power of each of the statements in Column A with the explanatory power of the corresponding statement in Column B:

Column A	Column B
1. All men are mortal.	All living things are mortal.
2. Everyone has a wife.	He has a wife.
3. People dislike bores.	People dislike other people who bother them.
4. Everyone loves someone.	Most people love someone.
5. 80 % of all people love someone.	70 % of all people love someone.

H. Show that all of the following sound, nonvalid inferences are not inferences to the best explanation:

1. He tossed the burning paper on the dry wood; therefore, there will be a fire in that wood pile soon.
2. Practically everyone in this room hates Joe; therefore, the guy next to me hates Joe.
3. 30 % of the first large, randomly drawn sample feel that way; therefore, about 30 % of the next such sample will as well.
4. He really hates him; therefore, he will try to get him fired.
5. We almost always end up going to the Rialto to see the movie; therefore, we will wind up there tonight.

Part II

1. Critically evaluate the following claim: Explanations show that the unfamiliar is really due to a more familiar phenomenon, and the more familiar it is, the better the explanation is.
2. Consider the following objection to the covering-law theory of deductive explanations: One can deduce from the length of a shadow cast by a flagpole, the position of the sun in the sky, and the laws of optics, the height of the flagpole. But this deduction, although it meets all the

requirements of the model, is not an explanation. For it is the height of the flagpole that explains the length of the shadow, and not vice versa. So the covering-law model is incorrect. Is this objection sound?

3. The covering-law theory of deductive explanations is incomplete since it fails to rule out as unsatisfactory self-explanations like 'all ravens are black because all ravens are black'. Show that this claim is true. How would you modify the theory to rule out self-explanations?

4. Consider the following argument: Inductive explanations are not satisfactory, because the explanans do not show why the explanandum must be true. Is that a good argument against inductive explanations?

5. It is generally believed that far-reaching scientific theories provide us with deeper explanations than are provided by superficial generalizations. Is this belief tied up with the mistaken views about explanatory power? If not, what lies behind it?

6. Is the extent to which an explanation fits in with our other explanations of other phenomena an additional factor, and one that we have left out, in determining the satisfactoriness of an explanation?

7. We have claimed that the explanan of an explanation must be true in order for the explanation to be satisfactory. But is this really so? Don't we often satisfactorily explain phenomenon by using approximations that are not really true?
   Give an example of such an explanation. Critically evaluate the objection.

8. Consider the following objection to our procedure in the text: We could greatly simplify our account of inferences to the best explanation if we evaluated explanations as being more satisfactory if their explanans were more likely to be true. Is this objection correct?

9. What, if anything, would be accomplished if we could show that all sound inferences are inferences to the best explanation?

10. What explains the fact that valid inferences are not (and cannot be) inferences to the best explanation?

CHAPTER 11

Our Three Controversies Re-examined

In this final chapter we will return to the three controversies with which we began. We will re-examine the arguments on both sides, analyzing them in light of all that we have learned in this book, and decide whether either side has actually proved its case.

11.1 *The Rationality of Faith Re-examined*

As we saw in Chapter 1, the arguments of both the adherent to the strict position and the adherent to the permissive position rest upon some general claims about when it is rational to believe that something is the case. Let us first look, then, at these general claims,

The adherents to the strict position rest their case upon the general claim that it is rational to believe something only when there is evidence that makes it likely that such is the case. Now, we can symbolize their claim as follows (in which 'R' represents the property of being rational to believe, and 'E' represents the property of being evidence that makes it likely that):

(1) $$(x)[Rx \supset (\exists y)Eyx]$$

On the other hand, the adherents to the permissive position rest their case upon the general claim that as long as there is no evidence making it likely that something is not the case, then it is rational to believe that it is the case. We can symbolize their claim as follows (in which 'R' and 'E' are as defined previously, and 'N' represents the property of being the negation of):

(2) $(x)([\sim(\exists y)(\exists z)(Eyz \cdot Nzx)] \supset Rx)$

Before we look at the arguments for their general claims, we should point out one thing. Although it is possible that both of these general claims could be true, the truth of both has certain unlikely consequences, as can be seen by considering the following proof:

(1)	(1) $(x)[Rx \supset (\exists y)Eyx]$	Assump.
(2)	(2) $(x)([\sim(\exists y)(\exists z)(Eyz \cdot Nzx)] \supset Rx)$	Assump.
(1)	(3) $Ra \supset (\exists y)Eya$	UE (1)
(2)	(4) $[\sim(\exists y)(\exists z)(Eyz \cdot Nza)] \supset Ra$	UE (2
(5)	(5) $\sim(\exists y)(\exists z)(Eyz \cdot Nza)$	Assump.
(2)(5)	(6) Ra	CE (4)(5)
(1)(2)(5)	(7) $(\exists y)Eya$	CE (3)(6)
(1)(2)	(8) $[\sim(\exists y)(\exists z)(Eyz \cdot Nza)] \supset (\exists y)Eya$	CI (7)
(1)(2)	(9) $(x)([\sim(\exists y)(\exists z)(Eyz \cdot Nzx)] \supset (\exists y)Eyx)$	UI (8)

What does (9) say? It says that if there is no evidence making it likely that some statement is false, then there is evidence making it likely that that statement is true. In other words, for any statement, either there is evidence that makes it likely that that statement is true or there is evidence that makes it likely that it is false. Why is (9) an unlikely claim? Because, it rules out the possibility that some statements are such that there is no evidence that either makes it likely that it is true or makes it likely that it is false, and this is a mistake. Indeed, we are working on the plausible assumption that the statement that God exists is just such a statement.

This all means that if (1) and (2) are both true, then (9) would be true, and since (9) is not true, then (1) and (2) cannot both be true. So, by use of De Morgan's law for conjunction, we could prove that either (1) is false or (2) is false. Consequently, we know that one of the leading principles on which rest the arguments we are considering must be false. The only question remaining is, Which of the principles is false? Is principle (1), the basis of the argument used by adherents of the strict position, mistaken; or is principle (2), the basis of the argument used by adherents of the permissive position, false? Or are they both false?

We will begin our attempt to answer this question by looking at the arguments offered by both sides in Chapter 1 for their general principle about rationality. The argument offered by the permissive position for its general principle, (2), comes down to the following. As we see from the case of Joe's continuing to believe that Mary loves him, even though there is evidence that (at least) makes it very likely that his belief is false, it is certainly irrational to hold a belief when there is evidence making it likely that the belief is false.

But when there is no such evidence, then, even if there is no evidence making it likely that the belief is true, it is still rational to hold this belief. Now, this argument is invalid: its conclusion does not follow from its premise. For its premise,

$$(x)[(\exists y)(\exists z)(Eyz \cdot Nzx) \supset \sim Rx]$$

says that a certain condition is sufficient for its being irrational to hold a certain belief. Its conclusion,

$$(x)([\sim(\exists y)(\exists z)(Eyz \cdot Nzx)] \supset Rx)$$

says that that condition's not obtaining is sufficient for its being rational to hold the same belief. Such a conclusion does not follow from such a premise.

On the other hand, the argument offered by the strict position for its general principle, (1), comes down to the following. A rational man does not act capriciously or hastily, and he therefore waits until there is evidence that what a statement says is true before he believes that it is true. This argument leaves entirely unclear how one gets from not acting capriciously or hastily to waiting until there is evidence.

So far, we have seen that although one of these two general claims about rationality is false, the arguments offered in Chapter 1 do not show us which is true (and, of course, which is false). Let us, however, approach the problem from a different angle, from a consideration of the meaning of 'it is rational to believe that'. For it might be claimed (plausibly, as we shall see) that, given the meaning of 'it is rational to believe that', (1) [or (2)] must be true.

How would such arguments run? One might argue for (1) as follows. 'It is rational to believe that' is a symbol used before another symbol that expresses a statement to produce a new symbol which expresses a true statement if and only if there is evidence making it likely that the original statement is true. This is the rule governing the use of that symbol; this is its meaning. Therefore, if there is some statement which it is rational to believe, there must be evidence making it likely that the statement is true; that is, it must be the case that (1) is true. One might argue for (2) as follows. 'It is rational to believe that' is a symbol used before another symbol that expresses a statement to produce a new symbol which expresses a true statement if and only if there is no evidence making it likely that the original statement is false. This is the rule governing the use of that symbol; this is its meaning. Therefore, as long as there is no evidence making it likely that the original statement is false, then it is rational to believe that that statement is true; that is, (2) is true.

The dispute, then, about (1) and (2) has turned into a dispute about the meaning of 'it is rational to believe that'. Given one account of its meaning, (1) is true and the strict position about religious faith is also true. Given another account of its meaning, (2) is true and the permissive position about religious faith is also true. The question, therefore, is, Which is the correct account of the meaning of 'it is rational to believe that'?

We saw in Chapter 2 that when we are offered two alternative accounts of the rules governing the way a symbol is actually used, when we are offered two different descriptive definitions of that symbol, the question of which is correct is a purely empirical issue. The correct definition is the one giving the rules that actually govern the use of the symbol. So it might seem that we are near the end of our problem; all we must do is run an empirical investigation to see how 'it is rational to believe that' is used, determine thereby which of the descriptive definitions is correct, and infer whether (1) and the strict position or (2) and the lenient position is correct.

Unfortunately, the matter is not so simple. To begin with, the very plausibility of both these definitions seems to suggest that something is wrong here. Secondly, the author's own investigations have revealed that people's usage on this matter is very unclear. They behave sometimes as though the first account were correct and sometimes as though the second account were correct.

What does this all mean? We are considering three types of cases:

(a) There is evidence that makes it likely that the statement is true.
(b) There is evidence that makes it likely that the statement is false.
(c) There is no evidence either way.

Now, there is no doubt that the rules governing the use of 'it is rational to believe that' are such that it is true that it is rational to believe the statement in question in cases of the first type and false that it is rational to believe the statement in question in cases of the second type. What is left unclear by the rules governing the use of that symbol is whether it is rational to believe the statement in question in cases of the third type. In this important way, 'it is rational to believe that' is vague. Both these accounts of the meaning of that symbol are plausible (and people do sometimes behave in accordance with one of them and other times in accordance with the other), simply because they help us eliminate this vagueness. In other words, it is much more illuminating to view our two accounts of the meaning of 'it is rational to believe that' as alternative explicative definitions of that symbol, introduced to eliminate this fundamental vagueness.

If what we have just said is correct, then our whole issue turns on the question of which of these explicative definitions is to be preferred. This question is not so easy to answer. For both these definitions meet our two requirements for explicative definitions; they both solve the problem they were introduced to solve (since they both offer a clear, although different, answer to the question of whether 'it is rational to believe that' should be applied to statements in cases of the third type), and they do so while preserving all that can be preserved of the rules which have until now governed the use of the symbol (they both imply that, in the first case, it is rational to believe the statement in question, while in cases of the second type, it is not).

How, then, are we to decide between these two explicative definitions? The only suggestion we can offer is as follows. We need to approach this issue at a much deeper level. We must first inquire why rationality is so highly desired and what goals we hope to obtain by having only rational beliefs. If we could answer those questions, we would be in a position to decide which of these stipulative definitions is preferable. For if these goals are obtainable by our believing, in the third type of case, that the statement in question is true, then we ought to call such beliefs rational, and adopt the second account. But if they are not so obtainable—if these goals are obtainable by believing, only in the first type of case, that the statement in question is true—then we ought to adopt the first account.

In conclusion, therefore, none of the arguments we have considered resolve the problem of the rationality of faith. This problem is only resolvable by a deeper investigation into the goals of rationality. There are some cases in which a reasoned examination of an issue reveals that our discussion was not properly focused, and this is one such case.

11.2 The Marijuana-Heroin Relation Re-examined

As we saw in Chapter 1, the main argument for the claim that there is a causal connection between heroin addiction and previous marijuana use is based upon statistical studies of the extent of previous marijuana use among heroin (and, more generally, among opiate) users. Our statistics showed that a much higher percentage of heroin (and opiate) addicts had a history of prior use of marijuana than the percentage of nonaddicts who had a history of marijuana use. The only question is whether or not these statistics show that there is a causal connection between the two.

Those who claim it does not show a causal connection between the two offer two reasons. The first is that, on the contrary, these studies show that there is no causal connection between the two. For even these studies show that there are many heroin (and opium) addicts who have never used marijuana, and it is well known that large numbers of (perhaps even most) marijuana users do not later use heroin (or any other opiate). So, it is claimed, there is no causal connection, despite the statistical evidence.

There is one point that must be granted immediately. Since there are heroin addicts who have not previously used marijuana, the use of marijuana is not a necessary condition for heroin addiction. Similarly, since there are marijuana users who do not later use heroin, the use of marijuana is certainly not a sufficient condition for the use of heroin. Therefore, it is certainly not the case that the use of marijuana is either unconditionally necessary or unconditionally sufficient for later heroin addiction.

Does that mean, though, that there is no causal connection between the two? It certainly does mean that marijuana use cannot be the cause of every case of heroin addiction. But it does not mean that it cannot be the cause of many cases of heroin addiction. For example, consider Joe, the heroin addict, who has a history of marijuana use. In order for his marijuana use to be the cause of his heroin addiction, it must be the case that his marijuana use (e_1) belongs to some class of events E_1 and that his late heroin addiction (e_2) belongs to some class of events E_2 such that E_1's are unconditionally necessary (and/or unconditionally sufficient) for the occurrence of E_2's. Now, all we have seen so far is that the class of events E_1 cannot be the class of all events that are cases of regular marijuana use if the class of events E_2 is the class of all events that are cases of people becoming heroin addicts (and vice versa). But it is certainly possible that there is another class of E_1's (perhaps the class of regular use-of-marijuana-under-certain-condition events), and another class of E_2's (perhaps the class of becoming-heroin-addicts-under-certain-conditions events) which are such that e_1 belongs to E_1, e_2 belongs to E_2, and E_1's are unconditionally necessary (or sufficient, or both) for E_2's. So e_1 can be the cause of e_2.

Therefore, the first objection to the statistical evidence has not shown that there is no causal connection in any case between marijuana use and heroin addiction. Despite what it points out, taking marijuana in some cases may be the cause of later heroin addiction. We are not yet done with the first objection, for its defenders might argue that they have at least shown that the statistical evidence proves nothing. For everyone concedes that taking-marijuana events and becoming-heroin-addicts events cannot be (jointly) the classes E_1 and E_2. No other candidate has yet been proposed. So how can statistics prove that there is a causal connection between events of type E_1 and events of type E_2 when we don't even know which type of events we are talking about? In short, there may be a causal connection here, but the statistics don't show it.

Even this very plausible version of the first objection must be rejected. For we do know, on the basis of our statistics, that an unusually large percentage of heroin (and opiate) addicts have used marijuana previously. How is this to be explained? It certainly does not seem accidental. A very plausible explanation of this statistical phenomenon is that there is some class of events E_1 and some class of events E_2 such that most cases of becoming-a-heroin-addict events belong to E_2 and a good many cases of regular-use-of-marijuana events (particularly ones involving people who later become addicts) belong to E_1, and that E_1's are unconditionally necessary (or sufficient, or both) for E_2's. Since no other, better explanation is forthcoming, we can infer, by an inference to the best explanation, that this claim is true. Consequently, even though we do not know what type of events these classes E_1 and E_2 are, we can still infer, from our statistical evidence, that in certain types of cases there is a causal connection between the regular use of marijuana and later heroin addiction.

The marijuana-heroin case, as we have seen so far, is not unlike the case of the relation between cigarette smoking and lung cancer. Not everyone who smokes regularly gets lung cancer, and there certainly are many people who die from lung cancer although they never smoked. Nevertheless, there is good reason to believe that, at least in some cases, the cause of a person's getting lung cancer was his smoking. This is so because it is just this hypothesis—that there are some classes E_1 and E_2 which are such that a large number of cases of getting-lung-cancer events belong to E_2, and a large number of cases of smoking-regularly events (particularly those involving people who later get lung cancer) belong to E_1, and in which E_1's are unconditionally necessary (or sufficient, or both) for E_2's—that best explains the statistical evidence observed there: that a larger percentage of people dying from lung cancer have smoked regularly than would be found in a normal sample of the general population.

To summarize, then, we see that the first objection to the statistical evidence that is supposed to show that the causal connection exists fails. Although many people become heroin addicts without previously smoking marijuana, and although many people smoke marijuana and don't become heroin addicts, there still may be a causal connection between them in some cases. Since the assumption that there is such a causal connection seems to offer the best explanation of our statistical evidence, we are probably entitled to infer from that evidence—by an inference to the best explanation—that, in at least some cases, there is a causal connection between a person's having smoked marijuana and his becoming addicted to heroin.

Is our explanation, however, really the best explanation? Aren't there other equally good (if not better) explanations of our statistical evidence? To ask these questions is, of course, to bring us to the second objection raised in Chapter 1 against the argument from the statistical evidence to the conclusion that there is a causal connection between use of marijuana and heroin addiction. The second objection actually raised alternative explanations of our statistical evidence in light of the knowledge by marijuana users of how to obtain heroin and their presence in a subculture that makes it easier for them to get initiated into the use of heroin. It could even be argued that these alternative explanations are much better than the causality explanation. For as we saw in our examination of the Ball-Chambers study, the percentage of heroin (or opium) addicts that had previously used marijuana was much larger in those areas (the Northeast and Southwest) where such drug subcultures are abundant than in those areas (the South) where they are not. Such additional facts about the relation between heroin addiction and previous use of marijuana are better explained by the alternative hypotheses raised in the second objection than by the hypothesis that there is a causal relation between the use of marijuana and heroin addiction. Looking, then, at all the evidence gathered in that study, we cannot say that the hypothesis that there is such a causal connection is the best explanation of the evidence gathered; therefore, it would seem, our inference that there is such a connection is not sound.

Another way of looking at this second objection sheds further light upon it. We were looking before at the analogy between the argument showing that smoking cigarettes causes lung cancer and the argument purporting to show that using marijuana causes heroin addiction. It seemed to us at the time that these arguments were quite similar. But the second objection has shown us that there is a vital difference. In the case of lung cancer, no alternative explanation has been offered that gives us an account of the statistical evidence as plausible as the hypothesis that there is a causal connection between smoking cigarettes and lung cancer. However, in our case an alternative explanation has been offered that provides even a better explanation of the statistical evidence than the hypothesis that there is a causal connection between the use of marijuana and heroin addiction. Thus, we are justified in inferring from the statistical evidence—by an inference from the best explanation—that there is a causal connection between cigarette smoking and lung cancer, but we are not justified in inferring from the statistical evidence that there is a causal connection between the use of marijuana and heroin addiction.

Therefore, the statistical evidence we have examined cannot be used to show that there is a causal connection between the use of marijuana and subsequent heroin addiction. This is so, not because of the many cases in which one is present and not the other, but because our statistical evidence can be better explained otherwise.

11.3 *The Morality of Civil Disobedience Re-examined*

We come, finally, to our two arguments concerning the morality of civil disobedience. One side argued that you should commit acts of civil disobedience, for if they were not done, then many injustices would continue to exist. The other side argued that you should not commit acts of civil disobedience, for if everyone broke the law each time he thought that doing so would correct an injustice, terrible consequences would result because of the breakdown in an orderly and peaceful society.

The first, and, in a way, the most important thing to note about these arguments is that they are formally quite alike. They both claim that if people frequently commit a certain type of action, then terrible consequences will result. Therefore, they claim that it is not the case that people should always commit an action of that type. And they conclude that it follows, in a given case, that a given person should not commit an action of that type. Now, we will grant the initial claims of both these arguments—that one's always, or never, committing acts of civil disobedience would have terrible consequences. Our reason for doing this is very simple: these claims are quite plausible. What we shall be concerned with is. whether these arguments validly entail the conclusions inferred from their initial claims.

To test the validity of these inferences, we must symbolize their premises and their conclusion, and, for reasons that will become clear as we proceed, this will be much easier if we introduce two new symbols. The first is '*t*', which represents the statement that terrible consequences will result. The other is the deontic statemental connective '*O*', which represents 'it ought to be the case that'. In addition to these symbols, '*C*' will represent the property of being an act of civil disobedience, and '*D*' will represent the relation of doing.

The argument for Joe (*a*) not committing a particular act (*b*) of civil disobedience comes down to this:

(1)	(1) $(x)(y)(Cy \supset Dxy) \supset t$	Assump.
(1)	(2) $O \sim (x)(y)(Cy \supset Dxy)$	? (1)
(1)	(3) $O \sim (Cb \supset Dab)$	? (2)
(4)	(4) Cb	Assump.
(1)(4)	(5) $O \sim Dab$	? (3)(4)

On the other hand, the argument for his committing that act of civil disobedience comes down to this:

(1')	(1') $(x)(y)(Cy \supset \sim Dxy) \supset t$	Assump.
(1')	(2') $O \sim (x)(y)(Cy \supset \sim Dxy)$	? (1')
(1')	(3') $O \sim (Cb \supset \sim Dab)$	? (2')
(4')	(4') Cb	Assump.
(1')(4')	(5') $O \sim \sim Dab$	? (3')(4')
(1')(4')	(6') $ODab$	? (5')

In both these inferences there are many steps whose justification is very unclear. But in most cases, although they cannot be justified by claiming that they are instances of the basic inference-forms we have used in constructing our systems, they can be justified by showing that they are instances of obviously valid inference-forms involving deontic connectives. Thus, the inferences from (1) to (2) and from (1') to (2') are both valid because they are instances of the following valid form:

$$\text{(I)} \quad \frac{p \supset t}{O \sim p}$$

The inferences from (3) and (4) to (5) and from (3′) and (4′) to (5′) are both valid because they are inferences of the following valid form:

$$O \sim (p \supset q)$$

(II) $$\dfrac{p}{O \sim q}$$

And the inference from (5′) to (6′) is valid because it is of the following valid form:

(III) $$\dfrac{O \sim \sim p}{Op}$$

We cannot prove here, without entering into a long discussion of the meaning of 'it ought to be the case that', that these are valid forms of inference. But their validity is plausible.

The situation is very different when we look at the crucial inferences from (2) to (3) and from (2′) to (3′). First, it is not a case of a UE inference, or even of two UE inferences (one to eliminate the first quantifier and the other to eliminate the second). For the symbols expressing the premises [the symbol expressing (2) and the symbol expressing (2′)] do not begin with universal quantifiers; so the inferences in question cannot be of the UE form. Second, it is not clear that there is some new valid form of inference, involving 'it ought to be' statements, of which the inferences from (2) to (3) and (2′) to (3′) are instances.

It might be suggested that the form of inference:

(IV) $$\dfrac{O \sim [(x)(---x---)]}{O \sim (-------a----)}$$

is valid; if it is, we can justify the move from (2) to (3) and from (2′) to (3′) by saying that they are accomplished by two inferences of this form, the first eliminating '(x)' and the second eliminating '(y)'. For we could then write the following instead of (2) through (3):

(1)	(2) $O \sim (x)(y)(Cy \supset Dxy)$	(1)(1)
(1)	(2a) $O \sim (y)(Cy \supset Day)$	(IV)(2)
(1)	(3) $O \sim (Cb \supset Dab)$	(IV)(2a)

We could also then write the following instead of (2′) through (3′):

(1′)	(2′) $O \sim (x)(y)(Cy \supset \sim Dxy)$	(1)(1′)
(1′)	(2a′) $O \sim (y)(Cy \supset \sim Day)$	(IV)(2′)
(1′)	(3′) $O \sim (Cb \supset \sim Dab)$	(IV)(2a′)

The trouble with this justification of the move from (2) to (3) and from (2′) to (3′) is that there are good reasons to suspect that (IV) is not really a valid inference-form. First, if we accept the truth of (1) and (1′), of (4) and (4′), and of the validity of (I) through (III) (and it seems that we should), we must conclude that if (IV) is a valid inference-form, then it is the case both that it ought to be the case that Joe does action *b* and that it ought to be the case that he does not. This consequence certainly casts doubt upon the claim that (IV) is a valid inference-form. Second, there seem to be invalid inferences of that form. Consider, as an example, the following inference:

It ought to be the case that it is not the case that everyone is a farmer.

It ought to be the case that it is not the case that Joe is a farmer.

The premise is certainly true. It would be terrible if everyone were a farmer (who would produce everything else?), so it certainly ought to be the case that it is not the case that everyone is a farmer. But if Joe loves farming, then the conclusion might well be false. So there can be inferences of this form that have true premises and false conclusions, and this form is not then a valid form of inference.

At this point it might seem as though we must conclude that neither the law-and-order argument against civil disobedience nor the argument favoring civil disobedience is valid. For they both seem to be of the unacceptable (IV) form. But saying that would be a bit rash, for there seem to be clearly acceptable inferences which are of that form.

Why ought one to vote? Clearly, it cannot be because one's vote will affect the outcome of the election. It has practically never been the case in any significant election in the history of the United States that the vote of one citizen has determined the outcome of an election. Instead, the obligation to vote must be based upon some argument such as: What would happen if everyone who wasn't in the mood to vote or was inconvenienced by voting didn't vote? The result would be that most citizens would not vote, and that elections would be determined by a relatively small group. This would lead to all types of abuses (crafty politicians could manipulate these groups easily, etc.), and, ultimately, to the breakdown of our democratic system. So everyone, including me, should vote even if we aren't in the mood or would be inconvenienced.

What is the logical structure of this argument? It seems that it is as follows:

Everyone's not voting when inconvenienced by voting would lead to disastrous consequences.
Therefore, it ought not to be the case that everyone who would be inconvenienced by voting does not vote.
Therefore, it ought not to be the case that I (you, he, she) do not vote when I (you, he, she) would be inconvenienced by voting.

When we look at this argument, we realize that its last step is an inference of the (IV) form. Yet despite the invalidity of this form, the argument we have just looked at is valid and does prove that we have an obligation to vote.

This example is not isolated. Similar arguments are used to prove that I ought not to litter and that you ought not to cheat on your income tax. Again, neither my littering nor your cheating on your income tax is going to make much of a difference. But if everyone littered or everyone cheated on his income tax, terrible results would occur. So it ought not to be the case that everyone litters or everyone cheats on his income tax; therefore, I ought not to litter and you ought not to cheat. Once more, these arguments clearly involve an inference of the (IV) form; yet they are surely valid. There are many more examples of this same phenomenon.

What does all this mean? Although (IV) is not a valid inference-form, and although there are invalid inferences of the (IV) form, there are a great many valid inferences of that form. Why are they valid? We don't know, but it seems a reasonable hypothesis (because it would explain the phenomenon in question) that there is some form of inference which is valid and which is such that our valid inferences (such as the voting inference, the littering inference, the income tax inference) are of that other form as well but that others (such as the farming inference) are not.

Now, returning to the question of civil disobedience, we can see why we cannot dismiss the two arguments we are examining. For one of them may be valid because it is of this new form of inference, which, unlike (IV), is a valid inference-form. But is one of them of this form? And if so, which one? We cannot answer these questions yet, because no one has yet come up with an acceptable candidate for this new form. The final fate of the law-and-order argument and the parallel opposing argument depends upon further research in deontic logic. As powerful as the systems we have developed in this book are, they are not a final and complete system of logic. Until further research is done on a great many issues in logic, no such system will be forthcoming.

INDEX OF KEY TERMS

The references in this index are to the chapter and section in which the term is first introduced and explained. To understand the term fully, a reading of the entire section is recommended. For references to *Appen.* see the Appendix to Part Two, pp. 195–199.